e returne   fore

Working-Class Culture, Women, and Britain, 1914–1921

Working-Class Culture, Women, and Britain, 1914–1921

Claire A. Culleton

St. Martin's Press
New York

ISBN 0-312-22541-5

Library of Congress Cataloging-in-Publication Data
Culleton, Claire A.
   Working class culture, women, and Britain, 1914–1921 / Claire
A. Culleton.
      p.   cm.
   Includes bibliographical references and index.
   ISBN 0-312-22541-5
   1. World War, 1914—1918—Women—Great Britain.   2. Working class
women—Great Britain—History—20th century.   I. Title.
D639.W7 C79   1999
940.3'082—dc21   99–27686
                                                                        CIP

Design by Letra Libre, Inc.

First edition: January, 2000
10   9   8   7   6   5   4   3   2   1

For Inkey,
who taught me by example to
respect the struggle,
that it's not about nothing

Contents

Acknowledgments   ix
A Note on Primary Sources,
   Archival Collections and Secondary Materials   xi
List of Illustrations   xiii

Introduction   1

Chapter 1   Women's War Work, 1914–1919   17

Chapter 2   The Cultural Response   51

Chapter 3   The Dangers of First World War Work   75

Chapter 4   Working-Class Women's Factory Newspapers   101

Chapter 5   DORA and Women's Social and
             Domestic Lives During the War   135

Chapter 6   Women's Work and Maternity   149

Chapter 7   Demobilization and the Cost of War   169

Conclusion   177

Notes   183
Works Cited   201
Index   215

Acknowledgments

I AM GRATEFUL TO THE KENT STATE UNIVERSITY Research Council for generous funding and leave time toward the completion of this project, and to the College of Arts and Sciences at the University of Miami for a generous postdoctoral grant that funded my early research; to staff at the Imperial War Museum and the Fawcett Library; to Mary Culleton, to Susan Darrah, and to members of the Kent State Women's Group who read and discussed early versions of this work one summer (Martha Cutter, Kathe Davis, Patti Dunmire, Zee Edgell, and Margaret Shaw); and to the American Association of University Professors and its Kent State chapter for professional and collegial support over the years.

My project began at the University of Tulsa with the inspiration and encouragement of Jan Calloway, Sid Huttner, Mary O'Toole, George Otte, Linda Palumbo, Celia Patterson, and Susan Millar Williams and grew after later discussions with Shari Benstock, Angela Ingram, and Jane Marcus. Without the hospitality, typewriters, and good cheer of the Slattery and Maher families in Ireland and (at the time) England, I could not have completed my early research abroad.

A special thanks to my family, especially my mother, to whom I dedicate this book. Like Rose, she made sure us kids had that "Sing out, Louise!" intensity and conviction. Owls to Athens, Ma. Blue firetrucks, "take a chance, Columbus did," and all that jazz. For my brother Chris and my sisters Kiki and Carole, let's continue to want everything for each other. And to my dad, who gave his girls that "Jake's daughter" grit, thanks for it, Pop. We pass it on. To my three little nieces—Amanda, Brigid, and Sean—as Joyce says, be ownkind; as e.e. cummings says, be nobody—but—yourself. XXOO.

I am especially grateful to Nancy Birk, Archivist and Associate Curator of Special Collections, KSU Library, for creating this book's index, and I wish to thank friends and colleagues throughout the years who have helped with this project in one way or another: Ann Ardis, Lorie and Mark Bednar, Nancy Birk, Jim Bolger, Brian Castellani, Donna Cherry,

Laura Davis, Tom Davis, Christian D. Evers, Michael Flamini, Christine Gallagher, Barbara Green, Pam Grimm, Betty Kirschner, Rocco Marinaccio, Patrick McCarthy, Sean Murphy, Frank Smith (who made me call the press back), and Shaaron Warne; to scholars whose work has affected and transformed my own; and to my students at Kent State.

Parts of this work have been published in earlier and different versions as "Irish Working-Class Women and World War I" (in *Representing Ireland: Gender, Class, Nationality* Gainesville: UP of Florida, 1997: 156–180), "Working Class Women's Service Newspapers and the First World War" (*Imperial War Museum Review* 10 [1995]: 4–12), and "Gender-Charged Munitions: The Language of World War I Munitions Reports" (*Women's Studies International Forum* 11.2 [1988]: 109–116). I am grateful to the editors of these works for permission to reprint versions of these essays, and I wish to thank the Trustees of the Imperial War Museum and McFarlin Library for permission to use and cite archival material.

A Note on Primary Sources, Archival Collections and Secondary Materials

A WEALTH OF SOURCES THAT DETAIL WOMEN'S WORK in the First World War are available to scholars. Under the curatorship of Sidney Huttner, Special Collections of McFarlin Library at the University of Tulsa developed an impressive collection of First World War materials, and is a collection that continues to grow. There also are vast and rich collections of primary sources housed in library special collections and archives throughout the world, such as those collections in the New York Public Library, the Fawcett Library at the London Guildhall University, and the Imperial War Museum, many of which are on microfilm. The Department of Printed Books in the Imperial War Museum (IWM) houses the Women's Work Collection, a microform documentary record relating to women's participation in World War I. The museum rightly identifies the collection as "undoubtedly the finest documentary record" available, and briefly describes its genesis as follows:

> Under the careful control of Agnes Conway, the Collection developed thematically and describes through diaries, correspondence, pamphlets, memoranda, photographs and press cuttings the considerable practical achievements of women in this period, as they permeated all sectors of employment. (Publisher's Note to Microform Collection)

Moreover, because of the monumental oral history collection kept in the Sound Archives of the Imperial War Museum, the voices of women workers during the war live on, both in the figurative and literal sense. We can still hear them. Their expressions can ring in our ears and continue to shape and redefine our thinking on women, on work, on culture.

Age Exchange, a London theater company, published and subsequently reissued a selection of 1985 interviews titled *What Did You Do in the War,*

Mum? Recorded decades after the First World War, the oral history interviews provide important narrative hindsight not usually present in the primary sources that have come to document women's work during World War.

List of Illustrations

2.1. Arsenal worker wearing a fur collar. Girl munition
      workers making primers and pellet plugs for shell
      fuses in a Birmingham factory, March 1918.   54

3.1. Women munition workers in Swansea mourning the
      death of a colleague killed in an accident at work. Her
      funeral was held on August Bank Holiday 1917.   96

4.1. Front cover of *The Bombshell*.   104

4.2. Front cover of *Carry On*.   105

4.3. Front cover of *The Shell Magazine*.   106

4.4. Front cover of *Shell Chippings*.   107

6.1. Erotic postcards of women riding shells.   157

6.2. "Bertha": a shocking image of women's
      participation in the war.   160

Introduction

Historians tend to divide the First World War experience into "those who fought" and "those who waited," but so many British citizens joined the work force during the war that a more appropriate division would be those who fought and those who worked, especially since the waiting inevitably was done by both groups. Those who worked, specifically the women who were characterized as working class before the war because they, their husbands, or their fathers worked in or outside of the home, joined ranks with millions of newly employed working-class women during the First World War to work in essential industries in the metal industry, in munition plants, in wood and aircraft trades, in china and earthenware trades, in the leather trade, in paper and printing trades, in the chemical industry, in the clothing and textile industry, and in food and drink industries. By mid-1914, more than two million women—2,178,600—were employed in British factories, and by July 1918, that figure rose to nearly three million according to the 1919 Report of the War Cabinet Committee on Women in Industry (Griffiths 13). By the end of the war, women munition workers alone numbered 900,000, and those in clothing and textile manufacturing numbered nearly as many. Nearly three million British women were occupied in industry during the war,[1] often working as much as 82 hours a week, such as those who worked at Greenwood and Batley's, a firm prosecuted by Britain's Labour Board for its long hours. After protesting dramatically and passionately at the beginning of the war for their "Right to Serve," thousands more British women marched in legion to Westminster to petition for their right to keep those jobs at war's end in 1918. Despite vigorous and animated participation in war service and industry by British women of all classes, analyses of the cultural legacy of the war have tended to marginalize the experiences of women in general and of working-class women in particular.

Working-Class Culture, Women, and Britain, 1914–1921 is a history "from below,"[2] a study of the cultural and social consequences of British working-class women's engagement in the First World War. As such, it aims to transform our understanding of the nature and scope of "war" as a cultural and social category, one that constructs myths of class and gender solidarity while manipulating class loyalties and fueling class distinctions and divisions. Following two lines of inquiry, I chronicle the cost of war on Britain's working-class women and relate a more subtle but far-reaching tale of how this cost created profound and irreversible upheavals in British society, no longer permitting sentimentality of hearth and home and no longer nourishing fin-de-siècle literary styles or late Victorian cultural prescriptions. While their variety of experiences make it impossible to claim a single identity for working-class women during this period, I draw from a variety of sources to provide what Clifford Geertz calls a "thick description" of the lives of skilled, unskilled, and semi-skilled working-class women during the First World War, using evidence from oral history collections, women's service diaries, factory newspapers, souvenir magazines, and critical studies, ultimately to disagree with Asa Briggs's assertion that British women during and immediately after the First World War "were not to transform politics" (*A Social History of England* 283).

"No one realized that the war that broke out that summer would soon be called a world war," Dorothy Goldman explains in *Women Writers and the Great War* (3). "Though the action was concentrated in France and Belgium, it would be a war that was fought in Central and East Africa, in Serbia, Russia, Egypt, Austria, and Gallipoli" (Goldman 3). To fuel the war, workers as well as combatants were needed desperately. Mabel Potter Daggett found a macabre serendipity in her country's call to arms, and noted in her 1918 book *Women Wanted: The Story Written in Blood Red Letters on the Horizon of the Great World War* that "Every time a man drops dead in the trenches, a woman steps permanently into the niche he used to hold in industry, in commerce, in the professions, in world affairs" (24). This niche was *rarely* a permanent one. By 1919, most of the jobs that had been available to working-class women during the war were being offered to returning soldiers. Women of all classes were shamed into giving up their work to returning "heroes," and working-class women in particular were urged to seek work in domestic service. But from 1914 to 1918, "it was like being let out of a cage," Lilian Miles says in her oral narrative housed in London's Imperial War Museum. As Gail Braybon and Penny Summerfield suggest in their comprehensive study of British women's experiences in the First and Second World Wars (allusively titled *Out of the Cage*), "women felt like they had been 'let out of the cage' even when they were critical of the pay and conditions they had to put up with, and the way that men reacted to them" (1). It was indeed a moment in history full of macabre felicities, especially for those working-class women whose introduction into paid labor—or, for the first time, well-paid and full-time labor—came on the heels of months of economic slump following Britain's declaration of war on August 4, 1914.

When British conscription was introduced in January 1916, more and more women entered the work force, first by substituting for an enlisted husband or father—"holding the reins against a male relative's return," as Malcolm Brown describes it in *The Imperial War Museum Book of the First World War* (192)—and then by becoming fully integrated into the work force, if skilled enough, as part of Britain's uncharitably named "dilution" scheme (the word "dilution" applied only to skilled work in industry). Whether recruited into war service by patriotism, pay, or propaganda, or seduced into supporting what was billed as the "war to end war," women of all ages and classes entered industry, nursing, agriculture, and clerical work, hoping to satisfy their own fantasies of enterprise and their nation's war fever at the same time. It is difficult not to conflate working-class and middle-class women's motives for wartime work, since motives ran from the patriotic to the economic; but as Virginia Woolf would argue in *A Room of One's Own*, it wasn't until the First World War that British women were allowed, indeed privileged, to participate so dramatically in the enterprises of their culture.

Many women paid their way in, such as the two million who worked in the First Aid Nursing Yeomanry, the Women's Land Army, the Volunteer Aid Detachment, and other paramilitary organizations, which drew members from the upper and middle classes, whose families paid for their costly uniforms, and supported their involvement in the membership.[3] Lyn Macdonald describes the "typical" VAD nurse, for example, in her Foreword to *The Roses of No Man's Land:* "She's called Elsie or Gladys or Dorothy, her ankles are swollen, her feet are aching, her hands reddened and rough. She has little money, no vote. . . . She is the daughter of a clergyman, a lawyer or a prosperous businessman, and has been privately educated and groomed to be a 'lady'" (xi). For working-class women, however, unless they joined the bulk of the Women's Army Auxiliary Corps (WAAC), and worked as "cooks, clerks, waitresses, driver-mechanics, and all kinds of domestic workers," compelled by the "good wages and uniform" that one WAAC recruiting poster advertised, doors to middle-class active service were closed to working-class women. The latter were directed into industry, and spent the duration on the benches of arsenals and ordnance factories, in the glass, leather, or textile industries. Given women's animated participation in the war effort, it is far from accurate to characterize the millions of British women who worked during the war as "those who waited." What follows is an examination of this vital episode of women's history—the private and the official, the domestic and the national experience.

Because historians are more frequently turning to literature to extract information about literate cultures, one might begin with an analysis of what already has been done by literary historians of the war. Long before Paul Fussell published his study *The Great War and Modern Memory* (1975), social and literary scholars discussed and documented the profound influence that the events, consequences and aftermath of the First World War had on the literature of the modern period. Important contributions focused on trench journalism or on trench poetry, on soldiers such as Wilfred Owen, Isaac Rosenberg, Robert Nichols, and Siegfried Sassoon; but because such studies privilege the male experience of war, they promote and sustain what Allyson Booth calls "the gendering of tragedy" (8). Until recently, much of the research into the literary legacy of the First World War has focused on the contributions of Britain's soldier poets who inscribed the experiences of a war in which more than eight and a half million people died, including 780,000 British soldiers. It was a war that was supposed to be "over by Christmas"; moreover, it was a war that was publicized as the "war to end war." But as early as December 1914, writers all over Great Britain had sensed an abridgment of hope and were beginning to inscribe in their war literature a sense of hopelessness and despair that would characterize, for many, the writing of the emerging modern period.

Any war affects more than its soldiers, and despite the valuable research into the experiences and literary responses of soldiers and military men to the First World War, until the 1980s, little research had been done on the experiences and literary responses of women who were wives, widows, and necessary workers for the war effort. They, too, were poets, novelists, journalists, and dramatists whose wartime publications, diaries, and journals went into third, fourth, and fifth printings. What was identified in the 1950s, '60s, and '70s as the literary legacy of the First World War is now changed and is changing to include a wealth of literary material such as newspapers, memoirs, oral histories, narratives, and testimonies by women writers. In the past two decades, scholars such as Allyson Booth, Gail Braybon, Mary Lynn Broe, Helen Cooper, Jean Gallagher, Dorothy Goldman, Margaret Higonnet, Angela Ingram, Nosheen Khan, Lyn Macdonald, Jane Marcus, Adrienne Auslander Munich, Sharon Ouditt, Pam Schweitzer, Susan Merrill Squier, Trudi Tate, Claire Tylee, Angela Woollacott, and myself have worked to enlarge our understanding of the First World War with particular reference to women's writing and to the concurrent and subsequent reconstructions of gender in Britain.[4] In addition, Sally Mitchell's 1995 book *The New Girl: British Culture in England, 1880–1915* contributes to our understanding of the culture that conspired to produce Britain's New Girl and concludes with a provocative discussion of how the war served to rupture "the old unity of girls' culture [by] sexualizing . . . and regendering young women" (182), turning the "girl" into an "adolescent" precisely at that moment when Britain reintroduced the cultural push toward pronatalism and race building it had begun at least as early as the Boer War; Martha Vicinus's work on women and industry in *The Industrial Muse,* and her 1985 study of work and community for single women from 1850 to 1920 in *Independent Women,* which describes opportunities available to or invented by unmarried middle-class British women, define the shaping and reshaping of Britain's cultural attitudes towards women and work; and Julia Edwards's *Women of the World: The Great Foreign Correspondents* details the bravery and the exploits of women war correspondents. The work and study of these scholars have shifted academic interest in the First World War toward questioning and examining women's participation in creating, shaping, and responding to nascent cultural attitudes, their participation in the literature of the war, in the image-making, in the allegorization of women's wartime experience, and in the forging of a cultural consciousness.

Continually negotiating and forging a cultural and historical space for their voices at a time when the boundaries between the working and middle classes fortuitously seemed blurred (though they were not), at a time when the public concept of the artist and writer was changing, when rich or poor, Irish, Welsh, Scottish, Australian, South African, or English, side by side they were participating in the articulation of a common and forceful experience, working-class women were able to take advantage of the public's receptiveness to new themes and forms. Importantly, they took part in establishing for their culture many of the characteristics that would shape and define literary modernism: irony, politicism, formal innovation, structural fragmentation, multiple narrative perspectives, non-linear chronology, self-reflexive commentary, parody, reconceptualized sexual categories, and a unique openness and a receptiveness to the literature of other countries, to the language of other art forms, and to the lives and writings of working women and men.

I have become increasingly aware of the treatment of class in publications on the First World War, of the chronicling of middle-class experiences over that of the working classes, of the voicing of middle-class frustrations over that of the working classes, of the numerous citations of middle-class women's writing over that of the working classes, and of the romanticized heralding of Britain's heterogenous work force during this period. However valuable such histories, studies, and anthologies continue to be, they cannot sustain lengthy discussions about the complexities of gender and class during the First World War. While the work of

Paul Fussell and others has forged a scholarly understanding of working-class soldiers' literacy during the war and has provoked scholarly analyses of trench newspapers and other wartime writing by ordinary working men, there is as yet no substantial study of working-class women's lives or their writing during the war. Claire Tylee, Margaret Higonnet, and others have drawn attention to the importance of the fiction and memoirs of privileged women, but analyses of working-class women's writing remain sparse.

In a recent collection of essays titled *Women's Fiction and the Great War* (1997), for example, editors Suzanne Raitt and Trudi Tate write "It is no longer true to claim that women's responses to the war have been ignored" (2). Yet their volume contains chapters only on middle-class women writers—Mrs. Humphrey Ward, May Sinclair, Vernon Lee (Violet Paget), Edith Wharton, Frances Bellerby, Radclyffe Hall, Katherine Mansfield, Virginia Woolf, H. D. (Hilda Doolittle), and Gertrude Stein. Another recent book, Heather Ingman's *Women's Fiction Between the Wars: Mothers, Daughters and Writing* (1998), discusses women's writing using Virginia Woolf, Dorothy Richardson, Ivy Compton-Burnett, Elizabeth Bowen, Rose Macaulay, and Jean Rhys to construct an historical and literary context that is also decidedly middle class. Similarly, Jean Gallagher's captivating book *The World Wars Through the Female Gaze* (1998) focuses on middle-class women Edith Wharton, H. D., Mildred Aldrich, Gertrude Stein, and Martha Gellhorn, who subjectified in their writing female observers of First and Second World War combat. These projects, while entirely fascinating, confirm Regenia Gagnier's comment in *Subjectivities: A History of Self-Representation in Britain, 1832–1920,* that "feminist scholars have largely been occupied with the struggles of middle-class women writers" (35). Though Trevor Wilson writes in *The Myriad Faces of War: Britain and the Great War 1914–1918* that "Too much, arguably, has been written about the effects of the war in enhancing women's status" (724), he grossly exaggerates the academic attention given to this subject and gives little attention to it himself in his mammoth history (this statement appears in chapter 65, for example). My project is one that focuses particularly on working-class women in Britain, their historical experiences, their literary experimentation, their cultural ideologies, and their evolving status. I concentrate specifically on working-class women who as volunteers, workers, or dilutees for the British war effort describe the cultural resonances of war that continually were shaped and mediated by issues of gender and class. Their ordeals emerge from distinct cultural experiences, ideologies, and social, political, and class constructions; but their experiences evince what Joan Scott calls "proof of their ability to make history" (53). If historians of the First World War have contributed to the "gendering of tragedy," they also have shaped the "classing" of it, too, by rendering invisible the working class and "evicting" it from history, as Trevor Blackwell and Jeremy Seabrook argue. Blackwell and Seabrook find this eviction "a particularly vengeful act, given that history is what was, in some accounts, supposed to have vindicated it [the working class]" (*Talking Work: An Oral History* 208).

What I aim to provide in *Working-Class Culture, Women, and Britain, 1914–1921* are discussions of the lives, oral history narratives, testimonies, and work-place writings of women workers during the war, how their experiences and writings affected their class and status, how their class and status affected their experiences and writings, and how their experiences and writings affected and were affected by emerging modernist sensibilities that sought to modulate and transform their culture, their attitudes, their national literature. My attention to the literary culture of working class women continues the feminist project of revising Fussell's portrait of a literary landscape dominated by men, but it revises the revisionists, as well, by moving the frame away from middle-class women writers.

"How did people imagine themselves as subjects in a period of 'total war'?," Trudi Tate asks in *Modernism, History and the First World War* (4). How did they "imagine themselves as subjects, or indeed as citizens, in a culture . . . mobilised around rumours, lies, and official secrecy?" (43). While texts of literary modernism, for example, were constituting and constructing distinct subjectivities for middle-class women, working-class women tried to construct their own subjectivities in the form of "counterlaw or out-law" writings, a fascinating term used by Caren Kaplan to describe autobiographical texts that defy traditional generic classification and definition ("Resisting Autobiography" 119). "Outlaw genres renegotiate the relationship between personal identity and the world, between personal and social history," Kaplan argues. "Here, narrative inventions are tied to a struggle for cultural survival rather than purely aesthetic experimentation or individual expression" (130). Autobiographical writing, then, generally considered bourgeois expressions of individualism, actually serve an important cultural function for a whole class of women when it is taken up by working-class writers. In their autobiographical writings, in their memoirs, diaries, oral history testimonies, and in the "out-law" industry newspapers I describe below and discuss at length in chapter 4, working-class women represent and situate themselves in the context of current history. Regenia Gagnier remarks that one of the important differences between working-class and middle-class autobiographical writing is that working-class writers do not (because they cannot) avail themselves of the luxury of private retreat when the going gets tough. They must situate themselves among the aggravation, she explains, and must write from a position that is constantly within the turmoil. They write, she adds, already mindful of those who have struggled with and before them. Gagnier explains:

> In these autobiographies, the self that cannot adjust to the status quo no longer retreats in the isolated aesthetic of a[n Antonia] White or a [Cyril] Connolly, but, like Victorian working-class autobiographers, rather draws upon many narratives of personal and public histories, situating itself always in history and always among others, both friendly and hostile. . . . They—like all autobiography—show that the study of autobiography is not merely a genteel (or gentile or genital) literary exercise but a gauge of citizens' degrees of social participation and exclusion, consensus and revolt. (*Subjectivities* 277–78)

The writings of working-class women—like their recorded interviews and oral history testimonies—do not exhibit that characteristic spiritual search for self, an aspect often featured in more typical middle class autobiographical and self-representational writing,[5] because the authors are more concerned with showing how the individual triumphed *in,* and not *apart from,* society. As a result, working-class autobiographical writings tend to tell stories about groups. *Working-Class Culture, Women, and Britain, 1914–1921* focuses on those stories about these groups of women workers.

Building upon and challenging the work that already has been done by social historians and literary scholars, I aim to arrive at a comprehensive analysis of the complexities that conspired to link women's lives, their work, and their writings during a period in British history when the working class popularly was maligned for its alleged disinterest in the war and in the war effort. At a time when women of the middle classes successfully were redefining their status and importance in British culture, working class women had additional burdens, restraints, myths, and ideologies to wrestle with, circumvent, or triumph over if they were to achieve similar popular approval.

Their responses to war work were complex and interesting. They wrote not only poems, novels, dramas, biographies, and autobiographies about their or others' experiences working for the war effort but also published and produced their own factory newspapers not merely to rival the newspapers and trench magazines written and published by soldiers at the front lines but to foster an imitative sense of community many of them had felt as schoolgirls reading popular school publications. Women's factory newspapers were astoundingly popular, and some, such as the weekly publication *Cardonald News,* boasted circulations of well over 2,000. Unlike working-class women's other published material, their fiction, for example, the factory newspapers and magazines showcase strong, political, female voices that continually are aligned with issues of *work*. When juxtaposed with the literature and with written or recorded oral narratives, they paint a picture of Britain in wartime that is different from and unlike anything middle-class women or soldiers might produce about the experience of war.

Equally important, women's industry newspapers and magazines, being written and published in a variety of regional districts and rural areas throughout Britain, represented a rather distinct type of British working-class woman, one who lived and worked outside of the city at a time when popular women's magazines neither addressed nor represented such a figure. Extremely popular at the turn of the century, women's magazines were not published in provincial centers outside of London, Margaret Beetham notes in *A Magazine of Her Own: Domesticity and Desire in the Woman's Magazine 1800–1914*. In fact, "most magazines targeted the middle-class and offered explicitly bourgeois models of feminine behaviour" (7). They "produced an exclusively metropolitan version of femininity. . . . Women's magazines were read across the empire but the identity offered in the magazines bound readers firmly into the culture of the capital. Even 'provincial' readers in Britain were at the margin of the magazines' world" (7–8). Thus, at about the same time that working class women were neglected as subjects in women's magazine discourse, those who worked in rural districts began to produce their own magazines and newspapers on the job in an effort to constitute and construct their own subjectivities and to thematize the significance of their stories, their work, their lives.

The women's work site publications also helped to bridge a cultural gap, a rift that had begun to emerge in British culture during the war. By 1916, before the war was half over, a new division had grown up in British society, not so much between class, as Martin Taylor explains, "but between the Nation at Home and the Nation Overseas" ("Smug-Faced Crowds" 88). Nowhere more than in the women's service newspapers can we see the domestic theater of war more clearly represented and detailed. In their service and industry newspapers, working-class women describe their work, assess their lives, and detail the dramatic changes affected by the war. Vilified by their own fickle culture either for fueling the war effort in Britain or for not doing enough to promote it, and shunned by their co-workers because they were working class or "factory girls" and often minimally educated, the women workers on whom I concentrate often had to dodge popular disapproval from a surprising assortment of sources: middle-class supervisors sought to refashion and reinvent them and offered friendly advice on how to dress, how to apply makeup, how to enunciate; working-class women either were parodied in the press or were sentimentalized as "Tommy's Sister," a child sucking on sweets with "kiss-curls twiddling over her temples," as Hall Caine describes the typical factory girl in his 1916 book *Our Girls: Their Work for the War* (71). Women workers in general found themselves targeted by the press and by the community, but the women's working class often was singled out for scrutiny or burlesque. And their behavior—especially where money was involved—was probed for manifestations of expected roguishness.

Whatever their class, whether they were "doing their bit" on the benches of local factories, for example, or working abroad with Queen Mary's Army Auxiliary Corps (QMAAC), whether involved in the suffrage movement or the temperance movement, whether driving ambulances or collecting tramway tickets, whether selling pins for flag days, lamps for lamp days, war bonds, or handing out white feathers, wartime women quickly became the objects of cultural scrutiny and scorn. British citizens were curious to know and quick to challenge the tasks these women performed on the job, how much money they made, how they spent their wages, and what they did during their leisure time—especially if they were married and receiving a separation allowance from the Home Office. Unmarried women did not escape scrutiny, either; their social actions were regulated by curfews, prohibitions, and a host of regulations invented on their behalf under the 1914–1915 Defence of the Realm Acts (DORA). Though some women workers admit that they relished the spotlight at first, they soon grew weary of the attention, and wrote and spoke disdainfully about their experiences under the magnifying and unforgiving eyes of their culture.

For these women, working for the war effort in Britain demanded a great deal of bravery: there were picket lines to cross, cross workers to pacify, pacifists to tolerate, intolerable war mongers to suffer, and insufferable critics to sidestep on the way to the factories or the front. Some of the most caustic criticism came from literature produced by combatants. Soldiers dispirited early in the war and no longer vainglorious about their participation in it soon aimed their attacks at a more familiar army, characterizing the civilian front as a pack of "dullards whom no cannon stuns," as Wilfred Owen charged in his poem "Insensibility," or specifically accusing women of turning them into shells, as Siegfried Sassoon wrote in his sonnet "Glory of Women." E. A. Mackintosh called them "harlots" in his poem "Recruiting," and taking his cue from Mackintosh, no doubt, historian Trevor Wilson refers to "a great regiment of tarted-up females" who conveniently enjoined the sacrifices of others at little self-expense.[6]

Even those who did not serve in the First World War found the mettle to translate their misogyny and discontent with home-front women into published writing. Rudyard Kipling, for example, published a collection of memorial poetry titled *Epitaphs of the War 1914–1918*. One couplet succinctly captures the cultural animosity for the working class, and since war factories by this time were made up by a majority of working-class women, we might extend Kipling's invective directly to them.[7] In "Batteries out of Ammunition," Kipling writes, "If any mourn us in the workshop, say / We died because the shift kept holiday" (314). Importantly, Kipling's epitaph begins with the allusive "If"—likely a self-conscious reference to his popular poem of the same name. Reprinted and recirculated continuously during the First World War, Kipling's 1890 poem "If" inspired soldiers and industry workers in many ways, as we shall see in chapter 4, because the poem urgently encouraged steadfastness among calamity. But the word "if" here also works to shed doubt on the women's sensitivity—"*If* any mourn us in the workshop"—calling into question the workers' loyalties, painting them as robotic, money-grubbing workers, interested in themselves first and their union contracts second. Kipling's epitaph is a classic and succinct illustration of a familiar tactic used to discredit organized workers. He shifts attention and cultural scorn onto the workers while ignoring the complicity of, and failing to ultimately inculpate, the parliamentary war machine. Moreover, as the Kipling epitaph suggests, women quickly became popularized as the *cause* of soldiers' deaths: we die because they keep holiday.

Ironically, in the beginning of the war women were celebrated and indeed monumentalized as a cause worth fighting for, though their celebrity ebbed as the war persisted. Countless early war posters pictured women who urged or shamed their men into joining up. "Women of Britain say— 'Go!'" shows a middle-class woman and two children looking out a window to admire the passing unit of British soldiers. Another poster, exported to Ireland, shows a peasant woman pointing a rigid finger toward a representation of burning Belgium. She asks her male companion, "Will You Go, Or Must I?"[8] Fashioned into moral barometers for their generation as well as for their class, women were represented pictorially as their nation's conscience, and their patriotism and nationalist conviction won them celebrity because they succeeded in goading their husbands, their sons, and their brothers to war, whatever their class.

Young, unmarried women in Britain were recruited into Britain's propaganda scheme as well. An early poster issued by the Parliamentary Recruitment Committee reads:

TO THE YOUNG WOMEN OF LONDON: Is your "Best Boy" wearing khaki? If not, don't *YOU THINK* he should be? If he does not think that you and your country are worth fighting for—do you think he is *WORTHY* of you? Don't pity the girl who is alone—her young man is probably a soldier—fighting for her and her country—and for YOU. If your young man neglects his duty to his King and Country, the time may come when he will NEGLECT YOU. Think it over—then ask him to JOIN THE ARMY TO-DAY. (Brown 192)

Reprinted and posted in Ireland to read "TO THE YOUNG WOMEN OF IRE-LAND," like many of the posters published and circulated in Britain during the First World War, this particular example preys upon a number of women's wartime fears, not least among these the fear of being neglected or cheated on. Importantly, Britain's sons were urged to see their patriotic relationship as a sexual one; numerous posters and placards worked to reinforce the equation of combat with sexual virility, supplanting the image of Mother Britannia with those of girlfriends or lovers. As Malcolm Brown notes of the above example, "Early in the war, the prime function of women was to persuade, cajole, threaten, moralize, until their man—or 'best boy'—got himself into uniform" (192). Women's complicity in the war effort at this stage maligned them later on, and women were made to shoulder the nation's blame for the war dead, especially women who worked in arsenals and ordnance factories, since they were seen as fueling the war effort in two consequential ways: with their weapons manufacturing and with their jingoistic blather, as I discuss in chapter 2.

Poet Margaret Sackville blamed women, in particular, for sowing and subsequently reaping the harvest of war, ending her poem "Nostra Culpa" with a condemnatory "What shall we plead? That we were deaf and blind?/ We mothers and murderers of mankind" (39). The polemic that Sackville underscores in her poem is similar to one identified in a Gnostic conundrum, namely, "How long will men make war?—As long as women have children" (Cooper, Munich, Squier 20). Like the Gnostic conundrum, Sackville inculpates women for their complicity during war, a complicity marked by their acquiescence to motherhood. In addition to being blamed and despised for fueling the war in this way, women also were criticized for participating in and upholding a home-front naiveté that soldiers and other combatants found thoroughly disgusting. Martin Taylor notes that unavoidably women were identified in the minds of the soldiers with the widespread civilian temperament, and that the women's innocence, or their patriotism or jingoism, was rendered completely unpalatable because of their ignorance of the realities of war. Taylor suggests:

Although many women served with distinction, and were killed in action, the enduring images of women from the First World War are of the 'Little Mother', the recruiting chorus girls and the ladies handing out white feath-

ers to men not in uniform. These were the women who became the particular focus of the soldier poets' attack on the home front. (92)

Like so many others, writer Robert Graves took particular exception to
the figure of the "Little Mother" whom he mercilessly censures in his autobiography *Goodbye to All That* (283–85). The "Little Mother," the
anonymous author of a letter published in the *Morning Post,* wrote

> I must say that we women . . . will tolerate no such cry as 'Peace! Peace!'
> where there is no peace. The corn that will wave over the land watered by
> the blood of our brave lads shall testify to the future that their blood was
> not spilt in vain. . . . They have all done their share, and we, as women, will
> do ours without murmuring or complaint. There is only one temperature
> for the women of the British race, and that is white heat.

The "Little Mother" letter was so popular that copies reprinted in pamphlet form sold quickly: 75,000 copies were bought in less than a week,
John Williams notes (125) and gave currency to a model of unbending,
unyielding female patriotism.

Clearly, women were in a no-win situation. Bombarded with cosmopolitan images of women "doing their bit," urged into domestic war
service by countless posters and placards and incited into a "white heat"
by the popularly canonized figure of the "Little Mother," women were
"cynically exploited by the propagandists" (Taylor 92); and whether they
were censured by other women for taking on male roles during the war or
condemned by soldiers for fostering with their enthusiasm civilian madness and unbridled patriotic excess, women war workers had to brave and
defy the criticism of conflicting and virulent forces.

Clearly, working-class women's entry into war service was significantly more than, and radically different from, what their culture expected of them. In addition to working well over 60 or 70 hours a week
and squandering precious free time standing on Britain's familiar ration
lines, working-class women had to brave malicious criticism from all
sides. The coarseness of their culture's response and the sordid and un-
pleasant experiences endured by the workers as a result of their mobi-
lized entry into well-paid labor are rarely chronicled in popular or
national histories, and it is a story that remains largely unchronicled.

For example, Dorothy Goldman notes that "what women wrote about
this period has been largely forgotten, or granted only grudging recognition, and its vision has been submerged under masculine myths about
the war and war literature" (Goldman x). Women workers recognized
what Goldman calls the "grudging recognition" early on in the historical

chronicling of the First World War, and addressed the issue frequently in their service newspapers, as I discuss in chapter four.

Moreover, in a 1919 pamphlet titled *What the War Meant to Women*, Dr. Anna Howard Shaw articulately challenged the histories of the First World War and demanded that the history of the war be written without submerging women's experiences and without excluding from history its devastating effects on women. Shaw argued,

> We have been able to count the men who died in the field. We are told that five million men in this war died in battle and that two million more died from wounds received in battle and that two million more died of disease in the hospitals, making a great total of nine million men who died. But when we speak of the cost of life in this war we enumerate only the men who died. We have made no enumeration of the women. We have made no enumeration of the children. We do not know the vast bodies of women and children who have been slaughtered, women who have been outraged and who today are filling the madhouses of France and Belgium and Serbia and all the other nations which have been overrun by the armies. We know nothing about the horrible results which have come to the lives of women or of the cost of this war in women as well as its cost in men. (5)

Although Shaw wrote to move her American public, acting as chair-woman of the Women's Committee for the Council of National Defense, her documents and speeches mourn for a generation of women whose lives changed conclusively when their countries entered the war. This book, I hope, satisfies Dr. Shaw posthumously, since it details "the cost of [the] war in women," and describes the losses suffered by women during and after the First World War when they were most susceptible to attacks against their health, their sanity, their spirit.

To reiterate, *Working-Class Culture, Women, and Britain, 1914–1921* details and documents the social, cultural and literary consequences of working class women's mass entry into and subsequent departure from Britain's labor force. This book does not pretend to supplant the fine and important work that already has been done on the topic but aims to enlarge further our understanding of the years from 1914 to 1921 and working-class women's experiences during those years. I situate my work firmly within the rapidly expanding field of scholarship on women's experience of war. One strength of this book is that it gathers together for specialists in the field as well as for general readers decades of research on the First World War, much of it from sources that are now out of print, difficult to find, or housed only in archival collections.

Chapter 1 describes Britain's dilution scheme and details the various jobs available to working-class women during the First World War; chapter 2 discusses their culture's often hostile response to their engagement in that work; chapter 3 describes the dangerous industrial and factory working conditions to which Britain's domestic and subject working classes were exposed (women died by the hundreds in war factories, working with, handling, and even deliberately consuming the deadly material they produced). Chapter 4 describes their on-site literary production and focuses on service newspapers written and published by women who worked in shell-filling factories, arsenals, and ordnance factories during the war. Chapter 5 details Britain's 1914–1915 Defence of the Realm Acts (DORA), which greatly affected women's public and private lives, redefining at first and then regulating their cultural and domestic spheres. Chapter 6 focuses on women's work and maternity, specifically the ways in which these items were linked in the popular consciousness by Britain's pronatalist drive, in 1916, to promote motherhood as a means to thwart racial suicide—a national campaign aimed at "reminding" women of the importance of their roles as mothers and nurturers. Chapter 7 discusses postwar demobilization, what Deborah Thom calls "the ease of eviction from war occupations once the war was over and women's own agreement with this process" (297). Here I discuss women's attitudes and responses to their war work after they were put off, after they were put back in "the cage." Indeed, to those women who worked during the war in or out of industry as munition workers, crane drivers, conductors, needlewomen, ambulance drivers, nurses, gardeners, aircraft dopers, varnishers, painters, elevator operators, cooks, clerks, waitresses, driver-mechanics, and policewomen, covering so many occupations during the war, giving back to their husbands, sons, or fathers the metonymic anchor and crown was a painful process. Its legacy, as Jane Marcus describes it, was a generation of "angry, depressed, and suicidal women who had lost their jobs after the war, and with those jobs the self-respect and financial independence that kept them going, a sense of their own history, with its heroism and its hurts" ("The Nurse's Text" 469). Yet because it would be inaccurate to represent these years and the women's experiences at this time as altogether degenerative to working-class solidarity, as devolutionary to women's status in the work place, or as aiding and abetting the proletarianization of skilled labor—as many historians have argued—chapter 7 attempts to tell the story of the aftermath of the war in a different way. Challenging the primacy of cultural myths about working-class women's victimization after the war, about women's complacent acquiescence in this process, and about the widespread depression or hysteria that affected British women workers after the war, I aim to replace these myths with alternative versions of history that focus instead on the collective strength of the women's working class after the war, on the lessons they learned from their work, on the solidarity it yielded, and on the information surrendered to them during and after the war about their right to work for pay. Chapter 8 serves as a conclusion and epilogue.

More than five million women joined the civilian call to arms within a year of Britain's engagement in the First World War. Ironically, those who weren't lured into the war effort by pay, patriotism, or propaganda were attracted by their sense of pacifism and believed that they were working for the "war to end war." Women who didn't want to participate in manufacturing weaponry and aircraft, or assist those who did by volunteering to work in factory canteens and local hostels that supported essential industries, turned to other sorts of volunteer or charity work. Others canvassed door to door collecting funds and selling bonds to support the war for peace. It was a war that was supposed to be "over by Christmas"; but as early as August 23, 1914, after the Battle of Mons, and especially after the Battle of Loos in September 1915, when British soldiers first fired poisonous gas at the enemy, women all over Britain were beginning to sense that they had been had, that the war had little to do with peace, and that their lives, like their culture, would never be the same.

What consequences these circumstances and perceptions had on Britain's working-class women would stay with them for generations and certainly would influence their and their daughters' participation in the Second World War, but they also would affect women's immediate lives in significant and unexpected ways: increasing on the one hand the health and life expectancy of the working classes after the war but affecting an immediate rise in work-related deaths during the war and an acute rise in maternal mortality rates after the war; affecting the size of the postwar family through political campaigns that successfully yoked the abstract notion of patriotism with maternity but criminalized women's sexual behavior via Defence of the Realm Act regulations enforced through 1921 that monitored and governed women's sexual and family planning practices; and refashioning at best and rescinding at worst, as we shall see, women's employment, educational, economic, and political privileges.

Chapter 1

Women's War Work,
1914–1919

*"It was all excitement. It was out of the humdrum. See—life was beginning
to be for living. Before that it was just working and sleeping and eating,
when you could get it to eat."*

—Jane Cox, Needlewoman, Schneider's Clothing Factory[1]

"LIFE WAS BEGINNING TO BE FOR LIVING," JANE COX recalls of the days
during the First World War in an interview for the Imperial War
Museum (IWM) oral history collection, a storehouse of hundreds of
taped interviews with civilians who had worked during the war.
Margaret Brooks, Keeper of the Sound Archive, described the history of
this important collection in her essay "Women in munitions 1914–1918:
the oral record," in which she rightly asserts that "the raw material of
oral history interviews can bring an historical episode to life" (4).[2] Jane
Cox, who worked as a needlewoman at Schneider's Clothing Factory in
London, preserves in her oral narrative the excitement of that historical
moment. But hers is an ironic statement set against the backdrop of war,
when to those at home, death seemed an inescapable and indiscriminate
enemy responsible not only for lost sons, brothers, husbands, and fathers but one who stole the lives of sisters, daughters, girlfriends, and
co-workers. Yet Cox's unexpected description of daily life during the
First World War—"It was all excitement"—echoes that of many other
women who felt themselves come alive during the war, newly animated
by temporary changes in working-class British culture that brought

with them an unaccustomed lack of male presence, supervision and authority,[3] an increase in social and sexual freedom, and important economic changes that rendered women more effective family participants or heads of households. It is important to point out, though, that the women's very real exuberance would not dissuade their culture from constructing them as "secondary and temporary workers," as Sharon Oudit reminds us (33), and that they would remain for the most part the unstable workers of Britain's primary and secondary labor markets, no matter how much they enjoyed the liberties of employment during the First World War.

For many, these liberties enabled working-class women not merely to endure the war but to alleviate a number of difficulties usually present in their lives: their unexpectedly high wages allowed them to manipulate household budgets to better clothe, feed, and care for themselves and their families,[4] to maintain and in many cases to improve their living standards. Some factories provided on-site savings banks, which made it convenient for workers to open and sustain savings accounts when they likely hadn't had substantial savings before the war.[5] A report on the savings bank at the Cardonald National Projectile Factory, for example, notes that the total amount deposited over the course of two years was £16,500, and that the highest weekly deposit during this period was £355 (IWM Department of Printed Books, Women's Work Microfilm Collection, Item MUN 12/4).

Other changes followed. In spite of the shortage of medical doctors at home during the war, women were able to procure better health services for themselves and for their children due to the proximity of on-site doctors and the establishment of supervised creches at the work place.[6] Women's health became especially important after 1916 when Britain's pronatalist drive was in full swing and motherhood became a nationally protected occupation, though maternal mortality rates would rise after the war, as I discuss in chapter 6. Working-class health improved in other ways. Those who worked outdoors, for example, found the fresh air and physical work invigorating, especially those working-class women whose previous wage-earning work was carried on in the home alongside other home-working family members. Those now working in arsenals and ordnance and projectile factories, as well as those who worked in other industries, joined team football clubs, choirs, and acting troupes that gave them regular recreation and extended their circle of friends beyond their parochial communities. The contribution such recreation had on their health was likely significant. Andrew Davies explains that working-class women rarely had the luxury of engaging in regular sport and leisure activities before the First World War.[7] Especially true for those women who worked, time after paid work was not normally "free" time. For those women who did plan leisure activities, the activities usually coincided with an annual day trip sponsored by their local pub: "Once a year, pubs organized a day trip for women, often to the Cheshire countryside, and for some working-class housewives and mothers, this was the only day in the year when they could take a break from family duties" (Davies 56). Having sport teams and singing troupes at work was a novelty that not only encouraged camaraderie but also worked to change the character of the women's workplace, and to modulate attitudes towards and among co-workers and their middle-class supervisors.

Though food shortages had become commonplace, and with that, alarming reports of rationing lines that exceeded 3,000 long,[8] or estimates by the Metropolitan Police that 80,000 Londoners were lining up for meat and 30,000 for other goods in early 1918,[9] working-class families were better fed during the war. Mabel Potter Daggett noted in her 1918 book, for example, that "in the East End, families are celebrating meat days that were never known before the war" (151); and war worker Laura Verity described in her oral narrative the Finnan haddock or kippers that many munitions workers would buy for their teas on their way home from work, adding, "Oh, they were definitely better off in the First War than they were before" (IWM Sound Archive, Item SR 864, Reel 7). Consequently, better nutrition during the war gave rise to what social demographer J. M. Winter calls "the Paradox of the Great War": an unexpected decline in mortality rates among the working classes after the war.[10] Together, these changes yielded healthy citizens, productive and entitled workers, and efficient heads of households—all of which contributed to a metamorphosing home front morale and worked to alter the physical, economic, and social situation of working-class women in British culture.

Whether on the bench, behind the plough, or baling textiles, the millions of women who entered the work force during the First World War quickly found a degree of satisfaction in their work; and when peace came, and with it women's demobilization from the work place, women feared what the future might hold for them: "I cried me eyes out when I left—that was the sort of life I led," recalled Amy Elizabeth May, a worker at Woolwich, one of three Royal Factories during the war (IWM Sound Archive, Item SR 684, Reel 4). May's comment, like Jane Cox's above, identifies in the women's war work something that made their lives more meaningful, more accountable, more valuable. If during the First World War women felt like they had been "let out of the cage," as Lilian Miles recalls, or felt as if life were "beginning to be for living," by 1918 millions of women feared being shut back into the cage and reassigned to what Cox called the old "humdrum": "working and sleeping and eating, when you could get it to eat" (IWM Sound Archive, Item SR 705, Reel 4).

We understand what kept working-class women in Britain's factories—national leaving certificate policies often straitjacketed workers and forced them to stay in essential industries under threat of penalty, and those who signed on for the duration were likely to stay as long to avoid reprimand—but what was it that drew working-class women to war work? High wages made all the more attractive by weekly bonuses, piecerate and overtime opportunities were not the singular draw, although contemporaries announced that motive for working-class women who entered the work force during the First World War, as I discuss in chapter 2. Patriotism, other contemporaries claimed, was another motivating force behind women's entry into paid labor, and it not only accounted for women's success in the factories but explained why they would put up with what was identified throughout the war as dangerous and sweated working conditions, as we shall see in chapter 3. Some propagandists focused on a biological draw and argued that women "naturally" were compelled to the factories to answer the "mysterious call of their sex," and suggested that women who produced munitions were redirecting their maternal instincts towards weapons manufacturing, as I discuss elsewhere in this book, since child manufacturing was becoming more and more impossible during wartime given the limits of male presence on the home front. Looming largely over the impulses and instincts popularly attributed to the women workers was their desire to participate at any level in their nation's war, and not to be idle for the duration.

To this end, on July 17, 1915, less than a year after Britain declared war on Germany, 30,000 women marched in London to convince the new Minister of Munitions David Lloyd George and his Cabinet "that so far as winning the war [was] concerned the women of this country mean business," Clara Butt, organizer of the demonstration, announced to the crowd from a platform overlooking Embankment ("Women Marchers Beg for War Work," *New York Times* July 18, 1917: 1). Emmeline Pankhurst, founder of the Women's Social and Political Union, led marchers through London's main thoroughfares while "thousands of banners were borne in the procession and a hundred bands played stirring music," the *Times* reported. Hats and flags waved enthusiastically to the strains of Britain's national anthem (3).

Insisting upon their "Right to Serve" (the title by which the march would later become known), women petitioned for prompt action that would exploit the intensity of their conviction and capitalize on their degree of readiness; and by their march, they hoped to mobilize an army already 80,000 strong to work. "Some months ago," Butt explained, "the Board of Trade published an appeal to the women of Great Britain asking them to register for war work. Over 80,000 women have registered up to the present, yet, on the board's own admission, not more than 8,000 of these have obtained employment" (*NYT* 1). Butt and her fellow marchers expected to see Lloyd George squarely behind new labor initiatives for women, and declared that "There is waiting to be drawn upon an army of women war workers which merely awaits demobilization."[11]

But the women's Right to Serve March was not a procession organized for or by the working classes. Clara Butt and Emmeline Pankhurst argued in their speeches for a national animation of women of the middle classes, and referred to the army of working-class women only after each was well into her address. What Butt and Pankhurst wanted, it seems clear from their speeches, was for Lloyd George to mobilize that army of middle-class women from which the country might draw the next generation of professionals—doctors, for example, and teachers. Butt argued:

> There are without doubt scores of women ready and willing to undertake the five years' training necessary to qualify as doctors, but they lack the means. Yet there can be no question as to the necessity of encouraging such women to enter the profession. Not only should more hospitals be thrown open to women. Fees should be reduced also, or even abolished entirely, to meet the crisis. At present it costs approximately £200 ($1000) in fees, &c., alone to be graduated in this country. (3)

"The teaching profession has also been hard hit by the war," she continued, and urged that special provisions be made in that field, too, to take national advantage of the class of women able to perform in education. She closed her speech by referring to an army of "non-professional" women who might be used in industry or who might be put to work serving in canteens.[12] While Butt's army did not expect or hope to engage in combat, they asked as a group for the right to participate in the war, and to emphasize their likely contribution, they waved banners that advertised their willingness to work, banners that read, for example, "Shells made by a wife / May save her husband's life," and "Women's Battle Cry is Work, Work, Work!"

To a culture already grown used to, and weary of, regularly scheduled women's suffrage marches, the monumental march for women's Right to Serve met with a variety of responses. Newspaper accounts of the historical march ranged from the serious to the sarcastic; but women who participated in the phenomenal demonstration noted the momentousness of the event differently, commenting in their diaries, memoirs, oral narratives, autobiographies, and imaginative literature on its significance to their lives, to their daughters' lives, and to their culture. Their march quickly was sensationalized: "The British Lion is awake, so is the Lioness," one newsreel caption pronounced, dramatizing for a national audience in 3,000 cinemas women's push for recognizable war service (Thom 303).

Because the First World War so dramatically changed women's lives in Britain, engaging them not only in culturally and politically important work but giving many of them the experience of financial independence, women's engagement in the workplace during the First World War is often treated as a momentous cultural beginning of sorts, as a time when history and circumstance conspired to lend a munificent hand to the women's working class, ushering in changes that would affect them through the coming decades. Many argue, as Shelley Saywell does below, that the First World War remains a starting point for tracing the roots of British women's social and cultural autonomy. Saywell suggests:

> If you ask British women today when their emancipation really began, they will tell you that it was during the First World War, when women took upon themselves roles that were extraordinary in those times—not only running society at home but also going off to the trenches of Europe to serve as doctors, nurses and spies. (*Women in War* 1–2)

But few working-class women "ran" society at home, and even fewer served at the front as doctors, nurses, and spies. To trace the beginnings of working-class women's social and cultural autonomy, one must begin at the factories.

Many working-class women worked before the war, albeit for lower wages than those paid during the war when more and more of them were invited into the factories during these years. For them, the transition from being a daughter or wife of a working-class male to becoming a member of the working class itself was rarely an easy one, often complicated by invective, criticism, and sabotage from parents, friends, neighbors, and male co-workers who saw women's mass entry into paid labor as a fractious phenomenon, one that would rupture family life, dilute the labor market, violate men's hard-won labor wages, and give most of the women workers a financial self-reliance they had never known before, especially since most working-class women worked before the war for lower wages. These attitudes and fears tie in with the larger cultural response to working-class women's war work during those years, which I discuss in chapter 2; but for those millions of women who worked during the war as munitions makers, dopers, varnishers, clerks, canteen operators, and so forth, the transition seemed less formidable than it was emancipatory.

Despite the enthusiastic entry of the working class to war work, their support was only slowly and grudgingly recognized by the middle class. Allegations circulated feverishly about the supposed passivity of the working class—of their refusal to leave their prewar jobs, of their reluctance to join the colors, of their resistance to substitute in essential industries or to work as dilutees for the war effort—and rumors were quick to paint them early in the war as a collectively stubborn lot who refused to engage in their nation's militaristic enterprise, even though their earnest involvement in war work as early as 1915 could discredit such charges and imputations. Trevor Wilson argues that the widespread and seditious belief that the working classes were not supporting Britain's war confirms that antipathies between social classes remained unchanged and unchangeable during the war. He writes:

> Among the middle and upper classes there was much readiness to believe in, and deplore, a supposed lack of enthusiasm for the national cause among the working classes. From this were drawn appropriate class conclusions, as when (according to Masterman) the headmaster of a great public school attributed "the 'prevailing apathy' of the lower classes in this war to the fact that they have not received that training in character which the public schools alone can give. . . . The workman has been told, and undoubtedly believes, up and down the country, that some employers and traders are making vast profits out of his necessities. The facts may be true or false; the belief in the facts is indisputable." (162)

Other damning sentiments followed: Sir George Young complained to his son Hilton in 1914 that "among the poor and ignorant, the uprising of the proper spirit is slow work" (qtd. in Wilson 164). Seditious reports that accused the working class of not supporting the war—either by joining the colors or by working in the factories—capitalized on cultural and class stereotypes, and obscured and even ignored the prevailing evidence that it was the working class specifically that was fueling the war effort at home. Moreover, after the introduction in 1915 of the National Register and the Derby scheme, and the subsequent move to compulsory conscription, it could be said that the working classes were fueling the war at the front, too.

Stanley Aronowitz points out in *The Politics of Identity: Class, Culture, Social Movements* that historically such charges against the working class during wartime are common and that the working class often is derided for its apathy and its lack of militancy or for its sheepish acquiescence to the policies of its government. He writes:

> Early criticisms of the centrality of the proletariat as historical agent of systematic transformation are centered, almost exclusively, on the practical activities of the working classes in major capitalist struggles for reforms and, most distressing, the support of socialist and labor parties for the war policies of

their own governments in both world wars (although the struggle against fascism was of a different kind than the First World War). (179)

Aronowitz notes that critics often generalize about a de-radicalized wartime working class because they expect the "really existing proletariat" to evolve ineluctably into a revolutionary agent, and then they scold it vigorously when it fails to meet those expectations.

A counterdebate affecting the working classes when they weren't maligned for their apathy toward the war was one that impugned them in other ways—and questioned their growing membership in labor unions. When trade unionists feared that characteristically underpaid women might take jobs away from the men at home, they solicited women's membership in the rank and file and sought to make their wages equal to men's so that women would not cheapen the market as "pocket-money workers." Most working-class women's salaries before the war were so low that they were precluded from joining unions because they were unable or unwilling to maintain the necessary dues schedules, especially since many working-class women already had regular commitments scheduled to "clothing and shoe clubs whereby a group of friends or workmates could pool slender resources for large purchases" (Thom 279). Women made up 10.6 percent of union membership in 1911, though in some unions— such as the General Union of Textile Workers—women made up almost half of the membership in the years leading up to 1914 (Bornat 208). Improvements in women's salaries by 1914 helped to increase the number of women in trade unions, which tripled during the war, rising from 437,000 in 1914 to 1,342,000 by 1920 (Braybon and Summerfield 73). Approximately one-sixth of women workers joined unions during the war, Margaret Brooks notes (15). By 1921, women's membership in unions would grow to 15.1 percent (Lewis 169).

During the war, 17 percent of women workers joined labor unions, primarily over wage or timekeeping issues. Though historians have wondered why so few of the workers looked to unions for support, Deborah Thom rightly asserts that the question should be "not why did so few organize, but why did so many, against such considerable odds?" (261). With one-sixth of the women in war work unionized, the women's working class gained collective bargaining power. Equally important, they acquired a sense of entitlement from their alignment with and solidarity in unions, and this would affect not only their work in the factories but their temporary sense of importance and status in the British workplace. Despite women's participation in Britain's labor unions, and their alignment through membership with the British Trades Union Congress (TUC), women's wages rarely equaled men's during the war. It seems clear that women's unionization was a measure designed to shield the large male membership from unemployment via displacement more than it was a benevolent safeguarding initiative for the women's working class. By the end of the war, women's wages, the hours they spent at work, and the conditions under which they performed were no longer negotiated by union leaders and representatives but were affected and circumscribed by martial law, by DORA restrictions, and by Ministry of Munitions regulations. At a time when women had the opportunity to make a real difference in the character and composition of Britain's national work force, when their membership in industrial labor and trade unions reached an unprecedented high, governmental control of labor swooped in to neutralize the power of the unions.

Since women's participation in unions rewarded them for working within and not against capitalist categories and patriarchal workplace structures, women's alignment with the unions may have contributed to their lack of grand-scale politicism during this period. Antonio Gramsci raised a similar point in 1919 when he pondered the complicity of organized labor in sustaining its own exploitation by accepting and working within the presuppositions of workplace hierarchies. If women were privileged with membership only because of male anxiety and paranoia, emotions made all the more intense by prewar miner's strikes and heavily publicized industrial disputes, one might argue that women were not going to benefit fully from union membership anyway, and that their numbers served only to allay the apprehension of prewar male wage-earners and would not initiate them into the hierarchies of organized labor or earn them the privileges usually associated with membership.

Another issue complicating women's alignment with unions was one circumscribed by their class and status within the factory—most working-class women needed to be aligned with unions for the collective power they offered them, while middle-class women workers could rely on a social power that extended beyond the factories and, just as important, that could rely on some source of income outside the factories. Joan Williams describes in her unpublished memoir how such circumstances worked to splinter groups of workers. While working-class girls at the factory relied on their weekly wages, she wrote, there was another faction of workers who went "out for all [they] could make, while expecting all the kudos of a war worker." For Williams, these were the typical and highly publicized "War-Workers," middle-class women "who were apt to make much more fuss when displeased and complain to the higher authorities, without being able to be frightened by any threat of dismissal" (qtd. in Braybon and Summerfield 76). These women didn't need the unions so much as did their working-class counterparts, who could not rely on haughtiness or right-eous indignation to make gains at the factory.

Women's mass entry into the labor force, as well as their alignment with powerful trade unions and with the TUC, mark the beginnings of what many have called "women's emancipation," though social and cultural historians debate the precise dates of said emancipation. Some would agree with Saywell's comment above. Others would date the emancipation after the war when all British women—not merely those over the age of thirty—achieved the vote. Others would date it earlier or later, and still others might question whether emancipation has yet been achieved by women in the twentieth century, but few would argue with the basic premise of Saywell's point: that the First World War introduced so many cultural changes, especially for women of the working class, that it would be difficult not to recognize its importance to women's history and its role in changing British women's cultural status.

Did such social ladder-climbing exist for women, though, or is the story of women's emancipation more mythic than real, Margaret and Patrice Higonnet ask. In their essay "The Double Helix" they replace the more traditional image of the escalating social ladder with that of a double helix, and suggest that while the labor expected of men and women during the war took them into new territory, work remained separated by gender and women continued to be treated as inferiors to men because of the "constancy of this systemic subordination" (34). They liken the double helix structure to a stock social dance in which "the woman appears to have taken a step forward as the partners change places—but in fact he is still leading her" (35). Penny Summerfield sees "the two sexes ascending the opposed strands of a double helix, keeping their distance, never converging, and moving down again at the end of the war" (5).

When Jane Cox was asked whether she thought the war accomplished anything, she replied "Yes. It learned women to stand on their own feet. It was the turning point for women. Men became a little bit humbler. They weren't the bosses anymore . . . but during the war all women learned and they're still learning" (IWM Sound Archive, Item 705, Reel 4). What exactly did they learn, that generation of working-class women? And what are we, inheritors of their actions and experiences, still learning?

Of their many lessons, one of the first must have been absorbed from their juxtapositioning at the workplace with women from other classes and with women from Britain's dominions overseas. One *Times* reporter prophesied a "social levelling" as a result of the women's mix and proximity at the work site, noting in 1916 that "There is . . . coming about a social levelling—a confraternity of sisterhood." The writer goes on to explain, but his diction—"thrown into contact"—sounds more like a description of middle-class women being thrown to the working-class wolves. He writes: "The titled woman has been thrown into contact with the girl at the lathe, just as Tommy has come into close and often affectionate contact with his officers. They find themselves on a new footing. Battle is a wonderful leveller; so is labour" ("The 1916 Woman," May 18, 1916). The writer's closing oxymoron, "wonderful leveller," appears crudely ironic when applied to battle, but its application is equally inappropriate as a description of the First World War labor site, where stratified hierarchies excluded the possibility of new or equal footing among workers, and where one's class firmly affected her role and work in the factories. Millions of British women entered the working-class labor force during Britain's war against Germany and worked side by side with a significant percentage of British colonial subjects—women attracted to Britain's arsenals and factories from Ireland, Wales, Scotland, Canada, South Africa, and Australia. While scholars such as Angela Woollacott point out the heterogeneity of the women's working class in Britain during the war and herald the fortuitous juxtapositioning in the workplace of different classes and races,[13] work sites often were distinctly hostile environments for those women workers who came from Britain's colonial territories, lured by promises of work, assurances of high wages, and intimations of cosmopolitanism and multicultural integration, as we shall see later in this chapter.

Those entering the work force as novitiates worked on the bench alongside a number of already experienced women industrial workers. It is important to remember that British women did not work en masse for the first time during the First World War, but because so many women were employed during the war in what Margaret Brooks calls "visible" jobs, "working on buses, trains, and delivery vans, in banks and post offices and—in uniform and heavily publicised—in munition and ordnance work," Britons wrongfully assumed that the class of women industrial workers was something new, something born out of the nation's militaristic struggle (6). Thousands of women were employed in textiles and industry before the war, most working part-time and poorly paid, though they soon lost their jobs when the war began, since "industries were disrupted, hotels closed and dressmaking orders were cancelled" (6).

Woollacott, for example, in *On Her Their Lives Depend: Munitions Workers in the Great War,* quotes from the September 1915 Women's Trade Union League report, a document replete with alarming statistics of unemployment and industrial depression brought on by the declaration of war:

Within a few days of the declaration of war tens of thousands of women were without work: in the middle of August whole trades, including the

cotton trade of Lancaster, were at a standstill: a fortnight later it is probable that a majority of women in all industrial occupations were affected,
and to the number of victims there were heavy daily additions. (23)

In July 1914, women made up 36 percent of the industrial work force and
29 percent of Britain's total work force. One month later, Britain's declaration of war would devastate and put out of work tens of thousands of
working-class women, and even as late as July 1918, women would claim
only a modest 1 percent increase (to 37 percent) in the composition of the
industrial work force, according to a 1919 Report of the War Cabinet
Committee on Women in Industry (Griffiths 13).

Important to our understanding of the temperament of the women's
working class during the war, Gareth Griffiths reports that in 1916, 3,000
British factory women were asked whether they wished "after the war to
return to [their] former work or stay in what [they] were doing now":
2,500 preferred to stay in their present jobs; only five hundred wanted to
return to their former work (30). Despite the women workers' overwhelming desire to remain employed in British factories after the war, by
1919 they were pressured to leave their jobs and to return either to their
prewar jobs, if these were still available to them, or to return to the hearth
and home, as Griffiths explains:

> the demobilization of troops forced women out of their jobs and back into
> their 'traditional pre-war areas of work' with their associated low pay and
> poor conditions. The pressure to leave their jobs was enormous, campaigns
> were run in the press to 'persuade' women where their work lay. (31)

With men returning from the front, women's wartime jobs were in
jeopardy—something that frightened and angered women, as the pres-
ident of the Women's Labour League Congress noted early in 1917
when the premonition disturbed her:

> After the war . . . was the woman going back like Joan of Arc to her plough
> and rough menial work? After delivering her country and laying down her
> armour was she going to leave the arena of commerce to lay down her uni-
> form and go back to her pots and kettles, to unpaid and unconsidered
> labour or to the lower alleys of factory work? (Griffiths 30)

No longer confined to the "lower alleys of factory work," women found
their work significantly more palatable during the war than it had been in
previous decades, despite the fact that many serious problems had been
identified in women's labor during the war. While chapter 7 of this book

deals with the women's last year of war service in the factories, what I'd like to examine below are reasons why the factory work might have seemed so palatable to begin with during the war. What did the women find, as early as 1916, so attractive about working in industry? What were their jobs like? What sort of salaries did they draw? How did they spend their money? What were the working conditions, the living conditions, and the social conditions of factory work? What was the character of their work? What was a typical day like for many of them? Why, above all, were they reluctant to leave their posts in industry when there they witnessed the injuries and deaths of so many co-workers, as I describe in chapter 3? Many workers found that their skin turned yellow from handling TNT at the job, or their pillowcases turned pink overnight because of the chemicals that remained trapped on their skin, or they coughed up blood, lost a limb, a set of eyes, fingers. Some saw their hair become bleached at the front from bending over hot acid fumes daily, or they became incontinent, convulsive, or sterile from handling explosive powders. Workers had to endure daily searches on the job, constant standing, dangerously poor workplace lighting, uncomfortably high (or low) room temperatures, and crowded living quarters, for which they paid disproportionately high local rents. Given this, why would more than 80 percent of those interviewed in 1916 prefer to stay on? .

One answer would be the metamorphosing character of women's employment during the war. Prior to the Great Munitions Push of 1915, when Lord Kitchener's call to arms conscripted hundreds of thousands of women into war factories and other essential industries, women's employment was restricted by a number of labor policies that moderated women's pay rates, their work hours, and their opportunities for advancement. Women usually were paid at a piece rate, not a time rate, and they worked part-time with rare opportunities for promotion. Moreover, many employers before the war refused to hire married women, since it was believed that married women didn't "need" to work to support their families but had husbands who could do that. Hiring a woman meant (as it still does) *not* hiring a man, and the unions kept a watchful eye on employers who hired women because their hiring, like that of boys, threatened the wages and the job security of the adult male work force.

Women who were hired in prewar industry worked part-time and received egregiously low wages for their labor, since the sex-segregated pay scales that would erode somewhat during the war were squarely in place and were "respected" by employers looking to save on employee wages. Women who worked outside of industry, but not in domestic service, often worked at home and were contracted workers who were paid piece-rate wages. Complicating this were wage fixing policies, Lewis explains in

Women in England 1870–1950, the "tendency to fix women's pay without particular regard to the skill or intelligence required but rather in relation to a notional women's rate (of about 10/- to 12/- [shillings] a week in 1906), or as a fixed percentage of the male rate" (167). What Lewis makes clear in her discussion of fixed wages is a point that Beatrice Webb noted in 1919 when she criticized the Majority Report of the War Cabinet Committee on Women in Industry, namely that "paid employment was assumed to be the prerogative of the male." Webb argued:

> To concentrate the whole attention of the readers of the Report upon the employment of women past, present and future and upon their physiological and social needs, without any corresponding survey of the employment of men and of their physiological and social needs, is to assume, perhaps inadvertently, that industry is normally a function of the male, and that women, like non-adults, are only to be permitted to work for wages at special hours, for special rates of wages, under special supervision and subject to special restrictions of the Legislature. I cannot accept this assumption. (Lewis 172)

In attacking the cultural assumption of male license, of male privilege to paid employment, Webb suggests that the issue of male entitlement deliberately distracts from issues of women's work in the factories, their safety, and the conditions of the workplace. While these issues were being debated—whether women should work at all, whether their labor should be physically demanding and exacting, what their wages should be, and so forth—women continued to perform extremely demanding and physical industrial work.

Like these debates, the onset of war had little effect on the difficulty of women's work in industry. It remained physically demanding. It was strenuous, laborious, exacting, and exhausting. Though women's work in industry surely had been difficult prior to 1914, the women's working class lacked the attention and the acclaim of the national press who, until the declaration of war, saw nothing sensational in the women's daily grind. To working-class women who made up 36 percent of the industrial labor force before the war, the strain of factory work was not so new as the popular congratulations were. The writer of a 1913 Factory Inspectorate Annual Report, for example, described prewar work in the china and earthenware trade as alarmingly strenuous: "The foreman at one of these works said to me," the writer notes, "'There is no work so hard as this throughout the country,' and I am sure he is right" (qtd. in Griffiths 83). The 1913 report describes women who carried wads of clay weighing 48 pounds each; in the brickworks, they were found pushing barrows weighing 306 pounds and 425 pounds. "These would be lifted as part of the work all day long," the report continues. Women who worked this hard in 1913 worked equally as hard in 1916; what was different, what was new, was the attention, not the strain. Though their work would exhaust them, and send them home after agonizing nine and three-quarter-hour shifts, women voiced a preference in 1916 to keep their present jobs rather than return to those they held before the war. Why?

The editor of the 1917 service newspaper *Bombshell: The Official Organ of the N[ational] P[rojectile] F[actory] Templeboro* sums up in the premiere issue of the in-house journal the exhaustion of factory work and the monotony of the women's daily grind: "For most of us, life has re-solved itself into a battlefield on which Shells and Sleep, Sleep and Shells alternately hold the mastery" (1.1 [Mar. 1917]:16). This description sup-ports one given in the BBC film *We Are the Arsenal Girls*, which also dis-cusses the exhaustion of women workers, noting that they often skipped their daily tea break so they might lie down on or under their work-benches to sleep. More examples abound. Dorothy G. Poole, in the ac-count of her career from a munition worker to a Dilution Officer at the Ministry of Munitions (IWM Department of Printed Books, Women's Work Microfilm Collection Item #MUN 17/1) wrote of the considerable strain exacted by the work: "girls came off the unaccustomed three-hour shift looking just as drawn as they did off a five-hour shift later on. For myself, I found the muscular strain worse than the standing and fatigue, and it was weeks before the stiffness wore off—stiffness that made every muscle tender to the touch" (1). Despite the arduousness of the work, women performed astonishing well, not only during great pushes or drives but working through weekends and bank holidays as well. Their production was nothing short of phenomenal.

Hall Caine, of the Munitions Contracts Department, Ministry of Mu-nitions, wrote on June 18, 1918 of the extraordinary output of women munition workers at the Newbury depot during Easter Week that year:

> During what was to be Easter holiday in 1918, the Germans commenced their 'push,' a push that broke through the 5th Army, pushing the men back and costing the British lots of materials. Charles W Segrave, Ministry of Munitions, wrote that the women stayed at work through the holiday working 9 3/4 hour shifts, handling 1.80 tons per hour each, for a total of 17 and a half tons per day for seven days. (IWM Department of Printed Books, Women's Work Microfilm Collection Item #MUN 5/2).

At the Sutton Glassworks, St. Helen's, workers known affectionately to other munitions factory workers as the "Lancashire Lasses" worked equally as hard, according to a memorandum on file at the IWM: "A gang of six girls will unload and stack in a day ten wagons of Shell equalling a hundred tons of material. They will stack 9.2″ Shells (each of which weighs 250 lbs.) on their bases to a height of three layers" (IWM Department of Printed Books, Women's Work Microfilm Collection Item #MUN 6/2; author's name blacked out). If these are accurate descriptions of the workers' lives—battlefields of shells and sleep, sleep and shells—why, then, did they say they would prefer to keep their jobs at the end of this war? Any why, in June 1918, did thousands of women march to Westminster to demand the right to keep their factory jobs?

In his discussion of the march, cultural historian John Williams focuses not on the historical significance of the 1918 event but on what the marchers were or were not wearing in the procession, highlighting one observer's remark about the women's lack of petticoats, for example. The women, Williams writes,

> marched through London, representing all branches of women's war work. The parade of uniforms—from those of the para-military and nursing services to those of the bus conductorettes, the brown-smocked, gaitered Land Army girls with their cockaded hats, the brown-jacketed girl foresters in their bright green caps, the white-gowned munitionettes—made a colourful sight. Amid all this workmanlike garb, feminine dress had sustained one wartime casualty. An observer noted that there was not one petticoat to be seen. (253)

Indeed, the pair of women's marches that frame the dates of the First World War tell a significant story and encase episodes of women's history in which the answers to the usual questions are often as complex as the questions themselves and emerge from the women's sense of accomplishment, their sense of cultural engagement, and their sense of work-site camaraderie. Most often, the rigors of factory work supplied the women with a sense of achievement and agency outside the confines of the home, something quite valuable and new to them in British patriarchal culture, especially since working-class women's roles had been culturally prescribed, economically imposed, and deemed historically listless. Theirs was most often a world that established men as primary historical actors, not to mention breadwinners, a world that was circumscribed by household drudgery, child bearing and child rearing, one that was complicated by inadequate nutrition, large family size, and lackluster overcrowded housing that gave them little privacy. For those women who worked before the war, their work was de facto exhausting and undercompensated, since they worked under labor policies that had been squarely in place by the nineteenth century, even though those policies had undergone some significant change by the early twentieth century. Each time a woman stepped into the work force, she tried and tested the limits of time-honored notions invented to keep her off the job and at home. Often, these time-honored notions stratified the male work force, too, and worked to justify wage hierarchies and salary indiscretions as well at the factories. With women's mass entry into skilled labor during the war, these stratifications extended to and affected their wages and opportunities on the job. One such abstraction was the apprenticeship myth, that a master worker needed to train a minimally paid apprentice for several years before that apprentice could replace him successfully. Women toppled the apprenticeship myth almost immediately once they entered the work force and quickly learned the ropes, the ins and outs, and the ways and whims of the heavy and massive machinery they operated. They learned quickly and mastered jobs that "normally required a term of apprenticeship which would exceed the period of the war," Griffiths notes (24). Walter Greenwood's novel *Love on the Dole* contains some discussion of the apprenticeship system, and points to the role working women played during the war to expose the inequities of the system. Greenwood wrote in 1933:

"You're part of a graft, Harry;" he said: "All Marlowe's want is cheap labour; the apprentice racket is one of their ways of getting it. Nobody teach you anything simply because there's so little to be learnt. You'll pick up all you require by asking questions and watching others work. . . . Your apprenticeship's a swindle, Harry. The men they turn out think they're engineers same as they do at all the other places, but they're only machine minders. Don't you remember the women in the war?"

"What women?" Harry asked, troubled by what Larry had said.

"The women who took the places of the engineers who'd all served their time. The women picked up straight away what Marlowe's and other say it takes seven years' apprenticeship to learn."

As Greenwood intimates, women's entry into and success in skilled labor clearly risked the exposure of labor practices that for centuries justified wage discrepancies in the workplace, policies that not only rationalized worker exploitation but exposed employer greed. More important, it would become clear that prewar workers complicitously upheld these structures, that it was oddly enough consensual, and that within the stable social order of the factories there existed a substratum of agreement so powerful that it counteracted the divisions and disruptions of outside forces—in this case, the conflicting interests of women workers. As Judith

Lorber explains, even "the not-so-privileged also have an investment in a going social order that gives them some bargaining power" (10).

Robert Roberts recalls in *The Classic Slum* the day the myth of his father's magisterial work skills was usurped by a young woman worker who pulled back the veil from the mysterious greatness of the job. Roberts writes that his father

> was wont to boast that, at the lathe, he had to manipulate a micrometer and work to limits of one thousandth of an inch. We were much impressed, until one evening in 1917 a teenage sister running a capstan in the iron works remarked indifferently that she, too, used a 'mike' to even finer limits. There was, she said, 'nothing to it.' The old man fell silent. Thus did status crumble. (215)

Even those workers who were not consciously undermining the apprenticeship myth succeeded in eroding notions of "indispensable" male workers. A *Times* reporter noted in 1916, for example, that "A woman has been placed in London as a guillotine cutter in the cardboard trade. This is particularly interesting, as cardboard box firms frequently report that the men in this work are indispensable and that without them the plant would be necessarily idle" ("Women for Men," *Times* Sept. 15, 1916).

In an effort to protect at all costs the apprenticeship myth, along with their complicity in upholding the substratum that regulated their wage earning in the factories, some male co-workers turned to sabotage and would steal women co-workers' tools, nail their work desks shut, or spill contents from desk drawers, as many women document in their service newspapers and attest in their oral histories, as I discuss in chapter 4. These boring unpleasantries complicated and confounded women's daily performance on the job and likely led to higher rates of employee lateness and to frequent dismissals. Griffiths, for example, reports that

> Although a range of agreements was made on the use of women throughout the war, opposition to women being employed in industries previously dominated by men continued and took many forms. A woman tool fitter reported several instances of harrassment by her fellow male workers: 'My drawer was nailed up by the men, and oil was poured over everything through a crack another night.' While another woman who worked in an engineering works recalled 'I was sacked. There was a man who chewed tobacco and kept spitting in my pocket and I hit him.' There is little doubt that the women had to contend with the strong feeling, largely shared by the employer and the male workers, that they had no business to be in the factories at all. Their failures therefore produced a far greater psychological

impression than their successes; and failures which were the fault of management or of the skilled supervision were readily attributed to them. (21)

Compounding these difficulties that readily attributed women's "failures" on the job to their lack of skills, initiation ceremonies and rituals also affected and hampered women's performance on the job. In the 1978 memoir of her years as a munition maker, Peggy Hamilton recalls in *Three Years or the Duration* a series of orientation rituals orchestrated by her male co-workers:

> I remember showers of steel shavings pouring down on me from the gallery above as I worked at my lathe. Another time, as I was bending over my machine, a great wad of cotton waste, stuck with shavings and dripping with oil, caught me right in the face. (51)

Scrupulous meanness, brought on by severe anxiety, likely moved to action these saboteurs, who feared the consequences of displacement, exposure, and cultural ridicule, and who jealously guarded and subsequently fought to protect their work privileges and their privilege to work.

Caroline Rennles explains in her oral history narrative that apart from her interaction with hostile men bent on protecting their strangely won privileges at the work site, and in addition to putting up with their shenanigans at work, the rigors of factory work kept her especially on her toes. Most difficult, she recalls, were the work schedules and the production expectations set for women in the factory. They rarely were forgiven for being late to the job and often were expected to exceed unsurpassable production quotas, Rennles says. These expectations, combined with threats of being let go, increased women's anxiety on the job. Rennles says:

> If we wasn't there by half past seven in the morning they used to send us back to London, throw us out for the day, you see. . . . Anyhow, now our wages as far as I can remember, love, was thirty shillings a week but I think they used to give us five shillings a week for our fare and five shillings bonus if you could fill sixty shells a day. So you had to fill sixty. If you didn't. . . . (Imperial War Museum Sound Archive, Item SR 566, Transcript 3)

The desire for higher wages and the pressure to perform often led to a sort of industrial frenzy, though such a phenomenon was often regulated and sometimes legislated in house, as one correspondent for the *Times* notes in 1918:

> The girls were so anxious to get the utmost output that at the beginning of the shift or after the midday break they would sometimes start a machine

cutting into steel before the main driving motors had reached sufficient speed to take the strain. [One particular shell shop posted the sign,] "Warning. Anyone starting a machine before the bell has been rung will be instantly dismissed." ("Dilution and Greater Output," *Times,* June 24, 1918)

The women's industrial frenzy, their "anxious[ness] to get the most output," was often the result of the way in which the women's pay rates were figured. Jane Lewis explains, for example, that pay rates often were calculated using complex piece-work rates; so complicated were they, in fact, that workers had no idea what their paychecks would look like at the end of a shift, and from Lewis' description of the calculation process, women needed to invent a logarithm just to anticipate their earnings:

> Women munition workers during World War I were allowed a certain number of hours for the job and the worker finishing it just in time received the basic rate. The worker finishing the job in less time received in addition a bonus on output, or premium bonus, equivalent to one half (or some other fixed proportion) of the basic rate for each hour saved. Thus the employer extracted from the worker a piecework effort at a timework rate without having to go through the difficult process of reducing the piece rate. Many women employed under these systems could only guess at what they might receive by way of payment at the end of the week. (165)

Whereas Caroline Rennles recalls that her wages averaged only forty shillings per week, other workers interviewed by the Imperial War Museum remembered higher salaries, often as high as £4 per week. As the great munitions drive moved forward under Lord Kitchener's direction, longer hours, mandatory overtime, holiday shift work and six-day work weeks benefited the women's salaries while contributing at the same time to their eventual exhaustion. Pressure from the government to produce escalated their exhaustion. Dorothy Goldman notes that "at the height of the war, Colonel Joffre remarked, 'If the women in war factories stopped for 20 minutes we should lose the War.' Nor was the situation any different in Germany" (*Women Writers and the Great War* 13).

As salaries climbed, so, too, did the number of women drawn to munitions work; and with higher numbers of women working in Britain's smaller, local districts, the demand for housing the workers became a growing problem, developing into a subject of hearty and animated discussion in the press, in public meetings, and among church groups. In the *Times* article "War-Time Housing Problems," one journalist describes a London meeting called to discuss the housing crisis aggravated by increasing numbers of temporary women workers in the community:

Lady Proctor spoke of the difficulties of housing women since the war, mentioning that in some munition areas the girls had to occupy the same beds that had been occupied by other girls on different shifts, and in some cases even those vacated by men. In London the housing problem was acute. At the beginning of the war there were 27,000 women clerks employed; now there were over 100,000. Many of these girls had come up from the country quite ignorant, and it was essential that they should have housing with an atmosphere of home. (*Times,* May 18, 1916)

With their number of residents nearly quadrupling during the war, many districts sought to accommodate workers in private homes or hostels. The *Times* reports:

> Where women are drafted into a new district in great numbers it is the business of these committees to see to their housing, and appeals are made to well-to-do people who have never let rooms to accommodate workers, some of these appeals being printed and distributed even in the churches. In a few centres, such as Coventry, there are big clearing hostels, to which the women can go on arrival. In one district where there were 6,000 women employed before the war there are now over 20,000, and they have come in parties from Plymouth, Bristol, Jersey, Wales and the Potteries. (*Times,* Sept. 15, 1916)

Apart from the overcrowding and its concurrent problems, many communities sensed another immediate danger and feared that the influx of women in the town, and more importantly, on the Common, might invite something more unpalatable—prostitution and its related complications.

The fear intensified. For example, in a *Times* article titled "Lonely Girl Workers," the correspondent notes that

> war work has brought large numbers of girls into Ealing and the neighborhood. They are only temporary residents, and many of them have no local friends or associations. The consequence is that they find a difficulty in spending their leisure time to advantage. The sight of these girls wandering aimlessly about the streets and on the Common during the evening has aroused sympathy among the inhabitants of Ealing. . . . There should be places where the girls can rest and be entertained. (April 17, 1918)

The writer continues, noting that at the Ealing meeting the town council reported that the "experience of the Common after dusk would suggest the possibility of the existence in the future of an undesirable state of things" (*Times,* April 17, 1918). Woollacott points out the irony of the widespread fear and notes that women's salaries during the war precluded many from needing to rely on prostitution to make ends meet (130–31). As I discuss in chapter 2, rumors of working women's sexual promiscuity circulated widely during the war and spread with such a degree of intensity that many women found themselves haunted by innuendo and suggestion long after the war had ended.

Whereas widespread cultural fear about women's sexuality made the housing situation one of the more frequently addressed problems on the home front during the war, there was also the immediate problem of women's health, a problem complicated by the diversity and heterogeneity of the new working class and its influx into many of Britain's smaller districts. Thus, one of the first experiences to which new industry workers were introduced was the institutionalized inoculation regimen.

Ruby Ord recalls in her oral history that "During the two weeks training we were also inoculated twice, and vaccinated—inoculated and vaccinated in one morning, so that quite a lot of the girls went down like ninepins" (IWM Sound Archive, Item SR 044, Transcript 4). The inoculation system looked as if it were patterned after familiar first-day-of-school routines and in many ways seemed invented under the same auspices; mass inoculation seemed the most efficient way to safeguard the health of Britain's heterogeneous work force, since so many of the women hailed not only from distant cities and districts but from other countries as well, including Belgium. Britain's call to work extended to women in Ireland, Wales, Scotland, Canada, and South Africa, and as colonial subjects populated local districts, hostels and work sites, mass immunization seemed a more pressing issue.

By mid-1914, over 2 million women were employed in British industry, and by July 1918 that figure had risen to nearly 3 million. By the end of the war, women munition workers numbered 900,000, and those in clothing and textile manufacturing numbered nearly as many (Griffiths 13–14). These figures, while startling, enumerate only England's women workers, and indicate little about women from Ireland, Canada, Australia, South Africa, and Belgium, for example, who joined the ranks of the working during Britain's call to serve from 1914 to 1918. Woollacott notes that "Britain's far-flung empire had made it possible for a small number of West Indians, Asians, and Africans to arrive on British shores and to form scattered communities," and adds that there were "at least a few women of color" working at the cordite factory in South Wales (39). These women emigrated to join a work force often hostile to and unforgiving of their race, dialect, manners, and level of education. They also found themselves maligned and "blackened" in the popular fiction of the day. Sharon Ouditt in *Fighting Forces, Writing Women* traces one such "coarse-looking, brown-skinned girl" who appears as a fictionalized villain in novels about the working class during this period (85–86).

Though dozens of women workers specifically were called to serve from Ireland, for example, lured into Britain's munition factories and its clothing and textile plants by a vigorous propaganda campaign aimed at Ireland's single women, remarkably little information exists on Irish working-class women's experience of the First World War. Attracted to the dangerous work by the promise of high wages—higher than those paid in the six Irish munition factories in Dublin or in other munition factories in the North (Woollacott 30, 38)—Irish women from the north and south must have found that working for Britain's war effort was an easily accessible mode of emigration from their troubled country, especially before the Defence of the Realm Acts limited and then restricted Irish emigration. In fact, that is how war work was marketed: Irish daughters were urged to leave their families so that they would no longer burden the finances of those at home, and they were promised enough money to be able to send a significant portion of the wages back to their Irish families across the sea. Romanced by poster images of the glamorous and cosmopolitan British war worker and by promises of wealth, independence, and world peace—World War I was billed as the "war to end wars"—unknown numbers of young Irish women were seduced into working for the war effort on Britain's behalf.

What Irish workers found upon their arrival in England was "sweated" labor supervised by hostile, racist, and cruel managers. Attitudes towards Irish working-class women no doubt were influenced by labor's general contempt for the Irish working class, who, since the 1840s, had been perceived as a substratum of the British working-class community. As Carl Chinn notes in *Poverty Amidst Prosperity,* even Friedrich Engels held the Irish working class in contempt for "surviving on the minimum necessaries of life and for bringing with them filth and drunkenness" (65). Though Chinn adds that some of the greatest Chartists and trade union leaders were Irish, and that "British incomes were little affected by Irish migrants" (66), those women who came over to England for war work had to brave centuries of anti-Irish sentiment and hostility.

Their work weeks of 82 and even 92 hours were common, though illegal, and rarely prosecuted. Like other workers, the Irish women worked six-day shifts and were scheduled to work at least one or two Sundays out of three. Compounding the workers' dismay were the rat-infested work areas often assigned to them, freezing work temperatures, lackluster on-site facilities, and inordinately expensive lodgings rarely closer than a 25–minute walk from the work site. *The Women's Dreadnought* throughout 1914 published allegations that women working for government contractors were working at sweated rates of pay, and printed the following condemnation that year:

Jamesons' of Poplar, Government contractors, pay women 2s. 1d. a dozen for making soldiers' shirts. One woman who has been making boys' shirts for 2s. 6d. a dozen, to be sold to private firms, tells us that she refused Government work until there was no more private work to do. She tells us that the soldiers' shirts, besides being paid at lower rates, are larger and more complicated than others, and are of harsh stuff that makes the women's fingers sore. The shirts are dark and the cotton black, and the work therefore tries the eyes a good deal. The women can only manage to do a dozen shirts a day, by working very hard and out of the 2s. 1d. they earn by this, they have to pay 2 1/2d. a reel for cotton—a reel does not do quite a dozen shirts . . . strange patriotism this, that allows the Government contractors who are making money out of this war to sweat the women workers in this disgraceful fashion. (qtd. in Griffiths 17)

Apart from these conditions at the job, outside the factory women's lives were no less severe. Housing, for example, was in such short supply that unscrupulous landlords often rented rooms to one group of workers by day, and another by night, irrespective of the workers' genders. Because the rooms were constantly in use they were rarely aired out. In specially designed hostels for immigrant war workers, the same beds were slept in almost continuously, and bed-sharing, too, was common. One English worker, Lilian Miles, described a housing scene she and her sister came upon in Coventry: "Girls were all over the place there, and a lot of Irish girls there. It seems as if they bundled in and didn't bother, you know. They just didn't seem to bother. There were six sleeping in that one bed, six, you know. And there was me and my sister got this single bed. . . . It was a filthy place" (Imperial War Museum Sound Archive, Item SR 854, Transcript 10). Though many of the Irish workers opted to stay in temporary hostels and huts built by the government near some of the larger factories, the lodging was expensive there, too, even in the wake of the 1915 Rent and Mortgage Protection Act.

Isabella Clarke, an Irish woman who left Ireland at age 16 to work at White Lund's in Lancashire making gas shells, soon transferred to the Royal Ordnance Works in the working-class district of Coventry. There she paid the disproportionate sum of 15 shillings a week for her hostel accommodation near the Coventry Ordnance Factory.[14] True to the advertisements that lured her, Isabella Clarke regularly sent £1 to her mother in Ireland as well as 5 shillings a week to her grandmother (Imperial War Museum Sound Archive, Item SR 774, Reel 2). When the war was over, Clarke returned to Ireland an experienced industrial worker, but unlike millions of her British female counterparts, she was hired in a permanent postwar position—a "man's job," she called it, dressing flax (Reel 4). Clarke's experiences as an Irish woman working in one of

Britain's Royal Ordnance Works have been captured and recorded by London's Imperial War Museum Oral History Collection on Women and Work. Though I will not focus specifically or solely on her experiences, Clarke's recollections are valuable because, though isolated, they represent the *Irish* experience, and her voice—joined below with the voices of other working-class women in First World War Britain—cautions us that there is still much we do not know about Irish women, World War I, and the patriate and expatriate women's working classes in Britain.

No one has yet explored, for example, how working for the war effort in Britain was a venue of emigration for young Irish women, nor has anyone linked the phenomena sufficiently with theories of Irish emigration or specified it as a *special class* of emigration, connecting it to appropriate statistics of the day. Whether the women served for the money or whether they were lured to Britain to work against the Germans in Britain's "holy war" (especially after the 1915 sinking of the *Lusitania*), manufacturing munitions, clothing, and textiles for Britain during the First World War was one way for Irish daughters to leave home as legitimately as their brother and sister counterparts had done during the surge of postfamine emigration. This is not to suggest that it was an easy decision or that it was culturally sanctioned: Britain's vigorous propaganda campaign in Ireland was heavily countered by Sinn Féin, for example, who distributed its own versions of the persuasive "5 Questions" and "5 Reasons" pamphlets in response to Britain's influential brochures, and who produced parodies of British war posters, defiantly renaming the British "Defence of the Realm Act" the "Pretence of the Realm Act," for example (O'Brien 256).[15] Antiwar sentiment, blended as it was in 1914 with vehement anti-British sentiment, produced in Ireland an atmosphere hostile to and unsympathetic toward emigrating Irish women war workers. Because of this, the Irish women's working class in Britain often had to negotiate between the criticism of two contentious and aggressive cultural forces; not only were they despised by those at home for their choice (a choice often equated in Irish anti-British propaganda with "taking the soup"), but they met with similar effrontery overseas and were derided and confronted regularly by their British co-workers, as I explain below.

It is important to contextualize the situation of the Irish working class even further, especially in light of the labor situation in Ireland leading up to the First World War. Just one year after the Irish Women's Workers Union had been formed and affiliated to the Irish Trades Union Congress (1912), the Irish working class suffered a year of tremendous upheaval. The year 1913, the "*annus terribilus* of the Dublin working class" (O'Brien 222), saw more than thirty separate labor disputes involving some 2,200 Dublin workers between January and mid-August, and the infamous August 26 tramway strike set off a series of strikes and lockouts throughout the city. Joseph O'Brien notes in *Dear Dirty Dublin, A City in Distress, 1899–1916* that "the remarkable thing about the strike of August 26th was not only the rapidity with which it spread to other trades but also the aggressive unity of the employers against [James] Larkin and the ITGWU [Irish Transport and General Workers' Union]" (225). Riots, including the notorious Sunday melée in O'Connell Street, spread throughout the city. By September 1913, some "20,000–25,000 Dublin citizens [were] out of work, representing along with dependents at least one-quarter of the city's population" (O'Brien 234). To minimize the likelihood of what was being called "settlement by starvation," shipments of food began arriving in Dublin at the south wall of the River Liffey in late September. The cargo of the S. S. *Hare*, for example, co-sponsored by the British Trades Union Congress, provided "some 60,000 packages of butter, sugar, tea, bread, jam, potatoes, fish and biscuits" (O'Brien 234) for starving Dublin strikers and their families, an act that continued through January, even though the British TUC rejected Larkin's call for a sympathetic strike in support of the Dublin workers. Dublin and Belfast bakeries donated some 12,000 loaves of bread, as well, to feed Larkin's union. So efficient was James Larkin in distributing food and strike pay (5 shillings per week) to his union members that the Poor Law Guardians of the South Dublin Union reported at their year-end meeting in 1913 that the local workhouse contained 355 fewer pauper children than it had in the previous year (O'Brien 237), a propitious but ironic statistic set among the others of 1913.

When the 22–week strike ended in late January, just seven months before Britain's entry into the First World War, Dublin's social and economic life had been crippled. Nearly two million days of paid production were lost, and the Irish working class was not only destitute but dispirited. As O'Brien further comments:

> The working class, or rather the 12,000 or so men and women of the Transport Union allied to several thousand more in other organizations, had . . . suffered cruelly. They and their families had endured loss of wages, lack of food, the abuse of their pastors, the batons of the police and, for the unfortunate few, the toils of imprisonment. Some others faced the choice of seeking work in England or continued poverty at home due to unemployment: as late as the end of March 1914 it was estimated that 4,000 workers still awaited reinstatement in their former jobs. (237)

Moreover, O'Brien notes that "Dublin, having emerged from a war of the classes, soon had to adjust to the war of nations" (239).

While some Irish women worked in Dublin making shirts under War Office contracts, employment opportunities looked increasingly more optimistic in England. Since there were no restrictions upon Irish movement or employment within the United Kingdom early in the war, Irish workers could seek English work abroad. Though protected by her declared neutrality, Ireland's engagement in the war at all levels affected her working class, and moved Larkin's successor, James Connolly, to argue that nothing but "A great continental uprising of the working class would stop the war" (*Selected Writings* 25). No such uprising occurred, but one similar in spirit took place on April 25, 1918, when the Irish working class responded to the renewed threat of Irish conscription by staging a general strike that proved so successful in its magnificence and bravado that the British government withdrew the threat. This, then, was the political and economic situation of the working class in Ireland at the onset of the First World War. Motivated by a host of social, economic, cultural, and political circumstances at home, empowered by their strength and size but disempowered by lackluster labor policies and British colonialism, Irish women and men sought work in England's war factories at a steady, though ultimately unknowable, rate. While wartime England had a seemingly built-in infrastructure for civilian record-keeping, and the money, too, to keep and maintain proper civilian records, the Irish had neither the British sense of "clerkishness" nor the finances to do the same. Many travel and employment records, if they were written at all, no longer survive today.

In addition to oral history recordings that describe the conditions and treatment of Irish working-class women workers, and police diaries that record narrative accounts of frequent and aggravated rioting between Irish and English workers at the factories, women workers also produced a variety of industry newspapers during the war, newspapers that were written and published in-house by women working for the war effort in Britain. Nowhere is the rift between Irish and English workers more clear than in the writings and literary parodies published in the women's service newspapers, service magazines, and souvenir issues; nowhere are the dangerous working conditions more acutely described; and nowhere exists a more heart-wrenching litany of the haunting memories that attended the years from 1914 to 1918 for Irish immigrant war workers, as we shall see in chapter 4.

From the oral histories and Irish testimonies that survive, for example, we learn that many of the Irish women war workers were considered by their supervisors and co-workers to be boisterous and disorderly. Importantly, the characteristic rowdiness in the munition factories often was blamed on the influx of women and girls who were recruited to England from elsewhere—Ireland, Australia, South Africa, and Belgium. Gabrielle West patrolled a number of British war factories while she was a member of the British Women's Police Service, and her diary (housed in the IWM) frequently describes the tension and hostility between British and Irish women workers in the factories. In the following passage, for example, West describes the immigrant women workers as a clamorous lot and suggests that they fled to England not for political or economic reasons but to avoid cultural, even criminal, reprimand. She writes,

> They had made things too hot for themselves at home, and were the roughest of the rough. [They are] a great trial. They steal like magpies, fight, get up scandalous tales about each other, strike, and do their best to paint things red. (Brown 209)

West describes the immigrant work force as "girls who stormed around, yelled, shrieked, threw mud, and so on" (Brown 209), and notes in her diary that the rows and the fights got so bad and became so unmanageable and unpredictable that the only thing to do was pack up the Irish women and ship them all back home.

Summoned to intervene when rioting broke out between English and Irish women workers at the Hereford shell-filling factory in 1917, for example, Gabrielle West later recalled the events in a diary entry dated August 30, 1917:

> Some time ago several lots of Irish girls were taken on to work in the Amatol. There has been a lot of bad blood between them & the English. The Irish sang Sinn Fein songs & made offensive remarks about the Tommies. The English replied in kind. Each side waxed very wroth. The Irish wore orange & green, & the English Red white and blue. This went on for weeks. . . . Last week during the dinner hour, an English girl accused an Irish girl of stealing her dinner. The Irish girl replied by spitting in the English girl's face. There was a battle, all the others standing round & cheering on the combatants. We were called in to separate them. . . . Next evening scenting trouble 8 or 9 of us went down to see the shift train off from Hereford station. A tremendous battle ensued on the platform between about 20 Irish & the rest of the shift. (Woollacott 43–44)

That the Irish women workers were singing Sinn Féin songs suggests that British "patriotism" was not one of the stronger motivating factors for Irish women's entry into the British work force. Clearly, the Irish women retained their allegiance to a country to which they were soon returned, as Woollacott notes, since "the trouble [at Hereford] was only settled by the Irish women being sent back to Ireland the following day" (44). Not all Irish workers were deported, though. Caroline Rennles recalls that in 1919, on the day she and thousands of other women workers marched to Westminster to protest losing their jobs, a young Irish worker assaulted a policeman's horse on Westminster Bridge. "We ran for our life," she said (Imperial War Museum Sound Archive, Item SR 566, Reel 4).

Hostilities in the British war factories, amply recorded by diarist Gabrielle West, as well as those described by ambulance driver Alice Christobel Remington who was in Ireland during the Armistice,[16] created tensions that not only resulted in fighting, rioting, striking, and mudslinging but also created traceable analogues in the published writings of the women workers, especially in their newspapers and souvenir magazines.

During the course of my research, I have become increasingly aware of the gap in the documentation of the contributions and experiences of the hundreds of Irish women who answered Britain's call to serve during the First World War. Already more than 80 years have passed without significant attention to this issue. It seems important to verify, for example, how the Irish women workers were transported to Britain and to note who paid for their passage. What evidence is there of their experiences in the form of popular songs or cartoons, newspaper accounts, diaries, memoirs, autobiographies? Have they left traces of their experiences in popular culture? How many of them lost their lives working in the "danger rooms" of Britain's arsenals, and where were they buried? How many died from TNT poisoning, from black powder, khaki, asbestos, tetryl, lyddite, or emery poisoning? How many of the dozens of transported Irish daughters lost limbs at the hands of impulsive doctors or heavy machinery and pressing lathes? How many of them fell prey to the flu epidemic that swept across Britain in 1917? How many of them contracted and eventually died from tuberculosis, the rise in which was noticed only a few years after the war? How many of them were "lost" in a broader sense to their families? And when the war ended, did the women return to Ireland, remain in Britain, or emigrate elsewhere—to the United States, for example? A genuine sense of urgency attends these questions, since the longer we wait to gather and collect this information, the more quickly it will elude us.

Women who entered the work force as Isabella Clarke did at the beginning of the war at the age of 16, for example, are nearly 100 years old if they are still alive today. Presently, there is no separate information available on Irish women who, like Clarke, emigrated to join the British work force. Without strong measures being taken to uncover the voices of those marginalized and particularly vulnerable expatriate workers, the character of their particular experiences will continue to attenuate until it is written out of British history, and what little information exists will serve only, and at best, to supplement the annals and chronicles rather than revise them.

To be sure, little is known about the expatriate women's working class in Britain during the war, and while much more has been written about the domestic women's working class in Britain, many historians continue to study and publish on the male experiences of the war. Searching the indices of First World War histories and studies, one can't help feeling a bit like Virginia Woolf, who scoured countless indices of books for information on women and came up with little to go on from the library's male sources. Woolf explains in *A Room of One's Own:*

> To show the state of mind I was in, I will read you a few of them, explaining that the page was headed quite simply, WOMEN AND POVERTY, in block letters; but what followed was something like this:
> *Condition in the Middle Ages of,*
> *Habits in the Fiji Islands of,*
> *Worshipped as goddesses by,*
> *Weaker in the moral sense than,*
> *Idealism of,*
> *Greater conscientiousness of,*
> *South Sea Islanders, age of puberty among,*
> *Attractiveness of,*
> *Offered as sacrifice to,*
> *Small brain size of,* . . .
> *Less hair on the body of,* . . .
> *Shakespeare's opinion of,*
> *Lord Birkenhead's opinion of,*
> *Dean Inge's opinion of,*
> *La Bruyere's opinion of,*
> *Dr. Johnson's opinion of,*
> *Mr. Oscar Browning's opinion of* . . .
> I could not possibly go home, I reflected, and add as a serious contribution to the study of women and fiction that women have less hair on their bodies than men. (28–30)

Where women are mentioned in male histories of the war, it is sometimes within a context such as John Williams places them, in which he describes their 1918 march according to what the women marchers wore or didn't wear; or they are mentioned briefly, or claim only one or two entries in an index. Where women's contributions are given thick descriptions, these segments normally make up a thin section of the books in which they are contained. "Histories" of the war, then, are likely to be male-centered and battle-centered. While a number of writers describe women's roles and enumerate their contributions, few focus extensive attention on the subject. Normally, such discussions are contextualized within a discussion of male roles and contributions during the war, as if women's performances could be understood only when one understands what men were doing, when we bounce one set of experiences, one set of cultural responses, off another.

Shuttlecock history writing of course serves a purpose—its aim is to be in many places at one time, to describe as many factors of historical action and experience as possible. Its lofty aim, ultimately, is omniscience. But this impulse toward omniscience invariably tends to equalize, at best, historical experience, or to obscure, at worst, the historical narratives from below. Jane Lewis closes her Introduction to *Women in England 1870–1950* writing, "Finally, it has been suggested to me that the text errs on the side of earnestness. . . . but when women's past has so often been either trivialised and/or reduced to a paragraph, I am not sure to what extent that is a bad thing" (xiv). Projects like Lewis's are not about how women's history has affected and continues to affect history but about the constant process of historical negotiation as to what is history, who makes it, who writes it, who obscures it, who thwarts it—questions that Brecht raises in his often anthologized poem "A Worker Reads History." By questioning the very constructions that animated the women's working class during the war, by challenging the very institutional practices that produced them, and by interrogating the very systems that rewarded, defamed, and scrutinized working-class women, I hope to harness a constellation of circumstances that conspired to license and empower working-class women during the First World War, and to analyze the conditions that subsequently worked to demobilize them.

The boundaries of women's lives clearly had shifted during the war, but their experiences would give them only a temporary respite from the bluntness of prewar culture, and afford them only a short rest before they would be urged to let life return to "normal." By 1920, Braybon and Summerfield point out, "Women . . . had the vote, if.they were over 30 and property owners, but they had not abandoned husbands and children for exciting jobs, they had not gained equal pay, they were not moving into skilled work" (130). Though during the war women found themselves the focus of home-front attention in the press and in the public square, and the frequent subjects of gossip, burlesque, and reprimand, by 1921 the reconstruction of women, their status, class, and societal roles, would become a national fetish.

The next chapter describes the larger cultural response of working-class women's entry into paid labor, responses that continue to affect the way historians and sociologists think and write about the working class. Just as allegations of working-class disinterest in the war surfaced as early as 1914, for example, those same class stereotypes temper the way the working class of the First World War is discussed today. That is, the working class continues to be maligned for its "failed" (or lack of) politicism during and immediately after the war, as if its disinterest in the war were not a stratagem in and of itself, or if it somehow were not a political enough stratagem.

Only two days after Britain declared war on Germany, for example, *The Labour Leader* posted on its front page a protestation of the war that read

> Down with the War! . . . THE WORKERS NEVER BENEFIT BY WAR. This is not your war. It is not the war of the German working class, or of the French working class, or of the Austrian working class, or of the Russian working class. It is the war of the British RULING Class, of the German RULING Class, of the French RULING Class, and of the Austrian RULING Class. IT IS THEIR WAR NOT YOURS. (August 6, 1914)

Dominic Hibberd remarks in *The First World War* that "such calls found few echoes"; because "workers of the world were not going to unite for peace[,] Marxism had failed its first great test," he argues (39). I question what makes this effort a particular "failure," though, and wonder why the act itself of rallying sentiment isn't considered proof of political activism on the part of the working class. There is a particularly alarming attitude among some scholars who work on this period who write as if the working class's lack of politicism or inaction were a real disappointment, and who tsk-tsk with fierce cultural hindsight the working class's excruciating "failures" and "missed" opportunities to force change.

Looking at the forces that operated against the working class during the war, and in particular the women's working class—that is, stratified male unions, DORA regulations, the constant watch of Home Office constables, middle-class supervisors and overlookers, the strength of public opinion to force resolutions, and so forth—it is quite clear that regardless of these conditions, and even despite them, the women's working class was tremendously politicized during this period. They organized dozens and dozens of strikes during the war, marched in as many protests, and fought vigilantly for workers' rights. Their political consciousness eventually would coalesce years later and would yield momentous events such as the infamous Jarrow Crusade, organized and led by working women. After the war, work—not *women's* work but *factory* work—changed as a result of women's entry into essential war industry. These changes were due in large part to mechanization introduced into factories during and after the war, and were affected, no doubt, by American Taylorism and Fordism. Yet these changes also were due to women's participation at all levels in the work force. If the war changed women by privileging them for the first time to engage in their culture, then women gave back as much as they took and made sure through their vigilance—however "unpolitical" it may seem to contemporary critics—that the work site would be a different one for future working-class women.

Because the war wakened most everyone's fears of cultural change, working-class women who appeared to be breaking out of their chains seemed to pose the greatest risk to established ways of life. As we shall see in the next chapter, they were scolded for daring to rise above their station, and as one working-class woman wrote, they were held in contempt for being in such a position as even to try to rise above their station. It was a time in British history that was rife with class tensions; and as working-class intensity mounted, middle-class resistance raged. Though neither group would yield in the severity of its conviction or resistance to change, propagandists continued to herald in the press the fortuity of their juxtaposition in the workplace and romanticized their camaraderie as esprit de corps, congratulated their production, and sensationalized their sorority. Inside the factories, though, and in local communities and churches, class barriers were firmly established and unbreakable, and for the next four or five years, working-class women would be vilified for their brazen attempts to break away from class constraints. When the war was over, they would firmly be put back in their place. Life would return to "normal," if normal meant a return to the "cage," and a revisiting of the humdrum old life, as Jane Cox characterized it—"working and sleeping and eating, when you could get it to eat."

Chapter 2

The Cultural Response

WOMEN AS A SPECIFIC CLASS WERE WATCHED MORE closely than they had ever been during the First World War: their working hours, salaries and terms were regulated by special laws, as was their absenteeism, which was investigated rigorously by welfare supervisors. Their drinking habits, if they had any, were modified by the Home Office, who governed pub hours and regulated liquor sales; and in an effort to curtail what seemed like a widespread and morally dangerous "When the cat's away, the mice will play" attitude among married women whose husbands were serving at the front, some towns enforced curfews for married women, while in other districts they were barred from local pubs. Most alarming was the growing support for what the *Manchester Guardian* called "the unwritten law," in which a soldier was thought justified in killing his wife for her infidelity on the home front.[1]

Women saw their clothing, accessories, and other purchases made subjects of frequent discussion in the press, and their spendthrift habits became the stock of jokes, public conjecture, and reprimand. Moreover, with the passage of Defence of the Realm Acts in 1914 and 1915, women were subject to cultural, military, and government scrutiny. Women who received separation allowances were often the targets of neighborhood spies who sought further to regulate and prescribe their conduct. Everyone, it seemed, had an opinion to set against the new working woman: there were insidious comments about her uniform, about how she spent her leisure time (what little she had), and about how she comported herself on and off the job. For four uninterrupted years, the social behavior of women was scrutinized under the probing eyes of their culture.

While some Britons trusted that women workers or volunteers were doing nothing more than making fools of themselves by entering into the paid or volunteer labor force, others regarded the situation with greater severity. They argued that it reflected poorly on the Crown and urged that something be done and quickly. The following anonymous letter to the editor of *The Morning Post,* for example, fuses communal anger with civic alarm. The writer argues:

> I do not know the corps to which these ladies belong, but if they cannot become nurses or ward maids in hospital, let them put on sunbonnets and print frocks and go and make hay or pick fruit or make jam, or do the thousand and one things that women can do to help. But for heaven's sake, don't let them ride and march about the country making themselves and, what is more important, the King's uniform, ridiculous. (Gould 119)

It was the self-mockery of it all that the public disdained: women workers were seen as parodies born out of the suffrage movement and were found just as reprehensible, as Jenny Gould explains in "Women's Military Services in First World War Britain":

> Although women's support for the war effort was widely approved, the idea that women might play roles other than those of nurse, fundraiser, knitter, or canteen organizer was not popular. This resistance was rooted in conventional attitudes about women's roles and was expressed most vehemently by those who also opposed women's suffrage. (116–17)

Though women's entry into the work force in 1914 was nothing new in Britain—hundreds of thousands of women had held jobs before the war, though few were unionized, skilled workers—their new roles poised them to unravel slowly the domestic, social, and political fabric of centuries-old conventions; and as such, their animated participation in the war effort became a source of constant challenge, offered a topic for frequent prognostication and conjecture, and yielded hyperbolic prophesies of cultural catastrophe.

Factory women's compliance in the manufacturing of war, for example, made them especially glaring targets both in the press and in the public square. Though women were urged into participation by a vigorous national propaganda scheme, many Britons did not support women's participation at any level in the war effort and claimed pacifism as the ground for their charge. Other Britons did not support the idea of women leaving their homes to work—whether working for the war effort producing munitions, aeroplanes, or tanks, or whether working in substitution, where women took over the jobs of male tram drivers, ticket collectors, operators, and so forth (that is, jobs that didn't necessarily fuel the war but helped the nation carry on). Motivated by traditionalism or chivalry, these critics argued that working women degraded the pedestal they had once glorified. For both groups, it was the women's behavior they were really criticizing—the way they spent their money, what they ate, where they drank, and what they did with their leisure time when they would no longer stay home and make babies, even "war babies."

A third brand of criticism waged against women came not from the home front but from the front lines—from soldiers who fought there and from volunteers and workers who worked there. They experienced the war differently and quickly became intolerant of the home front complacency they thought Britain's working women represented. Ignorance was the charge they leveled, and they held women in particular contempt because of their ignorance of the harsh realities of war. Invariably, these three forms of cultural response fueled each other, and all working-class women could do was "carry on" and do their bit, deaf to the charges leveled against them by their culture. To be sure, as the war went on, these charges became implicitly more complicated and disruptive, as we shall see, and challenged at every level the cultural right of women to work.

Women munitions workers in particular shouldered much of the cultural criticism, not only because of the sort of work they performed but because of the considerable enormity of their group, the sheer numbers of them. The transgressions of individual munitions workers, for example, often were held up by the press as behavior representing the entire women's working class. One particular photograph from the collection at the Imperial War Museum may help us understand one aspect of the cultural vilification of munitions workers, since it documents what many workers claim was a misrepresented and mass-produced image during the war: working-class women in furs. Figure 2.1, taken at a Birmingham factory, shows a group of girl munition workers making primers and pellet plugs for shell fuses. One of the young women wears a fur collar while working on the bench (IWM Department of Photographs Item Q 108402). Fur was banned in most factories and especially in the arsenals on account of its extreme flammability, and though many workers criticized the characteristically low temperatures in the factories and arsenals, a fur collar seriously pressed the boundaries of safety, regardless of the warmth and comfort it might have supplied to workers. Complicating this, the fur trade was "dying" during the war, not thriving, as the culture might have supposed from the mass-produced images of working-class women wearing furs. Gareth Griffiths notes that some relief came to the dying fur trade in late 1915, "with the placing of orders

2.1 Arsenal worker wearing a fur collar. Girl munition workers making primers and pellet plugs for shell fuses in a Birmingham factory, March 1918. Photograph Q108402, printed with permission of the Imperial War Museum.

from the War Office for fur and skin coats for the troops" (15). Thereafter, fur was being "saved" for the soldiers, he notes. Thus, an individual's fur purchase was deemed not only unforgivable but culturally and
militaristically irresponsible.

To be sure, women workers were *not* exploiting the fur market, as many
of their compatriots believed. Peggy Hamilton's 1978 autobiography of her
years as a munition worker, titled *Three Years or the Duration*, discusses the
popular misconception of those at the home front with regard to munition
workers and their exaggerated penchant for fur. Hamilton writes:

> The slums, grime and poverty of Birmingham had appalled me, the group
> of ragged little boys begging at the factory doors each night as we left work
> made me angry and miserable; so that when our new arrival said during
> dinner, 'I think it's disgraceful all these munition makers and their fur
> coats; they're getting too much money,' I told her that I was a munition
> worker, that no one I knew owned a fur coat, that we worked from seven to
> seven, six days a week, for £1 a week and what sort of fur coat did she think
> she could afford to buy after paying for her living out of that?'
> 'It's more than they ever had before,' she said, 'and they don't know how
> to spend it.'
> 'And do the rich always know how to spend their money?' I asked.
> 'It's nothing to do with the poor how the rich spend their money,' she
> answered.
> 'Well, it's nothing to do with the rich how the poor spend their money
> either.' (48)

Hamilton adds that it was fashionable during the war to protest against
the "huge wages" of munition workers and that she considered such a
view to be "most unjust" (100):

> No doubt many of the women workers were receiving more than they had
> before, nevertheless their pay was about half a man's wages and they were
> working very long hours for it. Many women had their menfolk at the
> Front and were keeping their homes going by their work while their men
> were giving their lives for a shilling a day. By 1917, many of the male work-
> ers were returned soldiers, wounded and battered. Needless to say, I never
> experienced the enormous wages we heard so much about. (100)

Like most women who worked in Britain during the First World War,
Peggy Hamilton received "about half a man's wages" (100), and such wage
discrepancies invariably led to bitterness. Thousands of women workers
looked to the unions for support, joining leagues and organizing themselves and other women workers in the factories. Although male workers

had been unionized in Britain as early as the eighteenth century, women's entry into organized labor seemed culturally distasteful—especially during wartime; and since their organization inevitably led to strikes, work stoppages, and slowdowns, the women were looked upon as a detrimental force that not only threatened Britain's success in the war but was consequently "responsible" for thousands of dead British soldiers. Although some of the strikes were quite successful and caused workshops employing thousands of workers to remain idle during the walkouts, most strikes were instigated by male workers or by nonunionized workers, as Woollacott shows in her survey of the first half of 1917.

Woollacott's survey of strike activity from January 1 to June 30, 1917, for example, reveals that job actions during that year were frequent and successful. During the first half of 1917, she notes,

> Out of 201 trade disputes, 129 were started by men, 16 were started by women, 15 were started by women and men together, and in 41 cases the sex of the instigators was not reported. One of the disputes begun by women, for example, was a strike staged by about three thousand women workers employed by Messrs. Greenwood and Batley Ltd. of Leeds on 31 January 1917. The women's protest was over wages, specifically a demand for a war bonus of 4s. a week, because their piecework rates had recently been altered. Six hundred men were idled by the strike because their work was dependent on that of the women. Surprisingly, the women were not members of a union. (104–105)

John Stevenson also reports on strike activity during the war in *British Society 1914–1945* and notes that "over five and a half million working days were lost in 1917, more than the total for 1915 and 1916 put together. The final year of the war saw no improvement: 5,875,000 working days were lost—the highest total for any year of the war—while the number of disputes was almost 50 per cent greater than 1919." Throughout the war, women's wages rarely equaled men's; and it was only after men's unions feared that women's entry into labor would threaten male wages that the unions voiced their support for fair—not equal—pay for women performing what used to be men's jobs.

Yet even these comparably low wages were contested by the public, and any example of a woman's "reckless" spending was held up to the public, and especially to her neighbors, as morally reprehensible. Laura Verity, a gas burner maker and munitions worker at the National Shell Factory, at George Bray and Company in Leeds, and at Greenwood and Batley, insists that money was scarce for everyone during the war, and that munitions women were no exception, adding as an example that if you paid for anything with a big bill—like a five-pound note, she recalls—you had to leave your name and address with the custodian and he would get the change back to you. "That was how money was . . . yes, scarce" (IWM Sound Archive, Item SR 864, Transcript 57). Elsie May Farlow, who worked polishing time fuses at the Royal Ordnance Works in Coventry, noted that most of the munitions workers' money went toward sending parcels to soldiers or toward one fund or another (such as the popular Bench to the Trench Fund[2]), noting with so many others that the extravagance ascribed to the women workers was insidious and inaccurate. In fact, the *Times* reported that when the Young Women's Christian Association (YWCA) opened its Dinner Club in Liverpool in early 1916, a special resting room was attached to the dining area "to avoid the need of walking about during the remainder of the luncheon hour," since so many women workers complained that they were "tire[d] of looking in shop windows" ("What is Being Done" *Times*, May 5, 1916). The image of the frivolous worker scurrying around shopping seems a far cry from the peace and quiet and rest that they really longed for. The success of the Liverpool attachment room led to similar developments in YWCA canteens and restaurants in Hull, Sheffield, Birmingham, Wolverhampton, and Leeds.

To be sure, some women spent, and spent beyond their means. Amy Elizabeth May, for example, recalls getting paid quite a lot—£4 a week— and remembers buying clothes, shoes, boots, and coats: "Oh yes," she said, "there was quite a little bit of fashion going on then" (IWM Sound Archive, Item SR 684, Reel 3). And unlike her contemporaries who challenged the accuracy of women's enormous wages, Elsie McIntyre, a munition worker, charge hand, and overlooker at the Barnbow factory in Leeds, remembers the "enormous wages" as well, and catalogues in her oral history a spending spree that must have looked unconditionally brazen to her contemporaries. Though McIntyre's rise in the Barnbow factory to the eventual position of overlooker suggests that she was probably a middle-class worker,[3] her purchases seem to have been motivated not by materialism but class shame, she explains, and the commodities she purchased helped her to blend in with the people at work who were "better" than she. "Being amongst better people than myself, I started getting clothes, silk stockings and a white fox fur but it was imitation because it kept coming off onto my clothes," McIntyre notes. She remembers purchasing "all sorts of silk stockings," stockings where the silk came only "half-way up, that's all. You see, you'd come half way up and the rest were cashmere, navy blue as a rule, sixpence a pair" (IWM Sound Archive, Item SR 673, Reel 6). The white "fox" fur that cost her 12s. 6d., she concedes, was most likely a rabbit skin, but there was nothing imitation about her next big purchase. She recalls the day she purchased a Price piano:

I remember buying a Price piano then because they all came in fashion, you know. Yes, I went up Chapel Town Road and got one, to pay monthly. I didn't [play the piano]. But at that time there was no entertainment. . . . I never learned. But it was fashionable to have a piano, you see. We got a little bit better off so I said to mother, "I'm going to get a piano." She said "You'll do no such thing. Don't bother me with a big debt like that. We're only just pulling ourselves round." Anyway, I went and got it because I was like that, you know, if I put my mind to anything. (IWM Sound Archive, Item SR 673, Transcript 51–52)

When the war was over, McIntyre still had enough money to afford to buy her mother a washer, "the kind you did nappies in," she said (Transcript 52). McIntyre's mother's comment—"Don't bother me with a big debt like that. We're only just pulling ourselves round"—comes as no surprise and deflates the campaign of disinformation being spread against women workers during the war. Many working-class families were "just pulling themselves round" by the middle of the war, having gotten some of their debt under control, having saved a few pounds in thrift schemes and taken full advantage of rationing and bartering systems that emerged during the war to help householders manage family care. Most likely, young women such as McIntyre had a say in matters of family finance for the first time and not only were seduced by their "disposable" incomes but were no doubt naive as well about the consequences of monthly-plan extravagances. To be sure, at the heart of the great debate about women's wages was widespread cultural alarm at the breakdown of centuries-old barriers; it was a time when the boundaries between the working and leisure classes were blurred just as systematically as the lines between male and female expectations and roles, and attending each reprimand or condemnation of working-class women was a regimental "How dare you?" attitude.

It is equally important to note that women not only displaced male members of the household as breadwinners but in many circumstances, daughters displaced reigning mothers who had managed family finances exclusively and had authorized family purchases for decades. It was a time when the confines of age and gender loosened their stranglehold on Britain's young working-class women; and the immediate consequences of a culture so quickly and so dramatically changed by war often were blamed on and shouldered by the women's working class.

The anonymous writer of "In Self-Defence, By A Munition Girl" suggested in 1917 that the cultural anger and scorn described above stemmed from a tyrannical attitude about the "place" of the working classes; and she suggested that what angered her contemporaries most was how "unseemly" it was that she and her co-workers "should be in a position to make such . . . investment[s]." She writes:

> Without wishing to judge unfairly, it seems to me that these critics grudge me this sudden improvement in my financial position. If I were to put every penny I make into war certificates there would still be those who considered it unseemly that I should be in a position to make such an investment. It is the old autocratic spirit, struggling in its death throes to make a last endeavor to assert itself. The same spirit which my efforts in war work are supposed to be helping to crush. (*Daily Express*, Nov. 1, 1917)

Workers' class aspirations commonly were tied to discussions of women's wages. Trevor Wilson, for example, recounts a characteristic anecdote about two munitions girls contemplating the purchase of a pineapple, a story that captures the burlesque and lampoon to which the women workers were subjected. More than that, it echoes the communal anger that the women should be in the "position" to make such investments. He explains: "The pineapple was such a luxury that, for special functions, families with aspirations outrunning their means would hire [that is, rent] a pineapple whose presence—though not taste—would add grace to the occasion. The two munitionettes, after eyeing the pineapple and learning its (exorbitant) price, informed the fruiterer: 'Well, we'll buy it if you tell us how to cook it'" (724), a punchline that parades the women's ignorance as well as their class aspirations.

Most of the opinions set against working-class women reveal a deep-seated anger and resentment, especially this next example, in which a contemporary journalist yokes women munition workers and their new economic status with that of prostitutes. He writes:

> Whilst Mrs Jack Tar or Mrs Tommy Atkins have found it a tight squeeze to stretch the money far enough to cover ordinary necessities, Mrs Nouveau-Riche of munition fame, and Mrs Dockyard Matey have been able to indulge in finery that never came their way before 1914. (De Groot 295)

The character names invented by this writer are striking in their criticism. While the first two women discussed are identifiable by name as wives of British fighting men—*Jack Tar* being the colloquial term for a sailor and *Tommy Atkins* for an army private soldier—they have no identity of their own other than that reflected off the names of their husbands. It seems clear that neither of them works, since each finds it a "tight squeeze" to manage on her separation allowance. The other two women characters, also married, are not identified in terms of their husbands or in terms of what their husbands do but are defined instead by what they do, how they behave, how they earn and how they spend their money. It seems clear to me that the name *Mrs Nouveau-Riche* condemns the working-class woman's new financial status, just as the name *Mrs Dockyard Matey* suggests she has been hanging around the docks making "mates" of all the sailors. By her association with Mrs. Dockyard Matey, Mrs. Nouveau-Riche is equally tarnished. The writer suggests that both women are prostituting themselves for wartime profit. Both women tastelessly announce their profit by wrapping themselves in self-indulgent finery. This short description, then, encodes a world of critical information in terms of the kind of women's behavior the journalist valorizes and the kind of women's behavior he condemns.

This notion of a parade of working-class women dressed "in finery that never came their way before 1914," fails to take into account several large-scale changes in commodity culture that had taken place before the war, changes that cultural critics such as Janet Wolff and Rachel Bowlby have documented in their work about women and turn-of-the-century metropolises. Wolff and Bowlby identify what Barbara Green notes, as well, is a glaring omission from the work of Walter Benjamin's tableau of the nineteenth-century metropolis, the notorious absence of that figure brought about through the development of the department store, the "strolling female spectator," the *flâneuse* (Green 38). Importantly, Green argues that the figure of the middle-class *flâneuse* grew from early twentieth-century suffragists who took to the streets in the first decade of the twentieth century and marched, performed spectacles, and remapped public spaces. "One might argue," Green writes, "that Virginia Woolf was emboldened to streetwalk because the suffragette marched first, that the suffragette's activism provides the missing link between the *passante* and the *flâneuse*, between woman-as-spectacle and woman-as-spectator. . . . In our efforts to reconstruct the history of women's relation to the city, there is no better source than the underread autobiographies, fictional accounts and manifestoes generated by the suffrage movement" (Green 38). It is important to note that though the middle-class *flâneuse* flourished in prewar Britain, it wasn't until working-class women participated in this sort of pedestrian behavior that the figure of a woman strolling and window-shopping became such a threat to the culture. In other words, once working-class women position themselves not only as strolling lookers and shoppers but invite others to look upon them as they stroll, once they call attention to their own leisure and flaunt their consumerism in remapped public spaces, traversing concourses usually traversed by the middle class, then the entire notion of streetwalking reverts to prostitution, and the image of the *flâneuse* reverts to the image of the *passante*. That they are in a position to look, to gaze, to call others to gaze at their spectacle—these actions upset what we might call the usual order of things and work to challenge class divisions.

But they work to challenge sexual divisions, too, since the proliferation of the figure of the strolling woman likely gave rise to fears of lesbian "cruising." Joseph Boone discusses the phenomenon in his work on sexuality and the shaping of modernism, suggesting that early twentieth-century pedestrian mobility suited (and even invited) a form of urban, pedestrian queerness. Topographical spaces became sites where mobility was paraded and sexual identities enacted. "Such an explosion of movement . . . renders all urban mobility, to use gay parlance, a form of cruising. Indeed, cruising may be said to become the 'pedestrian rhetoric' *par excellence* in the modern era, taking the place of the role Walter Benjamin attributes to the *flâneur* of the nineteenth-century city" (214–15). Such transformations of urban public thoroughfares by working women threatened to disrupt the privacy of sexuality, to undermine the privilege of heterosexuality, and to introduce sexual subcultures into previously privatized public space.

The story of Ellen Harriet stands as a good representative example of lesbian masquerade in war factories and the social threat it caused when introduced onto a public thoroughfare. A cross-dresser, Ellen Harriet went by the name of Charles Brian Capon and worked as a successful and skilled wireworker for some two years until she was seen out walking with a young woman and was coerced into registering at the recruiting office. Her gender discovered, Ellen Harriet's story made the headlines: "Girl's Masquerade: Two Years as a Male Worker" (*Times*, Jan. 21, 1918: 3).

It is important to note that the critique aimed at women is one that characteristically ignored their strength as workers but condemned their power as sexual beings and as consumers. Their presence in public spaces threatened to overturn the normal social order, and working-class women who weren't objectified as the loyal Mrs. Tommy Atkins type were vilified on account of their sexuality and new financial status, cast alongside the Mrs. Nouveau-Riche and the Mrs. Dockyard Matey types because they publicly displayed and flaunted their desire.

A consequence of women's mass entry into paid production, this sort of widespread contempt for and condemnation of their sexuality, their behavior, and their spending extended to most women, and the figure of the loyal and self-sacrificing Mrs. Tommy Atkins quickly gained currency in the press and in other manifestations of popular culture. During this period, women found themselves reproached for how they handled their money and censured for not being quite so prudent as they ought, whether their money came from weekly wages or from separation allowances that amounted to twelve shillings, six pence, plus two shillings per child. Lillian Gard's poem "Her 'Allowance'!" first published in 1915 in *The Country Life Anthology of Verse,* censures the free-spirited spending of her married counterparts and advocates a sanctimonious alternative to her contemporaries' alleged spending sprees. Gard writes:

> 'Er looked at me bunnet (I knows 'e ain't noo!)
> 'Er turns up 'er nose at the patch on me shoe!
> And 'er sez, pointed like, 'Liza, what do 'e do
> With yer 'llowance?' . . .
> I sees 'er long feather and trimmy-up gown:
> I sez, as I looks 'er quite square up and down,
> 'Do 'e think us keeps 'oliday 'ere in the town
> With my 'llowance?
> 'Not likely!' I sez. And I bids 'er 'Good-day!'
> And I kneels on the shabby old canvas to pray
> For Bill, who's out fightin' such brave miles away.
> (And I puts back a foo o' they coins for 'e may
> Be needin' a part—may my Bill—who can say?—
> Of my 'llowance!)
> (Reilly 41)

The language of Gard's poem—in particular, the dialect in which it is written—is no doubt a reconstruction of the speech of many of the working-class women who filled the factories during Britain's call to arms. Significantly, Gard's poem pokes as much fun at the speaker and her dialect as it does at the subject under analysis—what Peggy Hamilton describes as "how the poor spend their money" (*Three Years or the Duration* 48). Importantly, Gard's poem "Her 'Allowance'!" is more prescriptive than anecdotal, and it encodes the tsk-tsks of her culture, reminding us once again that the cultural indictments against women who were newly placed in a position to spend money issued from those who previously had enjoyed—and defined—these privileges as their own.

Madeline Ida Bedford, a contemporary of Lillian Gard, assesses the situation quite differently, however, and argues in her 1917 poem that because women's high wages compensate for the danger of the job, the women are entitled to the luxuries they allegedly seek. Her poem "Munition Wages," first published in a collection titled *The Young Captain,* begins with the decadent assertion that women's high wages are "dim sweet," and inventories the worker's purchases—silk stockings, bracelets, jewelry, theater tickets, and taxi rides. Bedford concludes the poem with something much more than a *carpe diem* embrace, since she introduces the element of women's "danger pay":

This is my verdict—
It is jolly worth while.
Worth while, for tomorrow
If I'm blown to the sky,
I'll have repaid mi wages
In death—and pass by.
(Reilly 8)

Bedford's speaker articulates a common fear among wartime factory workers, since British arsenals and munition factories not only were dangerous places to work but also were attractive targets during German Gotha and Giant-bomber air assaults that began in early 1915. The workers' mere presence in the factories courted disaster and would lead a number of women to address the issue of their likely fatality in industry newspapers, as we shall see in chapter 4.

Though Bedford suggests that a sense of mortality attended her speaker's purchases, other women workers attribute the spending to other sources, though they also suggest that accounts of their spending were greatly exaggerated. For example, munitions workers complain in their oral histories, their autobiographies, and in their memoirs about the maddeningly strict safety codes in the arsenals and factories: one steadfast worker was expelled from the job because supervisors found a match in her clothing; other women were expelled for carrying pins, sewing needles, hairpins, and the like, since sparks from these metal items could set factories alight. Perhaps the no-frills, overzealous, and often misappropriated safety measures of the arsenals accounted for some women's desire to spend their excess wages on luxury items instead of saving the money or using it to "further the cause." Lillian Annie Tuck, interviewed by a representative from the Imperial War Museum in 1976, said, "We had meant to send money home. We were going to work wonders. But it was another story when we got there" (IWM Sound Archive, Item SR 854, Reel 1).

Surely, the oppressiveness of the First World War, coupled with innumerable daily sacrifices, constant exhaustion, and prolonged discomfort at work, contributed to the women's spending and to some women's extravagance; but women munition workers often were vilified by the home front because their spendthriftiness was judged in poor taste and because their high-profile purchases made the women appear unforgivably whimsical. The majority of the workers themselves, however—with the exception of those like Elsie McIntyre, the woman who remembers buying the piano—categorically scoffed at the wealthy, *nouveau riche* status ascribed to them by journalists and the war machine. In fact, many women found national appeals for thriftiness insulting: "To advise us working women to be thrifty is about the limit!" one worker wrote to *Labour Woman* in 1916 (Braybon and Summerfield 99). Two short poems published in *Shell Magazine*, a factory newspaper out of Leeds, discuss workers' attitudes toward their wages. One worker, C. W. Wright, addresses the issue in his poem "On Munitions," where he justifies his piece-rate salary by pointing out how hard he works:

> Folks often say I'm paid too much,
> Which shows how little they know,
> For I'm a working man, and as such
> I reap just what I sow.

> It's puzzling to me that in time of war,
> I'm paid at a rate called "piece,"
> For I'm hoping in peace-time to get much more,
> Well, we'll see when hostilities cease. (32)

A. H. Ibbotson, in her poem "Making Shells," insists that her co-workers remain mindful of how their insufficient salaries compare with the soldiers', and writes: "If you sometimes think your rate of pay/ Is not sufficient, just quietly say/ 'Tommy for one and twopence a day,/ *Is risking shells*'" (*Shell Magazine* 46). Clearly, while the middle classes upbraided factory workers for their high wages and conspicuous spending, at the same time fearing and mocking what they saw as the working-class's aspirations, workers continued to insist that their pay was not so ample and abundant as the claims made against them.

To be sure, women's ignorance of the realities of war also made them easy targets. When they weren't being criticized for their spending, they were being reproached for their behavior, as Christopher Martin notes when he writes of the national appeal to housewives, "Act as you always act."[4] At other times, women were reproached for their noncombatant naiveté. Siegfried Sassoon, whose poetry often censures the oblivious home front, published in 1917 a sonnet titled "Glory of Women," which derides women as causes worth fighting for. He writes:

> You love us when we're heroes, home on leave,
> Or wounded in a mentionable place.
> You worship decorations; you believe
> That chivalry redeems the war's disgrace.
> You make us shells. You listen with delight,
> By tales of dirt and danger fondly thrilled.
> You crown our distant ardours while we fight,
> And mourn our laurelled memories when we're killed.

You can't believe that British troops "retire"
When hell's last horror breaks them, and they run,
Trampling the terrible corpses—blind with blood.
O German mother dreaming by the fire,
While you are knitting socks to send your son
His face is trodden deeper in the mud. (100)

Sassoon's poem perfectly captures the "damned if you do, damned if you don't" bind that women found themselves trapped in during the First World War. Precisely like the male soldiers, women, too, were performing in culturally assigned roles. Because women were touted in the press and in governmental propaganda as a "cause" worth fighting for and certainly worth dying for, women who obediently fulfilled these roles quickly were vilified by combatants and derided by poets such as Sassoon and Wilfred Owen.

A year after the publication of "Glory of Women," Sassoon published in 1918 "Suicide in the Trenches," a shorter poem with a brazenly censorious final stanza. Here, his net is cast wider as he directs his attack not specifically on women but on the home-front "dullards" Wilfred Owen impugned in his poem "Insensibility." Sassoon jeers: "You smug-faced crowds with kindling eye/ Who cheer when soldier lads march by,/ Sneak home and pray you'll never know/ The hell where youth and laughter go" (119). Sassoon's attack against the "smug-faced crowds" echoes one by many soldiers and combatants, especially by those home on leave, who found unrecognizable the sentimental "Tommy" of the journalistic press. Martin cites the following letter written by R. H. Tawney, a wounded New Army sergeant, who wrote in a fit of anger to the *Nation* magazine:

> This Tommy is a creature at once ridiculous and disgusting. He is represented as invariably 'cheerful' and revelling in the 'excitement' of war, of finding 'sport' in killing other men, or hunting Germans out of dugouts as a terrier hunts rats. We are depicted as merry assassins rejoicing in the opportunity of a 'scrap' . . . exulting in the duty of turning human beings into lumps of disfigured clay. . . . Of your soldier's internal life, the sensation of taking part in a game played by monkeys and organized by lunatics, you realize, I think, nothing. (69)

Tawney's attack here, obviously aimed at journalists who invented, fashioned, and refashioned the iconic British "Tommy," clearly extends to the gullible reading public as well; and his venom censures the naivete of the home front while implicating both parties for their complicity in imagining and then monumentalizing such a stage figure.

More contempt abounds in male service newspapers, as is evident from even a cursory look through the anthology titled *Made in the*

Trenches. Composed Entirely from Articles and Sketches Contributed by Soldiers. Published in 1916 and edited by Sir Frederick Treves, Bt. and George Goodchild, the collection fuses sardonic humor with cold social criticism, as in the following example that attacks the home front on many levels: one side of the page has an assortment of nine soldiers and officers who represent in their recognizable uniforms various allies (Scotland, Australia, etc.). They are pictured above a caption that reads "Those who *should* write about it!" Across the page, another caption reads "Those who *do* write about it!" and here the humorist has drawn six newspaper covers with mockups of individual war stories. The cover stories invented for this parody reveal a frustration and rage similar to Tawney's above and reinforce the rift between Those at Home and Those Overseas, a division that already was clearly marked by the middle of the war. The six headlines, each trivial and reductive of the realities of war, specifically ridicule the ignorance of home-front journalism: "'How I Would Win the Great War.' Stirring Message to the Nation"; "What is Kitchener Doing? What I Would Do"; "'My Great Scheme for the Conscription of Women.' Clever Article by Lance CPL Hotair"; "'Is the Humour of C. Chaplin Necessary to Win This War?' Patriotic Article"; "'What I Saw in Berlin When I was Secretary to the War Lord.'"; and "'The Strict Necessity for Economy in Paper.' Double Page Article" (*Made in the Trenches* 22–23). Each mock front-page headline carries with it an illustration. The illustration that accompanies "What I Saw in Berlin When I was Secretary to the War Lord" pictures a stylishly well-dressed woman wearing a fancy coat and flapper hat, as if to suggest that her article about what she "saw in Berlin" will contain fashion updates and advice for the smart set but will say nothing about the war or its horrors.

Since the public learned about the war through the filtered, censored, and dishonest eyes of the press and those who controlled the press, their innocence and naiveté is not something combatants can especially blame them for. Martin Taylor notes that "The representation of war as purveyed in Britain was unrecognizable to those who had actually fought. Indeed, to anyone who had seen action, the picture of the war as presented by such magazines as *The War Illustrated*, must have seemed a very poor joke indeed" (96), as there was such a discrepancy between civilian and trench journalistic accounts. Taylor correctly points out, as well, that

> Women were, without doubt, cynically exploited by the propagandists. In urging men to go and fight, they could only have earned the soldiers' scorn for their ignorance of what they were actually sending the soldiers to. And those soldiers who had enlisted to the strains of "I'll make a man of you," very soon realised that the only thing they were likely to be made was a

corpse. Some women, however, did embrace the cause with an appalling enthusiasm. What soldiers must have thought of the following [poem, "The Vision" by Katherine Tynan,] can only be imagined;

> They shot Flynn's eyes out. That was good.
> Eyes that saw God are better blind. (Taylor 92–93)

Taylor further explains that one of the reasons women were singled out by the soldiers was that women writers consistently published imaginative but "wholly inadequate" portrayals of trench life. And although their literary efforts were applauded on the home front, "the poetry of most civiliams [sic] invited cynicism and resentment from those who knew what the Western Front was really like" (92).

Nosheen Khan in her study *Women's Poetry of the First World War* also documents the western front's contempt for women. In a chapter on "The War at Home," Khan quotes from Andreas Latzko's 1918 story "Off to War," which articulates a growing cultural misogyny. Here, Latzko "indulges in a bitter arraignment of women, stemming from the disillusionment that women did nothing to dissuade men from going to war" (Khan 82–83). Latzko writes:

> What was the most awful thing? The only awful thing is the going off. You go off to war—and they let you go. That's the awful thing. . . . That was the surprise! That they gave us up—that they sent us. . . . Do you think we should have gone if they had not sent us. . . . The women sent us. . . . They sent us to murder, they sent us to die. (Khan 83)

Khan argues that "In his efforts to shift the blame onto women for man's indulgence in war, Latzko reminds one of Owen and Sassoon who also seek to come to terms with their own war guilt by suggesting women as the culprit; to them tradition inculcates in women the desirability of glory for their men and consequently women do not speak out against war. They disregard the fact that the 'heroic' ideals were inculcated in women by man himself" (83). Whether the contempt ushered from male war guilt, male hysteria, male envy at the women's safe footing on home territory, or male frustration at the general home-front naiveté, women were at once targeted vehemently by those who had experienced "real" war and abhorred at the same time because they hadn't.

Ironically, though, even those women who had experienced the war's harsh realities first-hand—in France, on the western front, or elsewhere— were not exempt from cynicism, resentment, or cultural scorn. "Fabulous rumor," according to Sylvia Pankhurst, followed women everywhere:

War-time hysterics gave currency to fabulous rumour. From press and pul-
pit stories ran rampant of drunkenness and depravity amongst women of
the masses. Alarmist morality mongers conceived most monstrous visions
of girls and women, freed from the control of fathers and husbands who
had hitherto compelled them to industry, chastity and sobriety, now ne-
glecting their homes, plunging into excesses, and burdening the country
with swarms of illegitimate infants. (*The Home Front* 98)

Most severely affected by rumors of this sort were the WAACs. Ruby Ord,
interviewed for the Imperial War Museum Oral History project, notes
that it was nearly impossible for ex-WAACs to find work after the war because of the way they generally were frowned upon. She explains, "We
weren't looked upon with favour by the people at home. We had done
something that was outrageous for women to do. We had gone to France
and left our homes, and all that sort of thing, and we had quite a job of
getting fixed up" (IWM Sound Archive, Item SR 044, Transcript 29).

Apart from the perceived "outrageousness" over their leaving their
homes "and all that sort of thing," during the war and extending well into
the 1920s and '30s WAACs suffered from exaggerated accounts of their
sexual promiscuity. Ruby Ord explains that while their shorter uniforms
may have invited some initial speculation and rumor (causing quite a
scandal during the war[5]), the short dresses were more utilitarian than anything else. She explains:

Really, the uniform was a disgrace to anybody—an orphanage is better
turned out, to my way of thinking, on average than we were. And of course
when we arrived in France it seemed to rain all the time. The roads were
liquid mud and trailing skirts in the mud—we asked if we could be allowed
to turn up the dresses, and we were told that they must be 9" from the
ground. A big notice was put up in the camp and we changed that to 9"
from the waist. . . . We decided amongst ourselves, the rebels—after all, we
were suffragettes, a number of us—and we said "We are going to cut them
off at the length we want them so that they can't make us let the hems
down." So we just cut them off at the length we wanted and bound them
round so that there was no question of letting them down. It was quite a re-
spectable length, believe me, but not to their way of thinking. But you see,
as you walked the mud splashed up and we had only the one dress. So if it
was filthy dirty, you had to wear a filthy dirty dress. (Transcript 5)

As is often the case, speculation weighs heavier than fact, and a good
many WAACs, Ord notes, found themselves haunted well after the war by
accounts of their alleged sexual promiscuity. Though a Commission of
Enquiry was established in 1918 to investigate accusations about women's

conduct, the commission reported, "We can find no justification of any kind for the vague accusations of immoral conduct on a large scale which have been circulated about the WAAC" (Braybon and Summerfield 113). The commission's findings weren't nearly as interesting as the public imagined: the rate of pregnancy and venereal disease among the WAACs was very low, Braybon and Summerfield add, "and just as the First World War was often described as a time of great sexual freedom in later years, so the poor reputation of the WAACs lived on to affect those women who wanted to join up 20 years later" (113).

WAACs weren't the only group singled out for their improprieties. Frank Bradbury, a munitions worker at Greenwood and Batley, described the working-class cartridge girls in his shop as "hooligans" and notes in his oral history that

> If ever they asked me to go to look at the machines in the cartridge shop where the girls were, I wouldn't have gone. And some of the boys, the young boys, they would get them down and lower their trousers with the girls. Oh they were terrible. They were scum, really. (IWM Sound Archive, Item SR 675, Reel 4)

George Ginns, a munitions factory foreman at Daimler and at White and Poppe Ltd. in Coventry, commented on his co-workers, too, noting how different they were from "the decent girls":

> A lot of them were too darned idle to look after themselves, that was all. When they got a lot of these rough types as we got—of course they were mostly in that in the loading—they'd go in the pubs at night and well, they never had time to have a proper wash and clean up like the decent girls. I don't say majority, we might have had about 10% of them like that, but the other girls were really wonderful, always smart [looking] when they went out in the evenings. (IWM Sound Archive, Item SR 775, Transcript 30–31)

While Bradbury's and Ginns' interviews describe a particular kind of outrageous conduct ascribed to women during the war, Ruby Ord's interview is important because it reminds us that not all of what was perceived as "outrageous" behavior took place at work sites, in pubs, or in canteens. For Ord, it was her flight to France—her gall in leaving home—that marked her behavior as scandalous and initiated her into a group of women whose lives persistently would be marked by innuendo and haunted by "fabulous rumour" years after they took the leap.

Like Ord, other women who took the cultural leap, deciding to go to France with Queen Mary's Army Auxiliary Corps (QMAAC), for example, often had to pass through barriers "manned" by hostile neighbors. Ivy

Kewley, for example, describes a tense moment on the day she left for France to join the QMAAC, the organization formerly known as the WAAC and renamed the QMAAC in May 1918. There were a lot of women down in the station, she says,

> seeing the boys off, you know, and of course, I happened to come on the station and was going to the barrier and two women got hold of me and a crowd got round. Well, I felt about that big and you know they weren't very educated and they kept saying, "Where you going, love? Where you going?" I said, "I'm going to France." "Ah, God lover [sic], Ah, God lover; she's going to France." . . . But there was a heart of gold in these women. And some of them went to the kiosk and brought me chocolate, oranges, oh, they stuffed me up with all sorts before I could get through the barrier—and you daren't refuse. There'd be really trouble if you had've been, but, um, that was very funny, that was very funny. I was glad to get through that barrier onto the train. (IWM Sound Archive, Item SR 3154, Transcript)

Women who weren't criticized for the sort of "outrageous" conduct outlined above were attacked for other kinds of wild behavior, notably, for abandoning their maternal "instincts" in the factories. As we shall see in chapter 6, a movement was initiated in 1916 to remind women of their maternal roles and to urge women to become mothers again—an echo of the cultural mandate to housewives, "Act as you always act," that Christopher Martin reported on during food rationing panics.

Sally Mitchell's book, *The New Girl: British Culture in England, 1880–1915*, for example, concludes with a provocative discussion of how the war served to rupture "the old unity of girls' culture" by "sexualizing . . . and regendering young women" (182), turning the "girl" into an adolescent precisely at that moment at which Britain began its cultural push toward pronatalism and race building, especially during the years when the resourceful inventions of National Baby Week and Mother's Day prescribed the national protection and cultural support of mother and child. But even these imaginative campaigns backfired against women who tried to satisfy both cultural mandates, building shells *and* building the race; and the incongruity of doing both raised a new charge, "The hand that rocks the cradle wrecks the world." This cry would become an increasingly familiar incrimination.

Clearly, British culture displaced and transferred its fears over the turmoil of war onto the assembly of citizens they could most easily watch and prescribe; and because working-class women seemed singlehandedly to be overturning what Joan Scott calls "the natural order" of things— male/female relationships, family values, and cultural acquiescence to the State—they were held responsible for the contemptuous reversals and upheavals, and charged with creating and fueling a culturally rampant "sexual disorder." Scott explains in "Rewriting History" that

> The turmoil of politics is . . . depicted as an overturning of the natural order: men are weak and impotent, while women are strong, ugly, domineering, taking over public life, abandoning husbands and children. War is the ultimate disorder, the disruption of all previously established relationships. . . . War is represented as a sexual disorder; peace thus implies a return to "traditional" gender relationships, the familiar and natural order of families, men in public roles, women at home, and so on. (*Behind the Lines* 27)

The promise of a return, however, to "'traditional' gender relationships" at the end of the war was neither attractive nor alluring to those women who entered the work force during the war.

Importantly, Woollacott identifies another essential crux of the argument against women workers: their spending and behavior called attention to their bodies and raised suspicions that again were linked to aggravated fears of women's sexuality and autonomy. Woollacott notes, "Criticism of women munitions workers' spending their wages on new, ostentatiously fashionable or expensive clothes, in this cultural context, suggest[s] that, like their nineteenth-century forebears, they were behaving like prostitutes. Such allegations therefore were overlaid with moral condemnation and represented fears of women's sexual behavior" (*On Her* 131). Woollacott suggests further that the women workers'

> [e]xpensive clothes not only implied aspirations to higher class status but also enhanced physical attractiveness. Women's alleged drunkenness signified their supposed indulgence in bodily pleasures and sensuality, clearly implying a sexual promiscuity that threatened to undermine both social order and the health of the troops. Charges of drunkenness and promiscuity raised the specter of prostitution, which had long been associated with women factory workers but which munitions wages in fact made unnecessary. . . . [T]he expanded leisure activities of women munitions workers, reflecting both physical liberation and urban mobility, exacerbated fears of what their increased autonomy portended. (133)

Wollacott's point is not unlike one made by Pierre Bourdieu, who notes in *Distinctions* that when working-class women's clothing calls attention to their bodies it becomes something of a class threat, since middle-class women and men have always paid attention to the body, and deliberately work to maintain its health, its slimness, and so forth. That working-class women were even in a position to flaunt such bodies and to make such choices—what to purchase, what to wear, what to do in their spare time—

seemed a frightening harbinger, one that predicted immediate and consequential dissolutions of class structures and moral strictures.

Not only did the culture find women's autonomous behavior alarmingly widespread and flourishing, but as Emily Rumbold explains, some even suspected that it was dangerously contagious. Rumbold, who worked as a forewoman, shopkeeper, and clerk during the First World War, describes in her IWM oral history interview an episode that occurred while she and her friends were on their first leave. Though her positions as forewoman, shopkeeper, and clerk identify her as a member of the middle class, Rumbold's experiences indicate that the cultural scorn extended well beyond class markings and likely were aggravated by her association with factory work, as well as with working-class co-workers:

> We were passing this house to go to our billet which we'd been advised to go to—and this lady came down the steps and we passed quite close to her—and you see skirts were long in those days—she literally gave us one look and drew her skirts aside like that . . . we should have contaminated her I expect she thought. (IWM Sound Archive, Item SR 576, Transcript 4)

Clearly, public speculation about working women's behavior was aggravated and fueled by something much larger than fears of the present state of things, and no doubt this anxiety was exacerbated by vexing images of the future. Governed by frightening suppositions about the postwar restructuring of British society—about how the returning soldiers might react or respond to the New Woman, for example—cultural concern focused on the working-class woman, an easy target if only for her perceived naiveté. But increasingly, the culture's charges fell on sage ears—these victims of scorn were not as gullible or unsophisticated as they seemed. Their entry into paid production had in fact tutored them about a host of certain truths: some were trained in the lessons of capitalism and learned that money was power and power was freedom; others were taught to believe in the moral value of work and learned that work was indeed good for the soul and for the culture; others learned the value of work place camaraderie and learned that belonging to and engaging in activities with a community larger and less parochial than the one at home could help dull the sting of loss and regret. Confronting the criticism, women carried on with their daily lives, braving attacks from the home front, the western front and the front page, looking cultural scorn squarely in the eye, as Rumbold further explains:

> At one particular canteen . . . the women there gave us one look and said, "We don't serve women here," and they sent a complaint to our officers at

the camp and said that they were not going to serve any Englishwomen at their canteens. . . . We were told not to queue with the men but to stand at the side, which we did, and this woman who was in charge said to the French girl, "Take no notice of the women, just serve the men." That was that, you see. (IWM Sound Archive, Item SR 576, Transcript 6)

While cultural criticism and the consequent maltreatment of women workers targeted aspects of the women workers' behavior, not enough attention remained focused on the women's work at the job site. As we shall see in the next chapter, dangerous working conditions in British factories and arsenals seemed a more real and legitimate threat to British culture and to the future of the empire than any amount of perceived misbehavior.

Despite a hefty campaign to promote maternity during the war, for example, and despite the slogan invented to encourage women to produce children—"Re-Build the Nation and Empire: The Race marches forward on the feet of little children"—women's work in the factories was poisoning their reproductive systems, rendering many of the affected survivors barren. Daily exposure to asbestos or TNT powder, for example, caused irregular or painful menstrual cycles, incontinence, terrible headaches, and unbearable cramping. Aircraft doping also led to fatalities. Workers who used the dope to varnish, tighten, and waterproof the wings of aircraft complained of nausea, headaches, dizziness, and fainting. Crane operators in the metal industries noticed the effects of acid fumes from pickling tin plates. A crane driver said, "You had to come down every hour and a half to drink milk to get rid of the effects of the fumes. You drank half a pint of milk to clear the fumes" (Griffiths 57). Had more attention been paid to *these* issues, instead of focusing on what the women wore, purchased, or drank, literally hundreds, maybe even thousands, of womens' lives might have been saved, and the image of the Empire marching forward on the feet of little children would not seem, today, such a cruelly ironic vision.[6] This next chapter describes the dangerous workplace conditions so familiar to working-class factory women during the First World War. As we shall see, though one of the great paradoxes of the First World War is that the health and living conditions of so many working-class families improved, the war also hastened the rising number of work-site injuries to and deaths of women workers.

Chapter 3

The Dangers of
First World War Work

D URING THE FIRST WORLD WAR, AN UNKNOWABLE NUMBER of women
workers died in industry accidents; hundreds of other women workers died from toxic jaundice or trinitrotoluene (TNT) poisoning; others
suffered from black powder poisoning, or were poisoned by cordite ingestion, one of the most dangerous explosives handled by the women, or
died from protracted exposure to acid fumes, varnish, asbestos, gas, and
emery dust. It is ironic, then, that as soon as women entered the work
force during the war, their health was reported as significantly improved.
The move from a sedentary lifestyle nourished by tea and bread to one in-
vigorated by fresh air, hard work, hearty fare, and camaraderie reportedly
strengthened the workers and enlivened their spirits. Dr. Janet Campbell
noted in a report to the War Cabinet Committee, for example, that "an
improvement in the standards of women's health had occurred during the
war years. Prior to the war, malnutrition had been one of the main causes
of ill-health, anaemia and stunted physique among women" (Griffiths
21). Mary Macarthur of the Women's Trade Union League supported
Campbell's report but added that "long hours, long standing, lack of fresh
air, [and] long intervals without food, are . . . detrimental to health, and
the low wages which attach to most women's employment involve insufficient and often improper food" (Griffiths 22). As the war carried on, the
women's physical strength and endurance were taxed, and their immune
systems became exhausted, weakened.

Signs of the workers' fatigue and exhaustion were noticed immediately by supervisors, co-workers, civilians, and journalists. Quoting her

supervisor grandfather, for example, Monica Cosens, a middle-class munitions worker, writes, "As Gran'pa once said: 'it makes me sad to see the young girls here; they come in fresh and rosy cheeked, and before a month has passed they are pale and careworn.' . . . Gran'pa is right. There is no doubt that the girls become shadow-eyed and pale, and the effect of working through the night under the glare of electricity adds many wrinkles beneath their eyes, ageing them beyond their years" (quoted in Braybon and Summerfield 83). A correspondent writing for the *Times* in 1918 noted similar effects on Parisian women and wrote about the results of hard labor on the Parisian female work force:

> Feminine labour in France since the war has interested everybody, and the tiredness which is the result of four years of incessant toil in the munition shops, aeroplane factories, on the land, and in the many other places where women have replaced men, is now a very real problem. . . . It is not so much the work that tires, as the conditions under which it is done.
>
> In Paris in 1914 there were thousands of women working from 10 to 12 hours a day in workshops anything but hygenic, and these same women are still working even longer hours and at harder work, which tires the strongest men. No pay, however, can compensate for the loss of strength. On the land much the same tale is to be told, especially where the soil is heavy. The women who drive the trains and punch tickets in the Underground must also be included in the over-tired. Another result of hard work in a bad atmosphere is an increased desire for alcohol and a constant wish for excitement. ("The Week in Paris," July 22, 1918)

Consequently, the women's perceived "constant wish for excitement" led to their cultural scrutiny, and their perceived lust for adventure quickly was curbed by Defence of the Realm Act regulations invented on their behalf.

Things got only worse. As the hours spent at the factories grew longer, the service lines for rations became proportionately more intolerable, and the commuting back and forth from work or from the ration lines grew more dangerous and unbearable, since lights were dimmed or put out at night because of Gotha and Giant-bomber airship attacks on Britain. Accidents in the street became quite common, and for the percentage of women who worked night shifts, the struggle was intensified. Social historian Caroline Playne wrote in the 1930s that "the dread of the evening struggle in dark streets hung over many workers all the time, adding considerably to the strain of life" (45). Compounding this, the potential dangers of traveling to night work often were ignored by arsenal supervisors and minimized by journalists. A writer for the *Times*, for example, romanticizes the dangerous trek and sentimentalizes the workers' surroundings for his 1916 audience:

Nightworkers at Woolwich Arsenal are not without their compensations. Darkness softens the hard, noonday ugliness of the mighty vibrating world of copper, steel, and iron. The branches of lonely, little trees, standing forlornly in the few patches of green still left (war-time necessities have absorbed most of them) dance a special minuet in the moonlight; and on the bordering Thames shrouded ships come and go in silence that is more lyrical than a song. ("Midnight at Woolwich Arsenal," Sept. 1, 1916).

It is important to notice how the writer concentrates on the outside world, which often was as treacherous to night workers as the indoor "mighty vibrating world of copper, steel, and iron."

Sir Hall Caine, who wrote after a visit to Woolwich that "the shadowy figures of women workers in their khaki gowns and caps, move noiselessly about like nuns," likened their workplace to a convent and endowed it with imagery that removed from the work site the realities of its looming dangers. The writer of "Midnight at Woolwich Arsenal" further romanticizes the activity in the arsenal by embellishing it with allusion, much in the same way that Caine seems to be alluding to Wordsworth when he describes the women workers being quiet as nuns. After describing one worker as a veritable "Philoclea of Arcadia," and arguing that "Cinderella's moonlight flight was not more nimble" than the workers' sprightly return from their lunch break to their work stations, the *Times* writer continues:

> With a Dionysian light-heartedness the girls "beat the floor in unison" as they hurry to and from the table to the counter. This backward and forward movement forms itself automatically into a fantastic teapot quadrille, for most of the workers are carrying little teapots, blue and brown and pink and green, which make a moving mosaic of colour as they come and go. (Sept. 1, 1916)

The writer concludes the article by sentimentalizing even the dangers of which he is aware, noting that "it is more like a scene out of the powerful pages of Jane Austen than a breathing space in the heart of high explosives." The writer could not be more wrong. Because of their working-class backgrounds, it is unlikely that the women he describes here would be forming anything along the lines of a quadrille (the allusion is an insensitive one), and they certainly wouldn't be characters in a Jane Austen novel unless they made up part of the domestic staff of servants.

Margaret Brooks's description of the particular plight of women munition workers on night duty at the Woolwich Royal Arsenal is boldly different from the reporter's account above, in that Brooks paints a picture of the protracted aggravations and dangerous nuisances that attended the women's daily grind. Brooks writes:

For public safety and to minimise damage or delay to munition manufacture, in general, the explosives 'danger buildings' were built at some distance from other engineering procedures . . . (Woolwich, for example, had its nearly 1½ miles from the main building). In winter months the women formed chains holding hands to walk from the railway station to their buildings as they came on duty in the dark. (13)

Also in contrast to the *Times'* lyrically embellished descriptions of the night work, A. K. Foxwell depicts the arduous trek to Woolwich in her 1917 book *Munition Lasses,* supplying the reader with seasonal descriptions of endlessly long morning hikes to the arsenal. Munitions factories rarely were situated in the locality from which they drew their labor; for much of the war, women were migrating from their homes to the munitions areas at a rate of 5,000 a month (Wilson 719 n. 5). Foxwell describes typical expeditions to the work site: "In the hot August days the heat was stifling and the dust suffocating; in the wet days of October, and the rampantly torrential nights of November, we waded ankle deep in mud and water, arrived with shoes, stockings and galoshes soaked" (30). The workers soon grew dispirited by the long hours, the seemingly endless and bitter commutes, the sleeplessness, the overexertion, and became disgruntled, angry, bitter, and tired, as evidenced by their writings in factory newspapers and magazines. Worse, their fatigue and exhaustion multiplied the likelihood of accidents on the job, jobs that for the most part were performed under hazardous conditions to begin with.

Women who worked in factories and in service on the home front, as well as those who worked as nurses, with the VAD, or in other facets of war service at the front, were susceptible to a host of dangers associated with war work. Those who worked in industry, for example, were vulnerable to dangers of all kinds, not least among these various kinds of poisoning they were virtually defenseless against: asbestos, TNT, blood, powder, khaki, gas, emery, varnish, and lead. Other workers were likely to be overcome by acid fumes or suffer skin complaints, vision problems, incontinence, constipation, or cramping. Women who worked at the glass works separating the shards from the glass, for example, wore no protective gloves when handling the razor-sharp raw glass pieces. Neither did the women who operated glass-cutting machines; they too, wore no protection on their hands or faces. Dopers—women who applied moistureproofing ("dope") to aircraft parts or to canvas gas masks and the like—worked without protective face masks or eyewear, even though the varnish fumes were dangerous and often lethal. Women in china and earthenware trades who were involved with dipping or aerography were required to undergo a medical exam every four weeks throughout their period of war work, but these requirements were not so rigorously enforced. Moreover, the machines women workers operated in industry were dangerous as well as fast. Industrial accidents were common and ranged from those that didn't affect the women's job performance to those that removed them permanently from the theater of war work, incapacitating them beyond repair.

Lisa Haddon worked during the First World War turning wheels on a lathe, making wheels of all sizes for trolley tracks. "It wasn't very safe," she says, "because there was a belt above you which worked the machine and that should have had a guard on it, but it never did. . . . We wore a hat but it didn't really cover your head. I had a bit of hair in the front of my face, and that caught in the machine. I was sent to the hospital, but I wasn't hurt, just frightened" (*What Did You Do in the War, Mum?* 52). Haddon's accident never metamorphosed into the likely nightmare because her hair fortunately jammed the belt, which caused the machine to stop. Other sorts of accidents prevailed. Braybon and Summerfield note that workers at the rolling mills in Southampton "cut their hands frequently, and remembered that they kept working; the blood ran away with the industrial effluent" (84). More serious were accidents of the sort Beverley Langford remembers. She worked in one of the gunpowder sheds at Abbey Wood and recalls the day the shed next to hers blew up: some of the workers were blinded; others were more severely injured (*What Did You Do in the War, Mum?* 70). Workers also were killed or injured on the job by industrial machinery that was badly guarded or poorly maintained, by runaway trolleys or wagons, or by falling equipment, too. Whether traveling to work, at work, or coming home from work, women were susceptible to a force of menacing dangers, dangers that many commentators and social guardians inaccurately deemed unavoidable.

Women's biographies, autobiographies, poems, diaries, memoirs, service newspapers, and oral histories reconstruct what it was like for working-class women during the war. As we shall see, many women tried during the war to articulate the dangers and call attention to the problems that threatened women who worked in industry, but their entreaties often were met with dangerously naive pronouncements, such as this one by Dr. Mary Scharlieb published in 1916 in the *Times*. Scharlieb argues:

Work alone never kills; conditions may tend to sickness and disease, but solid, useful work, such as the munition worker is doing to-day, is far less injurious to the health than the undue excitement of the bridge-playing and dancing of normal times. (May 5, 1916)

Clearly, Scharlieb's insipid pronouncement is informed by critically naive assumptions about the social and domestic spheres of working-class women, since she categorizes their world as one circumscribed by bridge games and dances. Contrary to her avowal, "work alone" can and did kill. Many readers may not be familiar with the serious health risks women took by working in the TNT powder rooms of many of Britain's arsenals, but women workers in the munition factories during the First World War died by the hundreds, poisoned from the factory work, especially during the first two years of the war when "inexperience of the dangers of working with TNT led to over a hundred fatalities" (Griffiths 22).

A writer for the *Times* noted in 1916 that "at the Woolwich Arsenal, welfare work is conducted not only with the head, but with the heart and the imagination, and therein lies the secret of its success" ("Midnight at Woolwich Arsenal," Sept. 1, 1916). Perhaps it was their noted imaginations that inspired factory officials to supply workers with cocoa or milk to allay the ingestion of toxins, albeit not very effectively, and to counteract the effects of toxic jaundice (TNT poisoning). While these efforts were solicitous, they were unsophisticated and, for the most part, inconsequential. Isabella Clarke told an Imperial War Museum interviewer that the workers "had cocoa about three times a day. What was in the cocoa we don't know but they reckoned there was something in it for killing the gas" (Imperial War Museum Sound Archive, Item SR 774, Reel 2). Similarly, Caroline Rennles, a powder girl in the Danger Building at Woolwich, recalls, "They used to give us milk to drink, you know, I suppose to counteract the poison or whatever it was, in our inside" (Imperial War Museum Sound Archive, Item SR 566, Transcript 9). Elsie McIntyre, who worked at the Barnbow factory in Leeds, also recalls that if the women went in to work at six in the morning, for example,

> well, we'd have a break about 10:00. You go down a long corridor into a place where, they call it a canteen today, there was just a counter and one person behind dishing the milk out; half a pint, go back and work again till about 1:00 and go down again for another half pint, go back and work till two. And then you'd come off the shift then, you see. (Imperial War Museum Sound Archive, Item SR 673, Transcript 6)

The milk and cocoa were thought so prophylactic that the Barnbow factory even kept its own cows and reportedly had 120 of them (McIntyre Transcript 11). Braybon and Summerfield note that like the cocoa, the "milk actually had no effect on the illness, but did encourage workers to believe that employers were looking after them—not surprisingly, many of them also thought that the drinking of milk offered them some protection" (95). It didn't, and many of the women who worked with TNT suffered from toxic jaundice even though they also were required to rotate their shifts: a fortnight on the powder and a fortnight off, working in another part of the factory.

Women who worked with the severely poisonous TNT powder were nicknamed "canaries" because their skin would turn a bright yellow, their hair a fluorescent bronze, an early result of the toxic effects of TNT poisoning. Other symptoms followed: "Women workers experienced nasal discomfort and bleeding, smarting eyes, headaches, sore throat, coughs, stomach pains, nausea, constipation or diarrhoea, skin rashes, anorexia, giddiness, drowsiness, and swelling of hands and feet" (Braybon and Summerfield 85).[1] Women who worked with other explosives, such as CE (Compound Explosive) powder, tetryl, and lyddite, also suffered yellow discoloration. Moreover, at the Woolwich Arsenal, "37 per cent of the women on shellfilling experienced abdominal pain, nausea and constipation while 'all workers complained of a metallic bitter taste.' . . . 25 per cent of the women at the Arsenal had skin problems, many found their periods affected and 36 per cent said they suffered from depression and irritability" (Braybon and Summerfield 85). Even while these symptoms widely were acknowledged and monitored by factory officials, women who experienced them often were dismissed by on-site doctors who failed to recognize the severity of the symptoms, and since there was no treatment for toxic jaundice during the First World War, could not administer to the women sufferers. Many of the sufferers withstood terrible rashes, facial swelling, and temporary blindness when the disease flared up at its worst, according to one canteen worker (Woollacott 82).

Lilian Miles, a munitions worker in Coventry, lost a sister to a different kind of poisoning, black powder poisoning; and although her sister showed many of the signs attributed to poisoning, her doctor's misdiagnosis most likely contributed to her untimely death. Lilian Miles explains in her oral history that her sister had been ill:

> She went to the doctor. The doctor said that she was under the influence of alcohol because she was falling about. And she couldn't hold herself up. She was falling about. So the doctor told her to come back again when she was sober, he said. Well I went down to the doctor and I said to him, 'She doesn't drink.' And he said, 'Well, I think she was under the influence of drink.' And I said, 'She wasn't. There's something wrong with her because,' I said, 'she's falling about all the while.' And of course she was only nineteen. She wasn't twenty. She died before she was twenty. Besides, she didn't drink. . . .
> She died in terrible agony. She died in terrible pain. And they said that the black powder it burnt the back of her throat away. (Imperial War Museum Sound Archive, Item SR 854, Transcript 18)

Miles adds that "The *News of the World* put it right across the front page 'Pretty Devonshire Girl Dies in Tragic Circumstances.' But they brought in an open verdict because they said they didn't know whether it was the work she was doing or what it was that caused her death" (Transcript 18–19). Whether protecting themselves, or whether genuinely ignorant of the dangers to which the women workers were introduced, on-site doctors could do little for the workers.

From frequently handling the TNT powder, most of the women turned yellow regardless of the milk or the cocoa supplied daily by the factory. What compounded the danger of TNT work was that other measures invented to protect the workers often worked against them. Regulation gloves and caps issued to the women for protection, for example, often trapped the TNT powder on the women's skin, and the repellant "barrier creams" they applied to their hands and faces attracted wanton TNT dust like flypaper. Just as they believed that the regulation milk or cocoa protected them or lined their stomachs, workers believed that the barrier creams spared them from the dangers of TNT poisoning, too. Elsie McIntyre, for example, explained that "whenever you touched yourself—oh, you daren't—you wouldn't do that with your glove on your face. It would turn yellow right away" (Imperial War Museum Sound Archive, Item SR 673, Reel 1). But some fifty years after her war work, McIntyre still insisted during her interview with an Imperial War Museum representative that the TNT powder did not penetrate the barrier cream supplied by the factory. She described her and the others' daily ritual:

> We had a cream as we went up on to the clean side. There'd be a little wooden bowl, if I can remember. And they called it barrier cream. And it was pink. I remember that's what you had to do before you went any further, rub this on your hands. Then put your gloves on. (Transcript 38–39)

Neither the cream nor the gloves protected the workers from the powder that quickly altered the women's appearances: "Those people you saw going about. You wouldn't remember. You wouldn't be born. They had yellow hands even through the gloves," McIntyre adds (Transcript 2).

Some contemporary cosmetic firms sought to profit from the women's conditions. While many wartime advertisers hoped to tap into a rich vein of patriotism in British consumers at the home front and began linking everything from bath soaps to bottled waters with national pride and British expedience—"Lifebuoy Soap will carry you to victory over the Germs and Microbes of Disease. Enclose a Tablet in your next parcel to the Front: he will appreciate it"; or Perrier's advertising slogan: "Fight to the Finish in war and trade" (Pugh 13)—advertisers soon aimed their promotions at women workers who suffered from toxic jaundice. Woolla-cott explains this capital idea:

> Some enterprising manufacturers decided that there was a potential mar-ket here for preparations promising to restore women workers' skin to its normal color, and advertisements began to appear in the papers and mag-azines that women workers read . . . "Ven-Yusa, The Oxygen Face Cream," admonished women workers to "remember, that while it is patriotic for girls to help their country with war-work, it is also patriotic for them to preserve the natural beauty of their skins and complexions with the help of Ven-Yusa." (Woollacott 82)

Patriotism, so often linked with women's gender roles, was invoked by cosmetic firms hoping to profit from the women's illnesses. Gail Braybon also notes in *Women Workers in the First World War* that "advertisers clearly felt that women workers were a good market to aim at, and also that war work had a good enough image to attract the notice of the gen-eral population" (164). Quoting from Ven-Yusa advertisements, and from advertisements promoting Harlene's Hair Drill, a product endorsed with testimonials from munitions workers (163), Braybon notes that the ads made it seem as if "war workers were also benefitted by Dr Williams' Pink Pills for Pale People, and regular consumption of Rowntree's Cocoa" (164). A notice placed in *Shell Magazine* by Moore's Belfast Linen Ware-house in Leeds advertises a "Pretty Georgette Blouse" available in a num-ber of delicate colors—"Sky, Pink, Ivory, Helio, Champagne, Rose . . . and *Sulphur*" (59, emphasis added). What a contrast the color sulphur brings to the pale, dreamy colors already listed in the advertisement. My guess is that manufacturers were hoping to legitimize as "delicate" the color sul-phur while making some profit off of it at the same time.

While cosmetic firms sought to define their role in allaying the women's skin conditions, other contemporaries believed that the canaries displayed their yellow skin proudly, since it identified them immediately as women who were "doing their bit." In fact, a number of factory songs celebrated and monumentalized the canaries' conditions, such as this chorus from "The Girls With the Yellow Hands," a song from an explosives factory at Faversham in Kent:

> The boys are smiling though they rush against a barb'ed trench;
> The girls are smiling though destruction hovers o'er their bench;
> And when the soldiers sweep along through lines of shattered strands,
> Who helped them all to do their job? The girls with yellow hands. (Wool-lacott, 193)

This sort of pride, according to Lilian Miles, was "ridiculous." Miles argues in her Imperial War Museum interview that the proud-to-be-yellow notion was "just something to say," a way of dealing with the daily horror, because the yellow was impossible to wash off: "It didn't make no difference. I mean, you'd wash and wash and it didn't make no difference. It didn't come off. Your whole body was yellow. You were yellow all over" (Transcript 15). McIntyre describes how the yellow covered every part of her body and notes that she was startled at the sight of her own yellow feet as she changed into white pumps one evening after work, saying, "and you'd have the yellow feet with that all the time because it used to go through the pumps, you know, and through gloves. Oh yes. I think I must have been six months getting rid of that yellow stuff" (Transcript 38). Woollacott is correct in pointing out that any glorification of the canaries' yellowing features was "presumably to arrogate whatever glamor [*sic*] was possible to a discoloration that must have been a social embarrassment as well as an indication of poisoning" (193). Celebrification, glamorization, and invocations of patriotism conspired during the First World War to explain or define the cultural expectations of British women, especially the canaries; and charges of patriotism, glamour, and celebrity seemed the clearest way of explaining the women's attraction to the deadly TNT work.

At least 349 cases of serious TNT poisoning were registered during the war, although many more cases must have gone unrecognized or unregistered. Regardless of factory-issue protective clothing, facial grease, barrier cream, milk, cocoa, or other measures, such as the "home" McIntyre describes below, 109 of the 349 registered cases died.[2] Though Woollacott estimates a larger number of deaths from toxic jaundice, Woollacott, Braybon, and Summerfield agree, as I do, that the number is essentially unknowable and ultimately unforgivable.

In some cases, women affected by TNT poisoning were sent away for two to three weeks to recuperate, McIntyre explains, and were rarely seen again on the job:

If you got TNT poisoning there was a home, I think it was Headingley way. I'm not quite sure about it. Was it Wheatwood Hall? Well, somewhere that way where if you got TNT poisoning you had to go in there for about two or three weeks while they cleared it up again. And very likely you'd never get them back again. The doctor would never allow them to come back again. You had to be very strong to stick this lot, you had. (Transcript 11)

The cultural consensus seemed to be that the women workers either had to "be strong to stick to" TNT work, be driven by a powerful sense of patriotism or on-the-job pride, or be desperate and "hard up," as Elsa Thomas notes in her oral history: "You must have been damned hard up to turn yellow, mustn't you?" (Imperial War Museum Sound Archive, Item SR 676, Reel 5). A writer for the *Times* referred to it as the kind of work that wasn't nearly prosaic *enough,* and wondered what it was that drew women to TNT work,[3] a subject of much conjecture during the war when attention focused itself more on the women's motivations than on their health and safety.

Importantly, the bravery of the women was overshadowed by a cultural assumption of greed on the women's part. Most contemporaries assumed that women were drawn to dangerous munitions work for the money, as George Ginns, a foreman at Daimler's in Coventry, and in White and Poppe's fuse factory, explains:

> Some of them, you know, used to make up decently and cover it up but a lot of them I don't think cared a hang whether they looked yellow or green as long as they got the money. That was all they were interested in. (Imperial War Museum Sound Archive, Item SR 775, Transcript 30)

McIntyre adds that she and her co-workers characteristically were shunned by women who worked in other parts of the factory, since the canaries had such base reputations:

> It was supposed to be so posh at A Factory, you know. It was supposed to be posh there. I don't know why. But they used to just kind of frown on the big factory because we were all yellow, you see. And they didn't used to get yellow in there. (Transcript 64)

What is ironic about all this back and forth is that the women who worked with TNT were anything *but* yellow—daily they faced the dangers of TNT work, mindful of the hazards, familiar with the discomfort, and conscious of the risks. Though they received high wages, the wages hardly compensated for the dangers. More than 100 of them never lived to spend their "fortunes." Clearly, the division that grew up in the factories between those who worked with the powder and those who didn't extended more from class hatred than anything else. That the canaries—looked down on, pointed at, made fun of on trains and trams, and frowned upon by co-workers—continued to do their bit at all testifies to their fortitude and integrity. They put their lives, besides their vanity, on the line for the war effort.

Class issues like those described above often were romanticized by the press, which liked to describe and thereby congratulate the benevolent camaraderie between classes. The *Times* journalist below, for example, uses the terms "society girls" and "factory girls" to distinguish between classes at the Woolwich arsenal, even though both groups by virtue of their work were "factory girls" and worked side by side on the bench: "The society girl likes a clean overall and cap and the factory girl, who began by calling it 'swank,' ended by wanting them herself when she discovered that the men liked to see the girls smart and clean" ("Girl Munition Workers. Health and a Twelve-Hours Day," *Times*). Even this short extract is pernicious because it mocks the slang ("swank") of the working-class woman and implies that while she may be unkempt, she harbors a real desire to imitate the society girl and to lure a man beyond her class. It is not the working-class woman's sexual ambitions that the writer condemns here but her social aspirations. Barrages of similar kinds of press clippings must have made their way injuriously into the minds and self-images of "factory girls" working for Britain during the war and most likely contributed to hostilities on the bench between the classes, though for the most part only a small percentage of women working in munition factories were from the middle and upper classes. The rift between the canaries and other factory workers—society girls or not—belies the myth of romanticized heterogeneity so often heralded as one of the wonderful incongruities of First World War factory work. Braybon and Summerfield refer to it as "one of the treasured myths of the war—the ready mixture of classes in the workshop" (75).

The extensive collection of photographs on Women's Work at the Imperial War Museum documents the working conditions described in the written and oral documents produced by women war workers. Hundreds of black and white photographs chronicle the in-house lives and spirits of the canaries. Ten years after the canaries' photographs were taken, however, 50 percent of the women were dead, according to Mr. Willis from the Department of Photographs at the Imperial War Museum. Most of the women worked without masks, he explained; the floors characteristically were dry when they should have been wet down at appropriate intervals throughout the day to minimize trafficking of the deadly TNT dust. Working conditions were better guarded during the Second World War, Willis explains. To reduce any daily carry-over of TNT dust, during the Second World War women were supplied with a new pair of skirted overalls every week and given a week's worth of different colored underwear. All of the workers would wear the same specified color each day—for example, white on Mondays, blue on Tuesdays, and so forth. In fact, mirrors installed on the factory floors during the Second World War enabled female arsenal supervisors to check and see whether the worker had on the specified color. If not, Willis explained, and if it was the worker's first offense, she was warned. The second time it happened the worker was docked two or three days' pay. The third time she was caught not wearing the scheduled color, she was sentenced to fourteen days in jail with hard labor. The punishments were, no doubt, extreme. Though workers were reproved for jeopardizing their own health and the health of others in the factories, offenders shouldered the blame for spreading the poisonous dust that factory officials insisted they work with in the first place.

Uniform precautions in the factories were inconsistent during the First World War, though some did exist. Although the Cardonald National Projectile Factory "looked after the supplying and cleaning of the different uniforms and overalls worn by the girls, [seeing that] each suit or overall was washed at least once a week, and in some operations where soiling was more frequent, as many as two to three changes per week were supplied" (Imperial War Museum Department of Printed Books, Women's Work Microfilm Collection Item MUN 12/4), those women not fortunate enough to work at a plant like Cardonald, well-equipped with a generous linen room, were threatened by the daily carry-over of TNT powder. It endangered the lives of not a few women workers, especially those who were too poor to wear a fresh set of clothes every day or too busy or too exhausted to make it home in time for an evening washload. As a result, many of them lost their lives.

Caroline Rennles's experience as a canary is important to our understanding of the context of much of the writing in the women's industry newspapers I discuss in the next chapter, especially since so much of the women's writing responds to the conditions she describes in her oral history. Though Eric Hobsbawm discounts the factuality of oral history narratives and argues that "most oral history today is personal memory, which is a remarkably slippery medium for preserving facts, [since] memory is not so much a recording as a selective mechanism, and the selection is, within limits, constantly changing" (*On History* 206), Rennles's testimonial narrative, precisely because it comes from a person rather than from a written document, brings this historical moment to life. She describes with great candor what it was like to be a canary during this episode, and because of this, her testimony is invaluable. Rennles recalls:

It was all bright ginger, all our front hair, you know, and all our faces were bright yellow. They used to call us canaries, of course, all over our clothes, like. We used to do aerial torpedoes. Well they were a good 2 feet 6 I should think, and oh they were heavy, heavy. So we used to fill 'em up with powder and we used to put 'em like that, between our legs, know what I mean, and, you know, swing 'em up like that. That's all you could do, swing 'em up in the front to where you had to like take them up the other end of the hut, you see. And I remember this doctor he was looking at us girls one day and he'd said, "Half of you girls will never have babies," he said. "You're pulling your stomachs to pieces. And the other half are too sick, God help you." (Imperial War Museum Sound Archive, Item SR 566, Transcript 8–9)

Rennles also tells of frequent encounters with "old boys" on the trains, saying that "They used to say, of course, they reckoned we had two years to live, you know. You see, the powder used to go into your stomach. They used to give us milk to drink, you know, I suppose to counteract the poison or whatever it was, in our inside. The old conductors used to say in the train, 'You'll die in two years, cock,' they used to say to us" (Transcript 9). Rennles outlived the conductors' predictions but suffered tremendously from her work at the factory and often was incapacitated on the job.

Lily Maud Truphet worked with Rennles and remembers the problems her co-worker suffered, describing them in her interview with the Imperial War Museum:

Rennles worked in the cordite in the danger building. . . . All her face and her hair was all the edges of her hair where the cap didn't go that was yellow. . . . She had trouble with her insides and she used to get biliousness. She used to be so bad I used to take her [home] about one, two, three in the morning. . . . You had to wait till after two o'clock before a train started again so if she was taken ill before that, we used to wait and take her, and sometime we were lucky to get a bus. (Imperial War Museum Sound Archive, Item SR 693, Reel 3)

Truphet explained that Rennles often would lie ill in the rest room and wait until the shift was over, when her friends could take her and see her home safely. Once a month, once in six weeks, Truphet says, the enfeebled Rennles became so debilitated that she doubled over at work.

Like Rennles, a number of women recall crouching under the workbench in agony or lying down in the ladies' room until shift was over, incapacitated by crippling abdominal pains. Other women recall characteristically covering for each other in these cases, since workers often got fired for "shirking" work duties. Dozens of women and men interviewed in the 1970s for the Imperial War Museum Oral History project vividly remember "going yellow." Lilian Miles, for example, notes that "The yellow powder turned us yellow all over. And our hair, I had black hair and it was practically green. . . . Well it wore off. Once you come out of it, it wore off. Within a couple of weeks it was gone. It wore right off very quickly. But while you were in it you were yellow" (Imperial War Museum Sound Archive, Item SR 854). Similarly, George Ginns recalls,

"There weren't a lot [at White and Poppe] suffered with the TNT but they all went yellow, you know, very yellow, as yellow as that on that towel. . . . The majority of them in the loading room on this TNT all went yellow— quite yellow they were. I don't think [they could've avoided it]" (Imperial War Museum Sound Archive, Item SR 775, Transcript 30). Listening to these oral history recordings, one cannot help being struck by the number of times interviewees point to an object in the room, as Ginns does, to indicate to their interviewer just how yellow the women workers turned—"as yellow as that on that towel." It must have been a color far removed from nature, a degree of yellow you had to see in order to believe. It is also amazing that after so many decades, interviewees can still recall the vividness of the shade.

Ellen Harbard filled bullets at the Abbey Wood munitions plant and remembers the canaries there. Importantly, Harbard also discusses the ghettoization of the canaries:

> I was working filling the bullets. You sat there with boxes of empty bullets, and you filled them with powder from a big thing like a dispenser. Then we put them into trays, and a couple of men came and took them away. There were people there working with lyddite and cordite. Their faces all went yellow from the yellow stuff. You wouldn't sit near them, because if your clothes touched them, all the yellow stuff would come out. They had to have a place apart from us. (*What Did You Do in the War, Mum?* 64)

The recovery process from toxic jaundice/TNT poisoning was a long one. In her own interview, Rennles says that when she left the powder rooms at Slades Green for a job at the Woolwich Royal Arsenal, she remembers that her skin was still a frightening yellow "'cos all the men said, 'What's the matter with you, kid?' and all that" (Transcript 54). After she left the factory at the end of the war, it took Rennles about one year, she says, to be rid of the yellow.

Indeed, canaries such as Rennles must have given first-time viewers a fright, as might have a number of other women on the site, too, women like Beatrice Lee, whose hair became bleached at the front from bending over hot acid every day, the bleaching a common side effect of the acid fumes (Imperial War Museum Sound Archive, Item SR 724, Reel 3). "It was a very unhealthy job," Lee remembers (Reel 3). Many of the workers also had discolored eyes, as Irish worker Isabella Clarke notes, and many of them died from their protracted conditions. Though Clarke lost a friend to toxic jaundice, her own poisoning was not so severe. She explains:

We were coming home for our Easter holidays and my friend was stopped and they noticed that both her eyes and mine, the whites of our eyes was discoloured a little bit but hers was badly. . . . I came home as usual on Easter holidays and then they come and informed me that she'd died. (Transcript 2)[4]

What a frightening spectacle some of these women must have made with their yellow skin, bleached hair, and discolored eyes—so frightening, in fact, that when Queen Mary toured the munition shops during the war, she reportedly was very scared by the sight of the women (Interviewer, Imperial War Museum Sound Archive, Item SR 854, Transcript 15).

TNT poisoning was only one of the hazards of munition work, as there were a number of related dangers. In addition to TNT poisoning, other women workers were overcome by toxic fumes in the arsenals; others had limbs removed either by doctors or by impulsive, impetuous machines or pressing lathes. Margaret Brooks, Keeper of the Sound Archives at the Imperial War Museum, notes that

> there were slow and insidious dangers as well. The workers were not well protected against toxic fumes or toxic substances. At least half of the contributors [to the Imperial War Museum Sound Archive] knew someone killed or injured by civilian work: gas poisoning, powder poisoning, asbestos poisoning, emery poisoning, varnish poisoning, even khaki poisoning. As a result of their war work, hundreds of women were killed and unknown and unknowable numbers injured. (13)

Whereas the canaries turned yellow after working even for short periods of time with TNT, other women workers had to cope with illnesses brought on by gaseous fumes or aggravated by working with asbestos. Isabella Clarke explained that "very little of this gas, once it got into your inside, I mean, it did affect you. Your hair didn't go yellow but when you went to bed, as you took your head off the pillow, the pillowslip was pink" (Imperial War Museum Sound Archive, Item SR 774, Reel 2). Laura Verity noted that she got "a bad throat" from working with so much asbestos at Bray's, in Leeds:

> Lots of asbestos at Bray's. When I think now, my sister was onto me she said it's a wonder you and me's living that all that asbestos, 'cos all these nozzles and things were made of asbestos, you know, and it used to lay on the floors and you could see your footprints in it. (Imperial War Museum Sound Archive, Item SR 864, Reel 6)

Compounding the dangers of the factory powder rooms was the fact that "there seems to have been little effective guidance on safety," Brooks writes

(13). She adds, "Workers were told not to breathe through their mouths but at some factories they sang a lot and TNT dust rotted their teeth" (13). Frustration was fueled by the maddeningly lax safety conditions at the factories. Though factory officials tried to protect the women workers by issuing protective caps, barrier creams, or beverages, dangers were often thought "unavoidable," and many descriptions of the health consequences in the factories characteristically begin by deflecting the blame or by minimizing the consequential aftermath.

Christopher Martin, for example, describes the working conditions of canaries in his *English Life in the First World War* by typically referring to a litany of institutionalized safety measures:

> Despite the use of masks or respirators and unpleasant facial grease, the fumes from TNT turned the girls' faces a hideous yellow. . . . The historian, Caroline Playne, saw a train full of them at a Midland Station. They were "Amazonian beings, bereft of all charm of appearance, clothed anyhow, skin stained a yellow-brown even to the roots of their dishevelled hair by the awful stuff they handled." Women varnishing aeroplane wings were overcome by the toxic fumes; they were seen lying sick in rows outside the workshops. Even more perilous were the "monkey" machines in which a heavy weight was dropped to compress the explosive into shell cases. (63)

Malcolm Brown in *The Imperial War Museum Book of the First World War* writes of "unavoidable" dangers, too, when discussing the typical accidents at Gwynne's munition factory, located during the war by the River Thames. In his introduction of Joan Williams, author of *A Munition Worker's Career at Messrs Gwynne's, Chiswick, 1915–1919*, Brown notes that "Minor problems were almost unavoidable—chips of metal would get into the eyes and once some grit from the grinding machine lodged on one of [Williams's] pupils" (211). In her memoir, Williams wrote that she had to go to the hospital to get her pupil scraped, and that both her eyes were so inflamed that she could hardly see, adding that she "had a weird journey home, running a few steps and then being forced to close my eyes for a bit till they'd recovered enough to run further. I expect the passers-by thought I was a sad case of intoxication" (quoted in Brown 211). The irony of Brown's statement is that these "unavoidable," "minor" problems easily could have been avoided if the workers had been issued protective eyewear. Elsewhere, Brown writes in a deadpan whitewash of culpability, "Inevitably there were accidents. Caroline Rennles recalled that one girl had her eyes blown out when some TNT exploded in her face" (207).

These "inevitable" dangers of industry work often were compounded by the women's lack of training on the power machines. One writer for the *Times* described the lack of training as "another burden to bear," explaining that the women "have no probationary and instructional period before they are wanted, but . . . have to take the places at very short notice" ("The 1916 Woman," May 18, 1916). Needlewomen, for example, like those who worked at Schneider's Clothing Factory in London, customarily were used to handwork, but they were given only two weeks to learn how to use the power machines. Those who weren't familiar with the technique of "guiding the work" often fell prey to sharp and dangerous needle cuts (Jane Cox, Imperial War Museum Sound Archive, Item SR 705, Reel 4). The "unavoidable" point that none of the historians makes is that the accidents they and the women describe were inevitable or inescapable only because of the bizarrely imprudent circumstances under which the women's work was carried out.

Characteristically poor ventilation and low, if any, lighting in the factories also compounded the dangers for the women. In the mending room of a Nottingham lace factory, for example, only natural light was used, so all the machines were arranged around the side of the room by the windows (Griffiths 162); at Schneider's Clothing Factory, glass roofs maximized the daylight but produced a disturbing and dangerous glare when coupled with the scant electric lighting (Cox, Imperial War Museum Sound Archive, Item SR 705, Reel 4). Jane Cox further explains that the factories weren't heated, and that there were no washing facilities. What's worse, she adds, toilets were located on the roof, making women an easy target during air raids.

Gabrielle West, who served in munitions factories as a member of the Women's Police Service recorded the poor working conditions at the Pembury factory in South Wales, noting in her diary the disgusting state of the factories and workshops there. She explains:

> The factory is badly equipped as regards the welfare of the girls. The change rooms are fearfully crowded, long troughs are provided instead of wash basins, and there is always a scarcity of soap and towels. The girls' danger clothes are often horribly dirty and in rags, many of the outdoor workers, who should have top boots, oilskins and s. westers, haven't them. Although the fumes often mean sixteen or eighteen casualties a night, there are only four beds in the surgery for men and women and they are all in the same room. There is another large surgery but it is so far from the girls' section of the factory that unless it is a serious case girls are not taken there. There are no drains owing to the ground being below sea level, but there could be some sort of incinerator, but there isn't. The result is a horrible and smelly swamp. There were until recently no lights in the lavatories, and as these same lavatories are generally full of rats and often very dirty the girls are afraid to go in. (Quoted in Brown 206)

One reason for the existing conditions is that when Britain's "substitution scheme" was introduced in 1914, women in industry entered factories that had previously been operated only by men. Toilet-sharing, then, was common, and in some factories men used the toilets from eight to nine, women from nine to ten, and so forth. Most often the factories quickly were converted for war work, and since there was little money available to restructure and reorganize the factories, many workers performed war jobs in factories that were neither built nor intended for that sort of work. A symptomatic example is that one of the most successful filling factories outside of London had been a brassiere and corset factory before the war. Woollacott notes that

> The diversity of workshops that had undergone conversion by 1916 astounded the writer Boyd Cable on a tour of munitions factories. He reported that, for example, a tobacco factory had turned to making shells, a gramophone works was making shell-fuses, and a magneto-maker, a piano factory, and a coach-builder had turned to the manufacture of one or another kind of munitions, all within the same area. (*On Her* 27–28)

Complicating the inadequacies of factory conversion, some factories were ill-equipped for harsh weather, since before the war they had employed only seasonal workers. The quick reorganization, then, often left little time and even less money for a restructuring of the building with adequate lighting, heating, comfort, or washing facilities.

Furthermore, factories that had been closed for some time prior to the war—run down and overrun by rats as a result—were reopened and quickly fitted for war work. Women factory inspectors, working with a Ministry of Munitions committee, reported on 1,396 factories during the war and found that "31 per cent of the factories were rated as acceptable; 49 per cent of the remaining factories were rated as second-class; and 20 per cent were rated as third class because they lacked adequate meal rooms, washing and first-aid facilities, rest rooms and 'suitable supervision'" (Griffiths 12). Because private factory owners often profited greatly from government contracts, many had the means to upgrade workplace conditions over the four-year war period, though some renovations may have been judged imprudent during national war. In a factory such as the one at Pembury described by Gabrielle West, however, where acid fumes caused "sixteen or eighteen casualties a night," moral responsibility would dictate that at least that many cots should be available. Since so little was done to ensure, institutionally, the safety of the women's working class, it is clear that it wasn't the accidents that were inescapable or unavoidable, as they so often were described; but it was the dangers that were inevitable.[5]

The dangers inevitably led to a sense of heroism among the women workers, who often occulted the figures of killed or wounded co-workers, such as the 69 who died and the hundreds who were wounded in the January 1917 explosion at the Brunner, Mond and Co. chemical factory in Silvertown, a factory located across the Thames from the Plumstead Marshes. The explosion was so forceful that "the noise and fires were apparent all over east London, and Woolwich [Arsenal] workers feared that their own factories were burning or threatened" (Brooks 13). An eyewitness to the blast said in the BBC film *We Are the Arsenal Girls* that the factory "went up just like the Prince of Wales' feather"— straight up, and shooting off to the left and to the right. Information on the explosion was never released to factory employees or to workers at other factories according to the BBC film, which fails to mention that "none of the [explosions] were reported in the press, which was censored under the Defence of the Realm Act (DORA): the government did not want to harm civilian morale, or put women off munitions work" (Braybon and Summerfield 84). Those who survived the Silvertown explosion were given £5 and 20 shillings severance pay. Apart from the workers' deaths and the damage the explosion caused to the factory and to contiguous factories nearby, the explosion also ruined a number of working-class houses in the neighborhood.

Factory and arsenal explosions were common during the First World War. Ellen Harbard recalls the day her munition factory at Abbey Wood blew up:

> Some flames started coming along the line toward us, and two men in the shop got hold of us and threw us outside onto the grass. It was raining like the dickens. They knew something was going to happen. The alarm was going, and Queenie, our supervisor, had to go back for her watch. She was blown to pieces. They found her corsets on the line. (*What Did You Do in the War, Mum?* 64)

Like the Silvertown explosion, news of Abbey Wood never reached civilians. Harbard was late getting home the night of the blast, and her father had already been to the police station asking about her; but since the police had no news of the occurrence, he assumed his daughter was out gallivanting. "They were waiting for me on the doorstep," Harbard recalls, "and my father said, 'Here she is. Take her in and give her a good hiding'"(64). Harbard remembers losing a brand new mauve coat, a tammy hat, and boots in the explosion. She also adds "They didn't give us anything, though. We never got a penny" (64). The next day when she and her friend returned to the factory, they spent the day outside on the grass separating the good bullets from the bad. Fourteen days later, she says, they lost their jobs and were "put off" (64).

A similar disaster occurred at the munitions factory at Pembury, where Gabrielle West worked as a policewoman. Her account details the flames of the G. Cotton section, and the subsequent explosions that followed on its heels. West describes the event in her diary, saying,

> Such a day! I came home at 3 to our rooms. At about 6 o'clock there was a tremendous explosion and then a whole succession of little bangs. I rushed upstairs and from the window saw flames and smoke coming from the factory in volumes. The landlady wept and flapped and said poor Miss Buckpitt was no doubt already dead, and all the poor dear girls blown to atoms, and all the women police and so forth. (Quoted in Brown 208)

Once the fire was put out, West remembers, the workers were ordered back to their sheds. Afraid, but commanded to re-enter, one worker called out to the others as she returned to work that her last will and testament was stashed under the carpet in her drawing room, and asked that they see to it that her mother received all of her money.

Danger and mourning extended to other factories in Great Britain, as well, during the First World War, including those in Wales, where women workers so mourned the death of a co-worker that her funeral had to be held on August Bank Holiday, 1917. Figure 3.1 shows women munition workers in Swansea mourning her death at the funeral (Imperial War Museum Department of Photographs Item Q 108452) where hundreds of grieving co-workers attended the service out of kinship and a shared sense of immediacy and loss.

In an effort to memorialize the hundreds of killed and wounded war workers, the Lord Bishop of London held a special service at St. Paul's on April 20, 1918, where he addressed the crowds who had assembled and packed themselves into the cathedral. According to representative letters on file at the Imperial War Museum—letters from bereaved parents, brothers, sisters, husbands and friends—there were not nearly enough tickets available for those who had lost loved ones to civilian war service. Those who were fortunate enough to get into the cathedral that evening for the six P.M. service most likely had to stand (Imperial War Museum Department of Printed Books, Women's Work Microfilm Collection Item MUN 34 2/5). Reverend B. Staunton Batty, Chairman, wrote in a letter to London's factories that

> the number of those who desire to be present at service has very largely exceeded our expectations, and the Cathedral could be filled five or six times

3.1 Women munition wokers in Swansea mourning the death of a colleague killed in an accident at work. Her funeral was held on August Bank Holiday, 1917. Photograph Q108452, printed with permission of the Imperial War Museum.

over. We are obliged therefore to ration the tickets and send you all we can spare for your workers. . . . If we sent the full number of tickets, it would mean that more than three-quarters of the factories in London would have none. Possibly those workers who wish to come could arrange to ballot for the tickets. (Imperial War Museum Department of Printed Books, Women's Work Microfilm Collection Item MUN 34 2/2)

The concept of a lottery to attend the service of a lost friend, daughter, sister, or co-worker seems inordinately cruel—but Batty's letter is important because it suggests the magnitude and number of those who had hoped to attend and memorialize dead or wounded civilian war workers.

Aside from special war services, such as the one at St. Paul's Cathedral and others held all over Britain during the war in distinct memory of war workers, civilians were memorialized in other ways. During the war Agnes Conway, for example, sought to erect a Women and War exhibit as a permanent installment at the Imperial War Museum, and received letters from anguished parents who praised her efforts to memorialize the women workers. Grieved mother Mildred Hart wrote the following letter in response to the Imperial War Museum's announcement of a permanent Women and War exhibit. Because her letter details her daughter's death in the munition factory, it can help us understand and place within an appropriate context the hazardous working conditions in industry. Mrs. Hart describes for Conway the daily conditions of women's munitions work:

> I have at last received a photo of my daughter which I hope will meet with your approval she contracted Blood poison through working in the Edmonton Munition Works using the TNT. She was a great-sufferer she only worked there 2 months and was taken to the Military Hospital at Edmonton then from there to St. Mary's Hospital . . . where she died she went under an operation when they took from her 14 pints of poisoned blood from her she rallied a few days longer then died she was 23 years old and left a little boy her husband was in salonica at the time so could not see her thanking you for your kind offer its' nice to know they are remembered by some one. Believe me to be yours respectfully, Mildred Hart. (Imperial War Museum Department of Printed Books, Women's Work Microfilm Collection Item MUN 34 2/5)

Two other letters accompany Hart's in the Women's Work Collection at the Imperial War Museum. Taken together, the three letters paint a horrifying portrait of the deaths of young women engaged in war factory work. Mrs. Sophia Brookes wrote to Agnes Conway on September 10, 1919, about the accidental death of her daughter. She writes:

[She was] wheeling clay in a dandy over a lift and the dandy wheel got fast and threw her down the lift. . . . She was 15 yrs and 4 months she was killed 15th day of November 1918 while wheeling clay for Gov't purpose's over a lift about 30 feet deep the weep of the dandy got fast and threw her down the lift she was picked up unconscious and died on her way to the Infirmary. (Imperial War Museum Department of Printed Books, Women's Work Microfilm Collection Item MUN 34 2/3)

Grieved father Mr. Bunce wrote the following note to Conway in honor of his lost daughter Mary:

Dear Sir or Madam I am sending you one off the Photo of Miss Mary Bunce which I think is very kind of you she met her death on September 3th 1917 at the Old Parks Works Wednesbury she was a Crane Driver her age was 19 Last buirthday.
thanking you very much
from Mr Bunce
(Imperial War Museum Department of Printed Books, Women's Work Microfilm Collection Item MUN 34 2/4)

These three letters are powerful because they are so spare, written without reproach or censure, lacking in reprimand and blame, even though Hart's daughter died after working only two months at the Edmonton factory, even though Brookes's daughter was too young to be employed legally in heavy industrial labor, and even though Bunce's daughter met with a similar accident while operating a government crane. A keen sense of frustration must have attended the losses of their daughters, but the controlled language of the letters suggests that the parents—like many factory workers, government officials, and journalists—may have thought that accidents of this sort were indeed unavoidable and even inevitable.

Sophia Brookes's 15–year-old daughter, like so many of her counterparts, joined the ranks of the working class at an early age during the First World War. Young women of 11, 12, and 13 dropped out of school during the war, lied about their ages often with parental consent, and were subject not only to hazardous dangers in industry and in other jobs but left themselves open to emotional damage and hysteria, as well. Dame Agatha Christie, who worked as a Red Cross VAD nurse, remembers that when legs or arms were removed or amputated in the hospitals, they had to be brought down to the furnace—this was an unpalatable job usually reserved for the youngest girls. Christie describes one of the young girls, saying: "This poor child was very very young for what she was doing. She was, I think, not more than eleven or twelve then. She used to go nearly into hysterics" (Imperial War Museum Sound Archive, Item SR 493, Reel

2). Moreover, Alice Proctor, a VAD driver, recalls that "one unfortunate girl threw herself over the cliffs, committed suicide," and adds, "If they did go, it was because they were worn out with the mental part of it, the strain" (quoted in Brown 197). Sometimes, school supervisors unwittingly conspired in the girls' signing up. Ellen Harbard recalls that she was only 13 at the start of the First World War but the headmistress of her school told her that she was 14, so she left to do a sewing job. "I thought my mum had made a mistake, but when I told her, she said, 'No, you're only 13, but go if you want to.' I said, 'Well, I shall earn some money, shan't I.' Anyway the lady next door knew I was only 13, and she gave me away. I had to go back to school" (*What Did You Do in the War, Mum?* 64). One Mrs. Jones recalls that in 1917 she, too, left school at fourteen to work at the Woolwich dockyard (*What Did You Do in the War, Mum?* 53). The cultural draw toward war work was fueled not only by patriotism or the need to "do one's bit" for the war, but in many cases women no matter how young were lured into war work by heavy propaganda campaigns in the press, or by placards and billboards that shamed them and other family members into war work, drawing women and girls into the factories not only from neighboring towns but from Britain's dominions, as well. Britain's large emigrant and expatriate work force certainly complicates matters and raises even larger questions about the consequences of dangerous working conditions. Because the call to work in Britain's arsenals and factories extended to many of her dominions, one cannot help wondering about the fate of women (and girls) from South Africa, Ireland, or Australia who came over to do their bit for "the war to end war," for the "War for Peace."

There still seems a great deal of unanswered and ultimately unanswerable questions about the women's working class in Britain during the First World War, though oral histories, such as those on file in the extensive collection at the Imperial War Museum, biographies, autobiographies, memoirs, and diaries of women who worked during the First World War, provide essential information for understanding the dangerous conditions of First World War factory work and stand as valuable sources for discovering and recovering women's history.

In the next chapter, we will see articulated again working-class women's concerns for their safety. Women workers wrote bitterly and articulately in their service newspapers about hazardous conditions on the job site, and though many of the service newspapers were published monthly, some even weekly, the women's interminable manifestos were neglected and often trivialized as recast versions of schoolgirl magazines whose political content characteristically was ignored. To be sure, the factory was no safe place by any means; and it is heartbreaking to see that women tried to articulate specifically in their service newspapers their anger and fear about the dangerous conditions described so vividly above. The next chapter details the genesis of the women's service newspaper and continues the discussion of working-class women, factory conditions, and cultural reproval.

Chapter 4

Working-Class Women's Factory Newspapers

'Twas not our part
To share the thousand fights
Nor spend in the one God-given chance
The life we call our own.
But toiled we through long days
And longer nights
With ever on our lips
A prayer or song
'Till victory was won.

So reads the inscription on the fly leaf of the *Cardonald Souvenir Magazine*, the final issue of a factory newspaper published by workers at the Cardonald National Filling Factory in January 1919. A weekly publication since 1916, *Cardonald News* is one example of the dozens of women's factory newspapers that flourished during the war, chronicling women's participation in Britain's war effort, and capturing the lives, spirits and concerns of working and working-class women. Unlike *Cardonald News*, now part of the permanent Women's Work collection at the Imperial War Museum, many women's factory newspapers, service newspapers and souvenir magazines have been lost to time, something the writers themselves predicted, as the following selection from the preface of *Shell Magazine*, a publication of the women workers at the National Ordnance Factory in Newlay, Leeds, suggests:

> The time may come when this magazine will be relegated to the bookshelf or the cupboard, but so long as our readers live they will retain vivid memories of their life and work at Newlay. . . .

When peace has folded the world in her garment of calm, that same conservation will always bear a note of triumph as we tell how we did our best to supply the grandest troops in the world with munitions. (1)

Similarly, in the *Cardonald Souvenir Magazine* we read, "Soon it will be but a memory. But there will ever remain with us the knowledge that while it was not ours to fight—*we worked*" (Jan. 1919: 24). And work they did: by 1918, nearly three million women worked in industry; and in trades such as munition and clothing manufacturing, trades where factory newspapers flourished, women made up more than three-quarters of the work force (Griffiths 13). To give voice to their production, to interweave their own personal histories with *la grande histoire* of the war, women factory workers almost immediately turned to factory newspapers, where distinctions of class, education, and gender often gave way to the coalescence of national and industrial vigor.[1]

While First World War scholars may be familiar with service newspapers published by soldiers fighting in the trenches (publications such as the *Wipers Times* published by soldiers in Ypres),[2] women's factory newspapers and magazines are not so well known, and most are available only in special collections and archives. Written and published in and outside London by a female contingent interested originally in mirroring the male newspapers in terms of column features and news items and then in one-upping the male publications in terms of news, humor, artwork, and overall quality, women's factory newspapers boosted morale and strengthened civic and national pride on the home front; but they also were sources of humor during the grimmest of times, and they stand as literary and historical documents enumerating the accomplishments of working-class women of the First World War. More than that, they are political manifestos, chronicling the voices and championing the histories of the women's working class in First World War Britain. Amid the pageantry and bravado of the publications, though, lie the tensions of the workplace, evident in the women's published literary parodies, editorials, poetry and plays recorded in the factory newspapers. Articulating the dangers of factory work, censuring labor hierarchies within the factories, attacking the class system and its inherent bias, and encoding an often severe distaste for the war and for the social and cultural consequences of it, such as infamous Defence of the Realm Act regulations, women writers began to turn factory newspapers into cultural documents that chronicled the dangers and unfair labor practices confronting the diverse women's working class.

What motivated the workers at home to produce factory and service newspapers was most likely the proliferation of trench newspapers that found their way from the battlegrounds of Belgium and France to the homes, kitchens, and breakfast tables of mothers, fathers, wives, sisters, and brothers of British fighting men. A notice on the cover of the June 1915 men's publication, the *Garrison Goat* (published in Malta), for example, urges soldiers to "SEND A COPY HOME." Civilians brought the trench newspapers to their jobs, and the notion caught on: women wanted to produce factory newspapers in response to those produced by men at the front, often driven by a similar sense of frustration and futility. Martin Taylor notes that humor was often a principal ingredient in the trench magazine,

> humour in the face of official deception, petty regulations, physical discomfort, mental exhaustion and the ever-present threat of death. It was one of the few means of imposing order on an otherwise disordered existence, especially after faith in glory and patriotism had disappeared, and one that enabled, against all odds, the survival of human dignity. (*"The Open Exhaust"* 24)

A characteristic trait of the women's factory newspapers, too, humor often disguised a similar sense of disgust and camouflaged the women's common outrage. Though humor became an important component in the women's literary articulation of the wartime experience, an important distinction is that while the men's service newspapers contained a tremendous assortment of original verses, poetry, and limericks, the women drew more upon parody, and often couched their despair in rewritten forms of recognizable and culturally familiar poems, drawing their inspiration from a variety of sources that included William Shakespeare, Lewis Carroll, Rudyard Kipling, and William Butler Yeats. Unlike the authors of men's newspapers, who resisted the impulse to engage in criticizing Britain's wartime ideologies, women were freer to challenge cultural assumptions and boldly address contemporary issues such as pacifism, racial suicide, feminism, the dangers of civilian work, and the ever-increasing social limitations of the Defence of the Realm Act, the legislative act that curbed social activity and prescribed the behavior of a nation. That the editors were able to skirt DORA section II.21, which regulated and censored all publications that "caused disaffection or alarm" among the civilian population, is a testament to the writers' cleverness.

Even though many of the writers predicted in editorials that their work would be forgotten, as early as 1917 a movement grew to create a museum to house assorted artifacts of the war—trophies, souvenirs found on battlefields, maps, music, flag-day souvenirs, medals, decorations, autographed letters, regimental magazines, and trench drawings

No. 4 Vol. 1.   Double Summer Number.   June, 1917.

4.1   Front cover of *The Bombshell*. Printed with permission of the Imperial War Museum.

"CARRY ON"

The Armstrong Munition Workers Christmas Magazine 1916

1/-

4.2 Front cover of *Carry On*. Printed with permission of the Imperial War Museum.

4.3 Front Cover of *The Shell Magazine*. Printed with permission of Special Collections, McFarlin Library, the University of Tulsa.

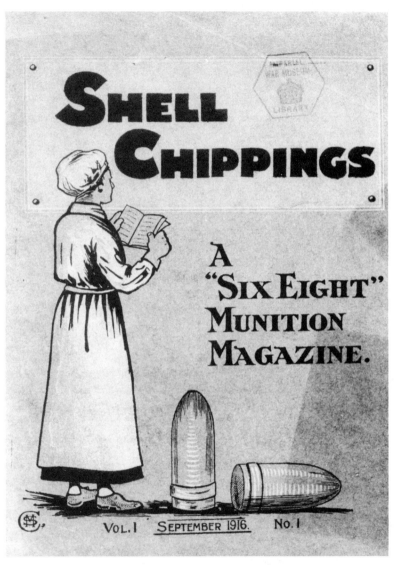

4.4 Front cover of *Shell Chippings*. Printed with permission of the Imperial War Museum.

(Griffiths 1). Out of this movement, Griffiths explains, "grew the foundation of the Imperial War Museum and a committee for recording the contribution of women to the war effort" (1). By October 1918, the Women's Work Subcommittee had collected enough material to hold an exhibition of women's work at Whitechapel Art Gallery, which attracted an astounding 82,000 visitors.[3] In his discussion of the event, Griffiths explains that the success of the exhibition reflected the extent to which, "due to domestic press censorship, the nation knew as little about the work being carried out by women in the shipyards and engineering shops as they did about what was happening in the trenches" (6). Because of the Subcommittee's early exhibition, and the interest generated by it, the Imperial War Museum now houses a unique collection of women's factory and service newspapers—publications such as *WAAC Magazine, WRNS Magazine* (published by the Woman's Royal Naval Service), *Cardonald News* (published by workers at the National Filling Factory in Glasgow), *The Whistle: The Journal of the Women's Police Service, The Georgetown Gazette* (published by workers at the Scottish Filling Factory in Glasgow), *The Woman's Leader* (published by the QMAAC), *Employees Quarterly* (published by the employees of Siddeley Deasy Motor Car Co., Ltd.), *NTF Souvenir* (a magazine published by women and men prison workers), *Shell Chippings. A "Six Eight" Munition Magazine* (an anniversary souvenir of women's work in the Bootle munition factory), *Home Service Corps Review, Carry On: The Armstrong Munition Workers Christmas Magazine, The Clincher: The House Journal of Castle Mills, The Clincher Magazine: The House Journal of the North British Rubber Company Ltd., Bombshell: The Official Organ of the NPF [National Projectile Factory] Templeboro, The Patriotic Gazette, The C. R. O.,* and *The Ladies' Field,* as well as some examples of postwar factory and service newspapers, such as the QMAAC publication *Old Comrades' Association Gazette,* and American women's service newspapers, such as *The Farmerette.*[4]

Many of these publications enjoyed an international readership, and often reached thousands of subscribers. When *Cardonald News,* a publication of the National Filling Factory (NFF) in Cardonald, Glasgow, published its souvenir issue in 1919, for example, its editor boasted an in-house circulation that exceeded 2,000 (13). First produced as exportable commodities—something to ship off to soldiers in the trenches to show how the women back home were helping the war effort—many factory newspapers reprinted testimonial letters from men in the trenches thanking the workers for their publication, as the following letter in the May 17, 1917 issue of the *Bombshell* attests:

Your little publication "The Bombshell" is very popular in the sector of the trenches occupied by men hailing from Sheffield and District. . . . We should like a few more as they are so eagerly sought after.

Yours, Q M Sgt. J R C Ashton, 6th Y & L Regt., A P O (8) 11, Base Details B. E. F. France.

(*Bombshell* 1.4 [June 1917]: 24)[5]

Though the workers savored the international popularity of their publications, their factory newspapers eventually began to serve a more personal office. When the war ended, and the women saw their work in the arsenals unwittingly drawing to a close, their factory newspapers became more like souvenirs, swan songs almost, missives containing the memories of years of service, documenting with an eye toward history, women's work in Britain's industries, in her arsenals, and ordnance and filling factories. A wealth of information can be discovered in reading the newspapers of women who worked during the First World War in police service, or with the WRNS, the WAACs, the QMAACs, the First Aid Nursing Yeomanry (FANY), the Forestry Service, the Women's Land Army, the Volunteer Aid Detachment, or in other facets of war service and factory work; but I focus in most of this chapter on the evolution of arsenal and munition factory newspapers published between 1914 and 1919, paying particular attention to the souvenir magazines published for Christmas 1918 and Christmas 1919, as the women workers were being relieved of their posts in the factories and "returned" to their homes. These particular publications register even more strongly than others working-class women's responses to the negative rhetoric with which the public assaulted them for their war work. Archival collections of these late factory newspapers and souvenir magazines are more complete than other collections, too, so they provide evidence of the range of responses that characterized women workers.

The most immediately striking element of women's factory newspapers is their appearance, the quality of their publication. In fact, everything about their production—from the quality of the paper, the varied selections of typeface, the sophisticated layout, the multicolor shots, the fancily wrought artwork, the reproductions of the many photographs, and the number of pages (often seventy or eighty in the souvenir issues)—seems to suggest that the factory newspapers enjoyed a wealthy patronage and that apart from the money generated from advertisements and sales, they most likely were funded privately or by subscription—an important point, since it differentiates the women's publications from the men's.

For the most part, soldiers' service newspapers were funded by circulation revenues: copies of the trench newspapers were sold to soldiers and civilians alike, and the money generated from the sales funded subsequent issues. What money was left over often went to the Chaplain's fund, according to Patrick Beaver ("Introduction," *Wipers Times* xvi). Indeed, the quality of the soldiers' trench newspapers varies: some were typed; some were hand-drawn; and others were "printed to a high professional standard"[7]—some, in fact, were shopped out for printing in London.[8] Unlike that of the trench newspapers, though, all revenue proceeds from the women's arsenal and munition factory newspapers and souvenir magazines were handed over to war charities. An announcement on page two of *Shell Magazine*, for example, reads,

> the whole of the work in connection with this Souvenir has been done voluntarily. . . . The committee . . . trusts that as a result of the combined efforts of all concerned, a considerable sum will be handed over to War Charities. (2)

One way to estimate the circulation of the women's arsenal factory newspapers, and thus gauge the severity of their weekly donations to war charities, is to note the increasing numbers in the papers' weekly contests. Many issues of the arsenal factory newspapers were hand-numbered to keep track of circulation and revenue. Each new issue published a winning number from the previous issue, and the holder of that particular number received a cash prize. Judging by the increase in prize value, and even by the numerical increases of the winning numbers, for example, we can see that *Cardonald News* enjoyed a weekly readership of at least 610 in 1918, since that was the number of the winning issue announced in the February 1 issue of that year. In fact, the cash prize at the *Cardonald News* jumped from 2/6 to 5/0 in less than one month in 1918,[9] a sure indication of the popularity, and the financial success of the publication.

Because the money generated from sales had gone over to war charities, as writers attest in their editorials, the cost of producing the factory newspapers may have been offset by published advertisements and supplemented by factory owners or by the workers themselves. This is important because in every issue there seems a great deal of editorial freedom. The factory newspapers are characteristically political in temper, pacifist in spirit, feminist in tone, and specific in their moral outrage. Clearly, the women workers suppressed their anger, their fear, their frustration, and their sense of injustice in the arsenals and ordnance factories for too long—and these emotions are given not only fair romp but fastidious attention in their factory newspapers, as we shall see.

A strong percentage of arsenals and munition factories published newspapers toward the end of the war, and many factories shared their publications not only with family and friends outside the job but with those from other ordnance factories and arsenals, since writers reported on events in other factories as well their own. One issue of *Bombshell*, for example, a publication out of the National Projectile Factory (NPF) in Templeboro, contains a piece on the Munitions Revue put on by workers at the Lancaster NPF. Some of the larger factories had competing newspapers and magazines and issued more than one souvenir or farewell magazine at the war's end. The editor of *Dornock Souvenir Magazine*, for example, proudly notes that "Until yesterday, our Cordite Section friends might have claimed with truth that the *Mossband Farewell Magazine* was the best publication of the kind which had been produced at the Factory" (1). Because editors of factory newspapers freely reprinted letters, features, and columns from other factory newspapers and often patterned their own material after popular columns found in another publication, each issue captures and documents more than the atmosphere of an individual factory or arsenal but appropriates the temperament and community of the women's working class. When examined together as a set of cultural documents, the women's factory newspapers reveal the encoded dialogues of a specific and underrepresented class. Similarities among these cultural documents, such as standard features in every issue, take on cultural significance.

Nearly every women's factory newspaper had its versions of Kipling's poem "If," for example, as well as versions of "Ten Little Indians," "Sing a Song of Sixpence," "The House that Jack Built," and "The Walrus and the Carpenter." Since so many factory and service newspapers had at least one version of Kipling's poem, an examination of the many varieties of the poem can be useful not only because of the literary and allusive merit they yield, but also because the writers successfully capture the spirit of the shop floor and describe the typical chaos, noise, and din of the factories. Important to our understanding of the version of "If" published in the first issue of *Bombshell* is that the writer addresses gender in the last line of her poem, pointing to the situational inadequacy of the conclusion of Kipling's poem, "You'll be a Man, my son!" She writes:

> If you can keep your head when all about you
> The belts are whirring and the hammers ring
> If when at first the stop and din astound you
> You try to learn and understand each thing;
> If you can learn, and not be tired of learning
> The name and use of all the different m's

And know the look and feel of every turning
And see the refuse sorted from the gems.

If you can keep your galleys clean and flowing
Without the loss of temper or of rake
Nor come back full of indignation glowing
When fruitless hunts for Izal take the cake,
If you can urge—and not be called a driver,
If you can push on work—you get a smile;
If you make each woman be a striver
And feel that what she's doing is worth while;

If you can bear to have your tools all taken
Each day, and never stop to curse the thief
If when your tubs want emptying, you're forsaken
By men, who prefer a plate of beef,
If you can get one mind in all your workers
And make them feel that if they persevere
Their shop will be the cleanest—even shirkers
Must know they've got to do their bit or clear;

If you can make your Brushes, Tubs and Trolleys
To serve their turn long after they are done,
And never think about the last turn's follies
Who *must* have scattered orange peels for fun;
If you can keep the Foreman and Machine girls
At peace with each one of your chosen few
And see that every red band at the bench hurls
Her orange peel far from public view.
If you last the Shift of eight long hours
At night and never turn a hair "pro tem.,"
You're a success, and—all the mighty powers
Will say you're just the Forewoman for them. (9)

Importantly, in the writer's third stanza, she alludes to hostility experienced by many women workers on the job: male sabotage. Many women
make reference to stolen tools, and point the finger at scornful male co-
workers who sabotaged their work by nailing shut the womens' work stations, for example, pouring oil over their tools, or refusing to answer
questions about the job. Couching her anger in the form of a playful parody, the writer calls attention to these charges and censures the offenders
while appearing to make light of the events.

WAAC Magazine also published a parodic version of "If," one equally
fastidious in its description of the chaotic workplace and its shortcomings

and mindful of the discrepancies between male and female members of
the auxiliary army corps:

If you can keep your cook when all about you
Are sitting up and begging for the lot,
If you can see the typists all around you
And snaffle all the best that they have got.
If you can treat a Gen. Dom. as a waitress;
And still elude Headquarters' eagle eye,
Or pay a clerk and use her as a housemaid,
By wangling the latest A.C.I.

If you can straf but always keep your temper,
Yea, even when deserters have their way;
If you can soothe the girls from Havre and from Paris,
And all who cause dispute about their pay;
If you can bear to see the hats you've issued
Just twisted till the wearers look like guys,
And find the clothes you've spent such hours in fitting
Bedizened with all sorts of coloured ties.

If you can spend a day in fruitless searching
For memo Z99 in every file,
But find it was undated and unnumbered
And had been left unanswered quite a while;
If you can force yourself to love the biscuits
The army likes to give for food and bed,
Or smile when you have ordered in some strawberry
But get some chips and carrots in its stead.

If you can laugh when leave is only granted
On condition that you pay for all your fare
And show no *wilful* damage was intended
When somebody has smashed up every chair;
If you can meet the Barrack Warden calmly
And tell him everything has gone astray
Yours is the Corps and everyone that's in it,
And what's more, you'll be a great U. A. [Unit Adm.]
(No. 3 [Jan]: 7)

The WRNS had a version, too, a short one that appropriates Kipling's
opening line but again addresses the gender distinction in its final line:

If you can keep your head when all about you
    Are losing theirs, and everything's a whirl;

> And not despair when brass hats simply doubt you—
> You'll be a coding officer, my girl!
> (*WRNS,* July 19, 1919: 30)

Other service newspapers published versions of popular poems such as Lewis Carroll's "The Walrus and the Carpenter." In the following two examples, both writers address the issue of substitution or "dilution"—the Home Office's word for describing women's entry into the skilled labor force, since it was assumed that three or four women would be required to do the job of one man. Because the work would be performed not by one but by a number of workers, or it might be broken down into various segments or tasks, the women workers would dilute the work force. To this end, a writer for the *Times* noted in 1916 that "to replace an ordinarily skilled man a more than ordinary woman is required" ("The Woman Who Works," Dec. 12, 1916). The following writer in *WAAC Magazine* parades that notion, and in her parody of "The Walrus and the Carpenter," mocks an M.P. who assumes that more than fifty women would be needed to do the work of one called-up man:

> England was glum as glum could be,
>   Labour was dry as dry;
> You couldn't find a man to work
>   There was no man to try!
> They'd all gone soldiering to France
>   Or else Gallipoli.
>
> A Red-hat and a sad M.P.
>   Were walking down the Strand.
> They wept like anything to see
>   The sad state of the land.
> "If we could only get some man,"
>   They said, "It would be grand!"
>
> "If fifty girls (or thereabouts)
>   Each took on one man's job,
> Do you suppose," the Red-hat said,
>   "'Twould be an awful blob?"
> "I think so," said the sad M.P.
>   And gave a bitter sob. . . .

[The M.P. meets up with a WAAC at the Connaught Club. She "administers" the following "snub":]

> "You thought it couldn't possibly

Help on the dear old War,
Simply because you'd never heard
Of such a thing before.

"Nicht Wahr?—Fritz and Hans would say—
You thought it wouldn't wash,
That we should try to do men's work
Was, simply speaking, Tosh.
But own it frankly—don't you think
We've helped you beat the Boche?"
(*WAAC Magazine,* 3 [Jan 1919]:3–4)

By the close of the poem, the M.P. agrees with the WAAC, and the two dine by his invitation on a sumptuous lunch reminiscent of prewar days, a feast no doubt inspired by the one described in Carroll's nonsense poem. That so many writers chose to imitate Carroll's poem suggests that it was more than the nonsense or the rhythmical meter that attracted them to "The Walrus and the Carpenter," a meter that Carroll borrowed from Thomas Hood's "Dream of Eugene Aram" (Gardner 233).

Carroll's poem, in fact, details the hoodwinking of innocent young oysters who "[hop] through the frothy waves/And [scramble] to the shore" because they believe that the Walrus and the Carpenter are calling them to take "a pleasant walk, a pleasant talk/ Along the briny beach" when in fact, they are leading them duplicitously to slaughter. The eldest oyster doesn't fall for their shenanigans; but the younger ones rush forward with all the zeal and ardor reminiscent of women's (and certainly men's) enthusiastic entry into factory work and war service. When Kitchener broadcast his civilian call to arms in March 1915, the response was immediate and more than 110,000 women registered themselves for war work. When the war ended, the demobilization of troops drove women out of their jobs and back into conventional prewar areas of work. Many of those workers felt betrayed and ill-paid for the integrity and intensity of their zeal.

"The Foreman and the Manager," a poem by E. S. Caley published in *Shell Chippings,* also appropriates Carroll's parody of Thomas Hood's poem. Here, the foreman eventually has resigned himself to women's entry into the work force and begins his lecture to the manager by admitting that "the time has come" for her to learn the tricks of the trade. The poem progresses as he passes along to her the secrets of industrial success:

"The time has come," the Foreman said
"To talk of many things,
Of Screws and Shells and overalls

Of clocking on, and Kings
And why the shaft gets boiling hot
And should the mandrels sing?"
(*Shell Chippings*, 1.1 [Sept. 1916]:5)

Importantly, this short piece takes its inspiration from what Martin Gardner identifies as the best known and most often quoted lines of Carroll's poem, the section directly before the Walrus and the Carpenter devour the oysters. The Walrus sits the oysters down and distracts them with a nonsense lecture about "shoes—and ships—and sealing wax—/Of cabbages—and kings—" to encourage them to let their guards down. Once he successfully wins their undivided attention, he and the Carpenter move in for the kill.

The importance of these parodies lies not so much in their frequent invocation of the original sources (Kipling, Carroll) but in the politicism of each imitation. The attraction that poems such as Kipling's "If" and Carroll's "The Walrus and the Carpenter" hold for the women parodists is clear: whereas Kipling's poem encodes the magisterial entry into manhood, a manhood tested and proven in the cultural furnace, Carroll's upside-down and backwards world, with its uncanny sense of wartime shenanigans, seems applicable to the women's sense of the state of things—their seduction and their deception at the hands of their culture's duplicity. That the women rewrote the poems at all seems a political gesture enough in that their parodies highlight the cultural inadequacies of Rudyard Kipling's patriarchal rites of passage and apply Lewis Carroll's nonsensical whimsy to serious issues concerning women and war.

In addition to these or similar parodies of well-known poems, women's factory newspapers also included a series of amusing standard features which seemed benign but carried political messages, as the following examples illustrate: an "Alphabet" column—"A is the Ambulance, tidy and neat;/You can look in and see the Nurse binding up feet" (*Cardonald News*, Oct. 5, 1917: 23)—a "Things We Want to Know" column—"If the life of a Gauge in a Shop is one week, what is the life of a Gauger?" (*Bombshell*, March 1917: 4)—a "Contradicted Rumours" column—"That linoleum is to be put down on the shop floors for the benefit of those with tired feet" (*Shell Magazine*, Dec. 1917: 51)—Classified Ads—"Get rid of your Superfluous Hair. I can show you how to do it. Watchman" (*Bombshell*, June 1917)—and an "Overheard" column. Many of these were derived not only from the paradigms supplied by male publications at the front but were influenced by columns that appeared in London papers throughout the war, especially those in *Blighty*, a digest specially prepared for British soldiers at the front. One other common feature is the invented coat of arms. A surprising number of women's factory and service news-papers feature coats of arms or other insignia on their front or back pages. The arms add not only majesty to their publications but legitimacy, and they suggest by their presence the familial atmosphere in the factories.[10]

Indeed, women's factory newspapers were fashionable and successful; each issue was entertaining, informative, and packed with advertisements. Since munitions workers' salaries were the highest among the various wartime jobs, munitions women characteristically were accused of spend-ing their extra money on luxury items such as silk stockings, pianos, furs, or jewelry,[11] as I discussed above in chapter 2. Journalists commented reg-ularly on the women's monumentalized spending and voiced the nation's concern that the women were "going wrong"; but one reporter for the *Times* mildly defended the thousands of women employed at the Wool-wich Royal Arsenal by insisting that

> very few had gone wrong. The munition workers had been accused of buy-ing cheap jewelry and fur coats. A girl who had very little money before might buy cheap jewelry for the first three weeks and then she tired of it; if she bought a fur coat—she could hardly buy more than one—it was a good asset. ("Girl Munition Workers. Health and a Twelve-Hours Day")

Standard advertisements placed by local merchants in factory newspa-pers, however, gave substance to theories that the workers were spend-thrifts, and just as women would be courted as new voters after the war, they were enticed as new shoppers during it.

Advertisements printed in *Carry On,* for example, a 1916 Christmas magazine published by workers at the Armstrong Munition Factory in Newcastle-on-Tyne, appeal directly to the women workers, enticing them with Christmas gifts they might want to buy for themselves, their moth-ers, or each other, and certainly not for brothers, husbands, or fathers en-gaged at the front: page one advertises a "diamond necklace with pink coral drop set in palladium £35" and a "1916 diamond date brooch," also at £35—more than two months' salary for even the highest paid muni-tions workers. "Christmas Gift Suggestions," an advertisement by Schofields Ltd. in *Shell Magazine,* includes a "Fashionable Skunk Opos-sum Cape, a new style made from finest quality skins, and lined [with] soft Brown silk, £63. Melon-shape Muff to match, £59/6" (60). These prices are significantly higher than those advertised in *Vogue* magazine, which since its premiere in 1916, has tended to indulge the tastes of the rich, the beautiful, the famous, and the fantasies of their poorer sisters. Its September 1916 issue advertised "fur coats at 35 guineas, suits at 8 gns, nightdresses at 39s. 6d" (Dancyger 119). Merchants, especially jewelers and furriers, vigorously sought to attract working-class women. Many of the women workers at Woolwich had their service badges gold plated, according to Caroline Rennles. She remarks that the extravagant gold plating tells only half the story: like many others you did not hear about then, she says, she "used to send pound parcels to the boys" at the front, instead (Transcript 53), a memory frequently corroborated by her contemporaries. Because of their implied outward extravagances, munition workers quickly became the objects of cultural scorn and contempt. To other women in war service who were not making nearly as much money, to the combatants on the western front, and to others at home, the women's exaggerated spending was culturally and morally reprehensible. Women munition workers address the topic of cultural vilification in their autobiographies and oral histories, written or recorded years afterward; but they also address the issue in their factory newspapers, where their accounts are not colored by hindsight and reflection but are spontaneous, preserving for us what Patrick Beaver calls "the thing itself: the slang, the jargon, the character of conversation, the depressing surroundings and the resolution and humanity" of Britain at wartime (xiii). Thus, the local advertisements run in the women's factory newspapers are important because they represent the proverbial carrot dangled in front of the mouths of women munition workers—an important difference here is that in this case, the women were vilified by their culture because being hungry, they bit.

As a result of their spending, working-class women faced what Pierre Bourdieu has identified as the usual "calls to order" from members in and outside of their class: the "Who does she think she is?" and the "That's not for the likes of us" that he suggests reaffirm the "principle of conformity—the only explicit norm of popular taste—and aim to encourage [that] 'reasonable' choices" be made when spending money (*Distinction* 380–81). These calls to order warn members of the working class "against the ambition to distinguish oneself by identifying with other groups, that is, they are a reminder of the need for class solidarity" (381). Advertisements placed in factory newspapers for diamond necklaces and brooches, fur jackets and muffs tantalized working-class women and sought to lure them to spend their money on material purchases that would mark them as members of another class.

Apart from the local advertisements and other standard features found in women's factory newspapers and souvenir magazines, the women's publications are refreshingly literary, especially in the published parodies that parade the original author's style and use the situations of the original poems as inspiration. The parodies and imitations show the women's familiarity with a number of classic texts, poems they might have recalled from their early school days or, more likely, picked up from working-class periodicals[12] and from visits to public libraries, since during the war the rise in the number of borrowers was "unprecedented," and the use of library reading rooms increased (A. Ellis 57), as Alec Ellis explains in *Public Libraries and the First World War:*

> Traditionally reading rooms were the most frequented feature of the Public Libraries. Long evenings, made longer and darker by the blackout, caused many to avail themselves of the public library who had never used it before. (46)

Importantly, women were freer to become members of local libraries during the war. Prior to 1914, women needed two sponsoring signatures for membership, but that requirement was dropped during the war, since those most likely to sponsor new women readers—husbands, merchants, and middle-class men—were called up to serve. A related change was that for children, the mother's signature was thought guarantee enough (A. Ellis 11–12).

Britain's public libraries were desperate for new members to replace those they had lost to war service. Though economy measures taken during the First World War affected Britain's public libraries in a number of ways—modifying the hours of operation, postponing necessary binding programs, displacing staff, and suspending funds for new books—some of these changes made it easier for the working class to frequent the libraries. The average number of weekly hours worked by librarians in 1911 was 45; this grew to 50 or more during the war to compensate for the working-class patrons who arrived home late from their shifts (A. Ellis 58). With public libraries for the first time within the grasp of the working class, particularly the women's working class, classics containing the texts of beloved poems were checked out with greater frequency, especially from the branch libraries in small towns and country districts (A. Ellis 17).

While many of the women working in Britain's factories during the war were minimally educated (some even left school for arsenal and other types of factory work), they most likely supplemented their education through the library, making the most of old and out-of-date sources thought useless and parochial to the scant 8 percent who frequented Britain's public libraries before the war (A. Ellis 42). In contrast to that 8 percent figure, the Adams Report showed that "approximately 48 million volumes were issued from England and 1,340,000 from Welsh public libraries" during the first year of the war alone (A. Ellis 43). Greater access, coupled with the regular increase in female staff—which before the war was only 30 percent (A. Ellis 55, 60)—drew women into Britain's public libraries and reading rooms. Information and statistics on public library use is worth noting especially here, since it explains the perplexing incongruity between the women's limited educations and their refreshingly literary and allusive workplace publications.

While the women's allusiveness may have been practiced and reinforced by those books they picked from public library reading rooms, many working-class homes had modest libraries of their own and usually had on hand copies of treasured classics such as *Robinson Crusoe, The Pilgrim's Progress,* a Dickens novel, a thrilling serial, the Bible, and perhaps a copy of a boy's or girl's magazine, since these were increasingly available and inexpensive by the 1900s. Gretchen Galbraith notes in *Reading Lives,* a history of reading activity across five decades in Britain, that many working-class families kept typical reading rituals, and the memories of these reading sessions stayed with the children through their adult life. One man, Galbraith notes, retained "a vivid image of his working-class mother's dramatic flare [*sic*] for storytelling" while "for J. M. Barrie, reading sessions with his working-class mother represented treasured intimate moments and the beginning of his own writing. Robert Roberts . . . remembered that his whole family would sit together, each reading from the *Harmsworth Self-Educator* that his father bought in parts and pausing to share a particularly startling piece of information" (28–29). This description of reading as a family activity is important to our understanding of working-class literacy and social practices, especially since these reading sessions enacted with parents, grandparents, and siblings contributed not only to the literacy level of all of the family members but to the family's sense of togetherness, as well. Howard Spring notes that it was only during these reading sessions, for example, that his working-class father would participate in family life. It was important for his children to read and pronounce words correctly, Spring says of his father. The old man would read a passage and "then each child would take a turn. If we mispronounced a word once, he would correct us irritably; if twice he would clout us across the head" (Galbraith 28). Though in the Board School debates of the 1870s and 1880s England wrestled with how best to educate British working-class children, parents who maintained reading rituals at home seemed to be managing quite well at it. These practices would instill in working-class children an allusive literacy that would define much of the writing in their factory newspapers and magazines, regardless of their education.

One issue of the service magazine *Bombshell,* for example, features a version of *The Rubáiyát of Omar Kháyyám* titled the "Workman's Rubáiyát"* (1.4 [June 1917]:15–16); and *Shell Chippings: A "Six Eight" Mu-

nition Magazine features a wartime version of Longfellow's "The Village Blacksmith" that reads:

> Under a spreading Motor Belt
> The village maiden stands.
> Her face is black, oil down her back
> And large have grown her hands.
> Toiling, rejoicing, sorrowing
> With scarce a moment's rest
> Her lathe she turns, her wages earns,
> But weirdly she is dressed.
> In cap and overall of blue
> She bends unto her task
> With shoulders bent, on work intent
> With goggles she is masked. . . .
> (*Shell Chippings* 1.1 [Sept 1916]: 12)

Most of the poems selected for parody or imitation are appropriate in their original contexts and meaningfully applicable to the women's wartime experience. Kipling's "If," for example, describes singularity of purpose amid calamitous upheaval; "The House that Jack Built" catalogues the importance of even the smallest architectural contribution in light of the monumental finished product; and Longfellow's "The Village Blacksmith" underscores the cultural importance of the simple figure. All of these situations apply to working-class women who daily had to keep their wits about them while performing small tasks of strict importance for Britain's success in the war.

On the other hand, Kipling's "If" details the passage into manhood; "The House that Jack Built" congratulates the male ego; and Longfellow's "The Village Blacksmith" praises the austerity and integrity of a male icon. Writers in the women's factory newspapers carefully emphasize in their parodies the irony of the sex distinctions, flavoring many of the rewritten versions with gender bravado, highlighting their own roles in the war, stressing the importance of their jobs as heroic laborers and manufacturers, and articulating a "for the want of a nail" attitude when writing about their positions crucial to the success of the war. The women's parodies are characteristically political—even when they take on treasured nursery rhymes, as we shall see—and the literary allusions couched within editorials and prose pieces reveal subversive and often seditious writers at work. None of the allusions is inconsequential or fortuitous; instead, each is stringently appropriate to the women's wartime experience.

The women's use of parody here works much in the same way that Paul Murphy has documented in his study of the poetry published and parodied in working-class periodicals of the nineteenth century. Murphy explains in *Toward a Working Class Canon* what it was that drove an editor to conscript one poem into service over another. He writes:

> If a work could not be read in a way that would empower a working-class audience of the time, if it could not excite that audience to proper thought and action, if, in short, it could not serve the exact purpose that almost every working-class periodical at this time held, then working-class journalists usually scorned or ignored it. (117)[13]

Editors and writers of women's factory newspapers also sought parodies that would excite their audience "to proper thought and action." As we shall see, in their articulation of women's wartime experience, the writers characteristically censure factories for unfair labor policies; they criticize the long hours and point to dangerous working conditions, hazardous materials, lackluster facilities, and insensitive or cruel superintendents; they poke fun at the national rationing system to reveal its inadequacies; they wax eloquent on what seemed to some the dissolving class structure in Britain; they mourn the loss of co-workers and loved ones and condemn gender discrimination. It is in this sense, then, that I argue that women's factory and service newspapers were political manifestos. Each issue instructed its working-class readership on what Murphy calls "the proper thought and action." Importantly, working-class parodists drew upon and exploited a number of recognizably middle- and high-brow texts, texts normally introduced to a culture through what Louis Althusser has called its ideological state apparatuses—churches, schools, the media—and that reproduce and uphold dominant class ideologies. To instruct their readers on the proper thought and action, women writers and editors relied on a constellation of nascent literary techniques that would come to define modernist literature—irony, irresolution, politicism, anxiety, self-reflexive commentary, juxtaposition and allusion, to name a few—and focused their wit and class consciousness on repenning beloved classics.

Criticism buried in allusion seems most common, as in the "As We Should Like It" column in *WAAC Magazine,* an obvious reference to Shakespeare's *As You Like It.* The parodist begins with the familiar "W.A.A.C. life is but a stage, and all the officials merely players" (8). Just as Shakespeare lists in Jaques's speech the seven ages of man—"And one man in his time plays many parts, / His acts being seven ages"(II.vii.141–42)—the writer in *WAAC Magazine* proceeds to enumerate seven ideal levels of rank and promotion, progressing from the "timid and shy" candidate to the full Controller. As such, her "As We Should Like

It" challenges existing procedures for advancement in the WAAC. But her critique takes on even more significance when read alongside the Shakespearean passage. Shakespeare enumerates the seven ages of a privileged, middle-class man and traces his life from his infancy in his nurse's arms, to his days as a schoolboy, a lover, a soldier, a justice, and ultimately a foolish old man, "Sans teeth, sans eyes, sans taste, sans everything" (l. 165). Shakespeare identifies each age with materialist possessions and class markings—the infant has his nurse, the schoolboy "his satchel/ And shining morning face," the justice his "fair round belly with good capon lined" (II.vii. 153), and the foolish old man, nothing. Shakespeare's parodist outlines a life no less consequential but a life whose successes are not measured by class markings or reproduced by materialist culture. She argues that such is "As We Should Like It"—not privileges assumed by *class* but privileges earned from *work*.

Equally important to our understanding of parodies in the women's newspapers is our recognition that the perspective of many of the papers challenges cultural ideologies instead of reproducing them. For example, Joseph Boone cogently argues in *Tradition Counter Tradition* that a distinctive feature of twentieth-century fiction is its persistent discontent with the marriage plot and with the sexual-marital economies scripted in fiction through the end of the nineteenth century (136–37). His observation is a useful one when reading through women's factory and service newspapers. That is, while publications appearing *after* the war were able to resuscitate the dying Cinderella fantasy in which a factory girl, downstairs servant, or other type of working-class woman successfully attracts the attention of a wealthy gentlemen (her husband-to-be), this sort of plot does not occur in women's factory newspapers during the war, though many of their pages were filled with original fiction and drama. We do not find in factory weeklies, for example, story titles such as those that would become popular after the war, "'I am only a factory girl,' she said, 'but I was determined to make you love me,'" or "'She was only an embroideress in a smart dressmaker's establishment, but a rich man loved her'" (Dancyger 125), even though the factory publications had the same audience in mind as a publication like *Peg's Paper,* which I discuss below. Such a rejection during the war in factory publications of this sort of maudlin, romanticized plot works to destabilize one of the most significant cultural expectations for women at that time: marriage.

The highly successful *Peg's Paper* aimed its ideology and rhetoric at working-class women and tried to resuscitate the marriage plot. Its creator Nell Kennedy reportedly sat for six weeks listening to the conversations of cotton mill girls in Wigan as they took their lunch breaks and shortly thereafter turned out in 1919 the first issue of *Peg's Paper,* "a sensitive and accurate reflection of what those girls wanted: emotional satisfaction, thrills, romance" (Dancyger 122). It is interesting to compare "what those girls wanted"—that is, how *they* should like it—with what the writer in *WAAC Magazine* wants—how *she* should like it—as evidenced from her allusive parody of the "All the world's a stage" speech. Clearly, she does not reproduce the marriage plot, as Shakespeare does, whose play dissects the problems of marriage though many of the characters marry at the end. Here the writer redresses it in her commentary by focusing on her work and not on her wedding, on her career and not on her class. In this sense she offers, like Shakespeare's heroine Rosalind, a rich "dramatization of a figure who plays endlessly with the limits and possibilities of her circumstances, . . . an unpredictable figure [who] continues to the end to defy the fixed identities and the exclusionary choices of the everyday world, offering instead a world of multiple possibilities and transformable identities, a world as perhaps we might come to like it," Jean Howard explains in her headnote to Shakespeare's play (*Norton* 1598).[14] Clearly, the women who wrote and produced these service and factory newspapers sensed the potency of the medium and through the use of allusion, put into effect destabilizing strategies that worked to upset, disrupt, or at the very least challenge the scripted futures of working-class women.

Just as Shakespeare's player plays many parts but winds up facing "second childishness and mere oblivion" (II.viii.164) nonetheless in the "last scene of all" (l. 162), writers in factory newspapers dreaded a similar fate, one that would predetermine their postwar obscurity. As in the example above, in which social commentary is buried in literary allusion, the editor of *Bombshell* wrote in 1917 that the workers at the National Projectile Factory were motivated to produce by their factory newspaper

> some record of these days of feverish bustle and activity for future years, some reflection—however inadequate—of life at the NPF on which, when we are old and grey and full of sleep, we can look back with happy remembrance. (1.1 [Mar. 1917]: 16)

Here, the editor alludes to Yeats's twelve-line poem "When You Are Old" (1892), a bitter poem that threatens his unyielding lover Maud Gonne with an image of herself old, disconsolate, and longing for his company and for his praise:

> When you are old and gray and full of sleep,
> And nodding by the fire, take down this book,

And slowly read, and dream of the soft look
Your eyes had once, and of their shadows deep. . . .

Yeats rebukes Gonne in his poem for not having paid attention to him while he courted her. The editor here does the same thing, as if to say to contemporaries beyond the Templeboro factory, "Twenty, thirty years from now, you'll appreciate our efforts, and when you read this, you'll come to see how you ignored the noble and industrious class of women war workers." Many women war workers despaired over not feeling appreciated, particularly as the war raged on, and more was being asked of them—increased production, longer hours, mandatory overtime, and holiday shift work. By November 1916, for example, 27 percent of the women workers in the Government's 36 shell factories were on overtime, as were 37 percent of the women workers in the Government's 13 filling factories, 45 percent of the women workers at 14 National Projectile Factories, and 90 percent of the women who worked in the three Royal Ordnance Factories—Woolwich, Enfield and Waltham (IWM Department of Printed Books, Women's Work Microfilm Collection Item MUN V/2).[15] In addition to the usual overtime, holidays, too, often were sacrificed to the bench or to the shop floor. During what was supposed to be Easter holiday 1918, for example, women at the Newbury Depot "worked nine and three-quarter hour shifts, handling 1.80 tons per hour each, for a total of 17 1/2 tons per day for seven days" (Caine, IWM Department of Printed Books, Women's Work Microfilm Collection Item MUN 5/2). The editor's allusion to Yeats's poem resounds with charges of cultural neglect, and because it is couched in a women's factory newspaper it projects the image of a once-vigorous woman, alone, "nodding by the fire," and gaining comfort only from souvenirs and memories of her years of war work, a scarecrow image that increasingly haunted women workers as the war drew to a close and one that emerges frequently in their later publications.

The women's sense of despair was not particular to munition or other factory workers just as it was not limited to soldiers who experienced the war as combatants, but the female articulation of the experience has not been privileged. Historically, women's experiences have been brushed aside to give voice to the male—the more "legitimate"—experience of war. Analyses of the cultural legacy of the war have tended to marginalize the experiences of women in general and of working-class women in particular. Working-class women's voices and experiences have particularly suffered cultural neglect, and while women writers acknowledge in their factory newspapers the cultural lack of interest, editors stress a characteristic perseverance and resolution. The editor of *Shell Magazine*, for example, urges her writers to be steadfast, and addresses in her column "Editorial Forgings" the historical difficulties of literary and cultural recognition:

> Remember, the way of literary success is proverbially hard. Browning was reduced to selling the glory of 'Pippa Passes' as a sixpenny pamphlet, and Dickens gave the world the treasure of the 'Tale of Two Cities' in a periodical magazine. (1)

Again, the writer's literary allusions are not inconsequential but dramatic and tinged with irony, since "all" was not "right with the world," as Browning proclaimed in "Pippa Passes," nor was it a romanticized and indistinguishable "best of times" and "worst of times," as Dickens so memorably characterized the burgeoning and class-torn era of the French Revolution. Moreover, it is essential that we realize *how* the Browning and Dickens allusions work in the above passage. Here, the writer tests the traditional uses and boundaries of allusion in that the allusions are used not merely to ornament or decorate a piece, but to augment themes in the editorial, to point to references outside the text that might enlarge a reader's understanding of the point being made in the particular passage. These allusions act as shorthand memos and are intended to remind a reader in capsule form of the full context from which the reference is drawn. Hence, the reference to "Pippa Passes" is not gratuitous; it is not a title selected at random but a carefully chosen example, as was her reference to Dickens's *Tale of Two Cities*. Like these two examples, the allusions work in two ways in the piece. They work as historical examples to remind readers that "the way of literary success is proverbially hard," as the editor suggests; and they also serve a larger purpose, by their titles alone, encouraging readers to summon up each text's most celebrated lines—"God's in His heaven / All's right with the world" and "It was the best of times. It was the worst of times." In doing so, the editor invites them to recognize the irony conferred upon those lines in their present allusive context.

In other words, many of the allusions in women's factory newspapers act as "pointers" that refer readers to a passage in a text that has more significance to the passage one is reading than the one cited by the writer; and the unarticulated parallels between the two texts are often more interesting and appropriate when fully explored or drawn out than they are in the encapsulated version introduced and suggested by a word, a phrase, a title, a name. These multiple allusions do not merely amplify themes but point instead to what needs outside explanation, inviting the reader not only to identify the source in the piece but to go a bit further and to "interpret the technique of allusion itself," as John Paul Riquelme suggests of the modernist technique (1). Because of the allusiveness and parody in these works, the women's newsletters playfully call attention to their own derivativeness, an aspect of modernist art that has been referred to as self-exposing plagiarism, which I have discussed elsewhere (*Names* 8–13). The editor's allusion to Dickens is an important one because it identifies the polemic of the women's factory newspapers. Juxtaposed with their descriptions of the best of times, the writers forcefully articulate the worst of times in their factory newspapers. Faced with the daily dangers of working in the TNT rooms, in the "danger zones" or "clean rooms," as they were called, having twice a day to stop work to "take the milk," or to apply barrier cream to their faces, or to engage in other prophylactic measures designed to protect workers from a variety of dangers, women arsenal workers quickly captured in their factory newspapers their keen sense of frustration and fear. Though factory newspapers originally were intended to boost morale, they quickly took on a political temper, and in addition to celebrating the women's production and their spirited collegiality and toil—as in the poem "The Munitioneers" published in *Shell Chippings*[16]—they began to document each other's heroism and to enumerate the steady rise in work-related deaths.

To this end, *Dornock Souvenir Magazine, 1916–1919,* one of the publications out of H. M. Factory, Gretna, contains a column titled "Things the Camera Missed," a mix of events undocumented by the press, such as "The explosion on the Nitro-Glycerine Spent Acid Pipe Line," "The R.E.'s being refused admission to the First-Class Dining Room of the Canteen," and "The fire at the Bag Washing Plant" (63). Ironically, while the women rebuke the press for not recognizing, documenting, or registering the dangers associated with their work, they also criticize published accounts that ran in local newspapers, since these reports tended to minimize frequent work site calamities or trivialize the aftermaths of the accidents.

A lengthy article in the *Dornock Souvenir Magazine,* for example, describes a serious rail crash that occurred somewhere between the Dornock and Gretna factories when chemists, guards, and women workers were shuttling a delivery on the "Up Express" to Rigg Power House. The article reports that the first coach of the "Up Express" had "left the rails, with one end in the bottom of a gully and the other resting against the bridge, the following two [coaches were] over on their sides, and a fourth [had] jumped the metals" (43). The writer revisits the scene, describing yells and screams that would "pierce the ear." She narrates seeing her co-workers crawling out from under the heap of mangled refuse. Some women had fainted, others were bleeding, and some had "violent blisters" on their cheeks. The essay closes with a simple conclusion: "We become heroes."

As a political gesture, this report is an important one, since it documents the workers' "transformations" into heroes; but it takes on even greater significance and bravado in its juxtaposition to an extract from a press clipping that describes the accident as one "of a minor character": "No lives were lost," the short extract reads, "but nine persons sustained cuts and contusions" (43). Juxtaposing the women's own account of the event with a poker-faced clipping from a local newspaper seems an early manifestation of the modernist technique of ironic juxtaposition. If the literature that has been called by the imprecise term "modernism" is characterized by frequent use of allusion, juxtaposition and collage, pastiche, irony, and manifestations of the artist's anxiety over or fear of being contaminated by mass culture, then we find in women's war industry newspapers evidence of all of these modern literary trademarks.[17] Certainly the presence and degree to which these characteristics are exploited differ from one factory publication to another; but it is important to note that because women's factory newspapers exhibit these modernist tendencies, their publications must be read alongside other examples of modernist literary discourse.

In an effort to memorialize or monumentalize their own heroes, even their own war dead, women workers often refer in their factory newspapers to the unflinching and selfless bravery of killed or wounded co-workers. A column in *Shell Magazine,* for example, is entitled "'Our' Heroes," with the word *our* in quotation marks suggesting that the women wanted to emphasize their own heroism on the home front, and to show that dead or wounded workers were an essential part of the cultural mythologization of the war, casualties to memorialize in the same mournful national spirit as dead or wounded soldiers. In "'Our' Heroes" the columnist M. Tiplady describes the particular courage of two women workers:

> In another case of a girl who had a badly crushed foot, her chief concern in nearing home, was her mother. Before one had hardly knocked at the door she was calling out, "It's nothing, mother; I have just hurt my foot a bit." Another girl who had her finger ends taken off declared, "It's nothing to what the soldiers have to go through." (*Shell Magazine* 46)

While men's trench newspapers characteristically supplied the troops with humorous and ironic treatments of the First World War—"local gossip in and about the units, humourous sallies at the officers and NCOs, good natured complaints about the billets and rations, poems, theatre reviews and sports results" (Taylor, "*The Open Exhaust*" 24)—the women's factory newspapers began to enumerate the losses and the dangers associated with war work, not merely calling attention to the ever-present threat of a factory explosion but documenting and criticizing as well a host of related hazards.

Margaret Brooks describes these related hazards and notes that despite precautions in the explosive workshops, where women worked with phosphorous, nitroglycerine, or TNT, dangerous accidents were inevitable (12). *The Dornock Souvenir Magazine, 1916–1919,* one of the publications out of H. M. Factory, Gretna, details the heroic conduct of foreman Edward Spencer at the hands of one of those inevitable accidents that might have killed thousands of workers:

> About 4:30 P.M. on November 5th, 1917, due to an oversight, spent acid was run from No. 2 Nitrator, Hill 4, into a charge of Nitro-Glycerine which was being prewashed in the sink. The natural consequence was that great heat was evolved, with the evolution of large quantities of red fumes of nitrogen peroxide and the probability of the charge of 2700 lbs. of Nitro-Glycerine detonating at any moment. ("One of *Our* Heroes," 10)

Spenser groped his way to the fuming charge and heroically "saved the day," saying later that "[he] was responsible for the House, and if it went up [he] was going with it" ("One of *Our* Heroes," 10). The Spenser piece is the first article in the *Dornock Souvenir Magazine,* appearing after ten pages of forewords, editorials, and photographs. Couched within the impressive 69-page souvenir are three short poems that also illustrate some of the "inevitable" perils of First World War factory work. "Through the Window," for example, describes how a bucket of "N/G" (nitroglycerine) catches fire and pushes a worker who "tried to be quick" through the window (58). "Through the window" becomes a refrain in the poem, a chorus repeated after each incident is described. The poem ends when one of the women hands the supervisor a petition for more cheese. He reads the women's signatures, crumples the petition, and pushes it "through the window," ironizing the poet's familiar refrain and suggesting with his indifference the dispensability of the women workers:

> The Super received it
> And when he perceived it
> He—pushed it through the window.
>
> *Chorus.*
> Through the window
> He pushed it through the window:
> He merely perused it
> Then quietly abused it.
> And—pushed it through the window. (58)

Another equally compelling poem published in the same factory newspaper is entitled "Ten Little Dornock Girls," a poem fashioned after the popular "Ten Little Indians." The ten-stanza poem describes how a group of ten women workers dwindled down to nine, to eight, to seven, and so forth, until there were none. It enumerates the deaths of ten Dornock girls, as in the following exemplary stanzas about working with nitroglycerine and acid fumes:

> Seven little Dornock girls did some N/G mix;
> One was overcome with fumes,
> And then there were six.
> . . . . .
> Three little Dornock girls went to work quite new;
> The Acid fumes did smother one,
> And then there were two. (18)

Characteristically, the women couch serious issues in rewritten versions of popular nursery rhymes, banking on the familiarity of pieces most likely to avert their anger and masquerade their grief, however temporarily. To be sure, the humor is part of the "irony" that Paul Fussell finds so characteristic of modern war literature, noting that a typical "irony of situation" distinguishes most World War I writing (7). While it is important to note, as F. J. Roberts did, that the "hilarity is more often hysterical than natural," or as Elizabeth M. Delafield noted, that humor and sentimentality, "the most powerful narcotic[s] in the world," had a palliative effect on the writers,[18] it is more likely that the women writers knew exactly what they were doing, and that "hysteria" or "palliative" social narcotics had little to do with their writing, especially since every literary allusion used by the women writers can be linked to a severe critical condemnation of the dangerous social, military, and labor conditions of First World War Britain.

It was not uncommon for writers in women's factory newspapers to veil their outrage and disgust with humor and sentiment, to cast their moral indignity in jejune verses, or to masquerade cultural criticism in the familiar rhymes of childhood. In *Dornock Souvenir Magazine*, for example, a worker writes "Little Miss Muffitt/ Sat on a tuffet/ She had just filled a bogie of nitre. . . . (62); and *WRNS Magazine* contains a parody of "Ten Little Indians" that begins by describing the death by explosion of one "Little Wren": "Ten Little Wrens stood looking at a mine;/ One poked her nose on a vital part/ And then there were nine" (Aug. 12, 1919). The severity of the dangers, so forcefully articulated in women's later testimonies, in their essays, memoirs, and oral history narratives, often gets deflated in the factory newspapers and souvenir magazines where the topics are treated with humor. The exacting intensity of the poem "Through the Window," for example, lessens once the workers incongruously petition their supervisor for cheese, since the cheese element seems jarringly inappropriate when juxtaposed to other serious accidents described in the piece. Similarly, the forcefulness of "Ten Little Dornock Girls," "Little Miss Muffitt" and "Ten Little Wrens" seems trivialized, since they are written after children's nursery rhymes, a form that might allow the workers' versions to be taken as innocuous.

But what makes the women's experiences and their published parodies unique is that the women most likely picked up their technique in the factories where many of them worked with cordite, one of the most dangerous explosives handled by the women. Ironically, cordite had an enjoyable, candylike taste because of its glycerine content.[19] Though mindful of its dangers, workers used to suck on the "sweets" nightly. Lily Maud Godber explains in her oral history:

> In the danger buildings . . . we were taking the cordite out of the brass cases. It was ever so nice to eat, we used to suck a bit and it was very sweet—but they used to say that you shouldn't do that because it would affect your heart. But it was nice—just like little thin pieces of macaroni to look at. You could suck it away; it'd more or less disintegrate. They said soldiers used to do that to affect their heart to get out of the Army. Perhaps we'd have one piece a night. (Imperial War Museum Sound Archive, Item SR 693, Reel 5)

Cordite is a recurring topic in women's factory newspapers and works as a particularly potent metaphor for the women's rhymes, since its deceptive sweetness veils its danger. Just as nursery rhymes are often highly politicized cultural texts—"Ten Little Indians," for example—and function to indoctrinate children and expose them to various cultural ideologies, the situations of the nursery rhymes chosen for parody and imitation are appropriate in their original contexts and applicable to the women's wartime experience. When transferred to the war experience, the rhymes take on profound historical significance.[20]

Clearly, by 1918, women's factory newspapers had adopted a political tone unlike that of the men's newspaper writings; working-class women throughout Britain's arsenals and munition factories not only actively challenged national labor policies and military practices in their factory newspapers but documented the dangers associated with war work. How they skirted charges of treason or prosecution under DORA can only be guessed at: they cleverly disguised their discontent in seemingly innocuous rhymes, masqueraded critical commentary in humor, and challenged cultural assumptions when they appeared to be making light of them.

Moreover, by suggesting the way things *should* be done—as in "As We Should Like It" or "The New Way," printed below—they outlined their designs for the postwar restructuring of British society, mindful of what would be their new roles.

It was difficult for women workers in 1919 not to look back on British women's involvement in other wars, proudly noting the contrast of their present animation and vigor, and resist envisioning their future cultural engagement. "The New Way," a poem published in the July 1919 issue of *WRNS Magazine,* for example, evaluates women's "new" roles in the war, contrasting their present spiritedness with a fitful and restless past:

> When to a joust or a crusade,
>   The medieval warrior
> With his fantastic cavalcade
>   Went medievally to war,
> He left a shield or sword behind
>   For his deserted Chatelaine to mind.
>
> The gentle lady turned her hand
>   To polish, and on duty bent
> She scoured the arms with Monkey Brand
>   Or its remote equivalent.
> But strange! although her lord was gone—
>   She never seemed to think to put them on!
>
> Our men today, who sweep the seas,
>   No longer bear the stamp of Gieve,
> But wrap themselves in wool or frieze—
>   No Continental could conceive
> Officials more ridiculous.
>   They left the anchor and the crown to us.
>
> And we, whom war has rendered wise,
>   Took, with the uniforms of men,
> The duties which they symbolise,
>   And gave our strength to them; That when
> We give them back, as soon we must,
>   The men shall see we have not let them rust. (12)

Hardly specific to the situation of the WRNS, "The New Way" champions women's mass involvement in the First World War and celebrates their active participation while criticizing their former listless, culturally assigned roles during wartime. To those women who worked during the war as nurses, munition workers, crane drivers, conductors, needlewomen, ambulance drivers, gardeners, dopers, varnishers, painters, elevator operators, cooks, clerks, waitresses, driver-mechanics, and policewomen, covering so many occupations during Britain's dilution scheme, "giving back" the metonymic anchor and crown was a painful process. Its legacy, as Jane Marcus describes it, was a generation of "angry, depressed, and suicidal women who had lost their jobs after the war, and with those jobs the self-respect and financial independence that kept them going, a sense of their own history, with its heroism and hurts" (469). Amy Elizabeth May commented on the despair in her oral history, saying, "I cried me eyes out when I left—that was the sort of life I led" (Imperial War Museum Sound Archive, Item SR 684, Reel 4). Their litany of despair continues in their oral histories and in their subsequently published essays, biographies, autobiographies, poems, novels, and dramas. But before the sense of an ending attended their writing, women's factory newspapers captured and chronicled women's roles in the war, adding their voices to a culturally silenced chorus, claiming their part and exacting their claim in the epic drama of their nation.

Anna Smith's poem, published in the *Dornock Souvenir Magazine*, succinctly appropriates the emotional and political temperament in the factories once demobilization set in, when so many of Britain's women hoped to ensure that their work would not be forgotten by a culture newly distracted by peace and eager to displace and/or supplant their heroic contributions with that of male counterparts returning from the front. Her poem substantially captures the sentiment and the emotional upheaval that attended women's dismissal from the work force. She writes,

Never, Dornock, never more
Shall I hear thy hooter roar:
The Hun has fled, and Peace has come.
The Factory Works have ceased to hum.
And I must seek for work afar
More suited now to Peace than War.
But where'er I go, I'll always mind
The friends I've met, both true and kind.

No more we'll be searched by the Bobby.
No more kharki trousers we'll wear,
No more will we breathe in the Acid,
That rose in great fumes in the air—
"No more!" "No more!" (65)

Not inconsequentially, Smith's short piece is schizophrenic—the first stanza is guardedly sentimental while the second is censorious and full of pathos. After the turn in the poem, the reader realizes that the refrain "No more" is both one of regret, illustrating Smith's reluctance to leave her friends behind, and one of castigation, as if she were saying "No more!—Never again!" Smith begins her stunted sonnet, a form usually preserved in the literary tradition for plaintants of unrequited, idealistic love, by describing the fond memories of her war work, the friends she has met, and the peace that has come; but the poem ends with a litany of the memories she'll be haunted by—the constant searches at work,[21] the corrosive smell of the acid, the ill-fitting trousers and overalls—in a particularly female version of shell shock, a kind of horror experienced only by women in the arsenals and one articulated time and time again in women's factory newspapers, service newspapers, diaries, memoirs, autobiographies, oral histories, poems, and novels.

What remains clear about the women's arsenal factory newspapers and magazines is that although they were begun in a spirit of imitation, as spin-offs of soldiers' trench newspapers, they never took on the irreverent tone of the men's writings, though they exhibit a type of irony characteristic of modern writing. Clearly, the male model of the trench newspaper was not sufficient for the women, so they developed their own version, their own way of documenting and writing themselves. Just as women shell makers used to stick handwritten notes and scribbled messages in the recesses of the cartons of shells they were about to ship off to France, secret, clandestine, sexy messages to the soldiers—"Just a little scribbled note I hope this found you well I hope you're so and so and so and so and things like that," as Amy Elizabeth May recalls (Imperial War Museum Sound Archive, Item SR 684, Reel 2)[22]—their factory newspapers remain as an extension of that desire to tell, to communicate not only with each other but with future generations, too, documenting women's work in the arsenals with an eye toward history. Reading women's factory newspapers now, more than 80 years later, we recover those muted messages stashed in the hollow nooks of shell packaging, lost to the recesses of time, and recover historically vital working-class voices.

Chapter 5

DORA and Women's
Social and Domestic Lives
During the War

"CIVIL LIBERTY IS EVER THE FIRST VICTIM OF WAR," Sylvia Pankhurst noted in *The Home Front* (36), and at no time during the First World War was civil liberty more at risk than it was under the iniquitous Defence of the Realm Acts (DORA). First introduced by Reginald McKenna in the Commons on August 7, 1914, and reportedly passed after only minutes of Parliamentary discussion on August 8, DORA was a "'skeleton' Act," Christopher Martin explains, "an approved general principle to which a multitude of amendments were added" (10), amendments that increasingly authorized governmental intervention in the lives of British citizens and subjects. It regulated strictly citizens' movements between the empire and the colonies, and later suspended emigration; it regulated governmental control of the engineering industry, bridled workers' strikes, fixed crop prices, and issued to farmers compulsory tillage orders; it forbade the hiring of men between the ages of 18 and 60 in nonessential industries; it restricted processions and public protests; it monitored and censored the public press and tightened regulations on private publishing; it enjoined stringent curfews for single and for married women; it imposed limited hours of operation for pubs and other social establishments; it introduced the daylight savings order; it prohibited the chiming and striking of London's public clocks; made it unlawful to whistle for taxis between 10 P.M. and 7 A.M.; and encouraged a civilian watchdog campaign that served to animate one segment of the civilian population while straitjacketing another. Specifically, DORA redefined the role and reprimand of the government during a period that teemed with chaos and emergency, and its hand touched—and often revoked— even the modest of civilian rights and privileges, introducing an element of compulsion into the daily lives of British citizens and subjects.[1]

"One of the most remarkable changes which the war brought with it was a novel addiction to the rapidity of action," Charles Townshend argues in *Making the Peace: Public Order and Public Security in Modern Britain* (63). Townshend adds that while "dispatch seemed in the mood of everyone . . . DORA itself should probably not be described as a panic measure, but it was a clear example of the haste-process" (63–64). Consequently, J. M. Bourne has argued that the extension of power through DORA was a "series of ad hoc responses," driven by a perception of urgency but with "no overall plan, no philosophy of action" (61); and Clinton Rossiter, an American political scientist, labeled DORA "perhaps the most radical Parliamentary enactment in the history of England, indeed in all the history of constitutional government" (61). As a cultural document that affected and restrained the lives of Britain's citizens, and as a document that often and specifically aimed its rhetoric and regulation at women and the carrying out of its mandates at the women's working class, a knowledge of the DORA is especially important to our understanding of working-class women, their social and domestic lives during the war, and their publications that describe this period.

That so little has been written on the subject even in general terms is a problem that puzzles many historians, since it generally is believed that the DORA significantly usurped civilian rights, and changed the way British citizens and subjects historically would be governed. B. L. Ingraham notes of the DORA, for example, that "what is surprising—if not shocking—to the foreign observer in the light of English history in the preceding century is the alacrity with which the English surrendered practically the totality of their cherished liberties to the discretion of government officials during an emergency" (*Political Crime in Europe* 295). Although cartoonists portrayed DORA as a spinster aunt, her powers were formidable, Christopher Martin notes, adding that "one contemporary said that it gave the State powers beyond that of the Stuart kings" (10). Noting the severity of cultural changes brought on by the DORA, then, Townshend scratches his head at the paucity of published discussions of the DORA and sketches the anemic nature of its critical attention, a neglect that has led me to devote a chapter specifically to the topic. He writes:

The Defence of the Realm Acts 1914 and 1915 (DORA)—the acronym coming to sound more cute than sinister as time passed—make only fleeting appearances in standard histories of the war. A. J. P. Taylor's *English History 1914–1945*, hardly an establishment view, contains a bare handful of passing references. Arthur Marwick's pioneering social study of the war, first published in the same year, went so far as to print the first DORA verbatim in its main text (something even legal textbooks do not do), on the ground that it would be 'so often referred to in the course of this book.' In fact, there follow a scant dozen references to it. His more general studies of the impact of war on society hardly touch on it. Sir Llewellyn Woodward's massive *Great Britain and the War of 1914–1918* does not mention DORA until page 464, and consigns its substance to a brief footnote. J. M. Bourne's otherwise luminous *Britain and the Great War* merely glances at it, as does Stuart Wallace's study of academic postures (though all his subjects were affected, and one—Bertrand Russell—was imprisoned by the Act). Trevor Wilson's gargantuan work has one sentence on it. Other histories of modern Britain have noticed the impact of DORA in the industrial sector, but not the constitutional. (56–57)

One could add many more titles to Townshend's list, since more recent histories are threadbare in their discussion of the significance of the DORA, too.[2] It is precisely this paucity of critical attention to the DORA that has led me to investigate the consequences of the acts with regard to women's social and domestic lives in Britain.

Townshend's 1993 book, though rightly critical of male historians' neglect of the DORA, slights women historians' discussions of its significance. Claire Tylee, in her 1990 book *The Great War and Women's Consciousness*, discusses the DORA at some length, reprinting and analyzing substantial extracts from it. In addition, Anne Wiltsher's 1985 book, *Most Dangerous Women; Feminist Peace Campaigners of the Great War*, discusses Home Office records of the period and notes the vigilance with which feminist peace campaigners were watched and reported on under DORA by British constables and civilian spies; Bland, Levine, Braybon, and Summerfield also discuss ramifications of the DORA and note in particular, how curfews imposed for women affected domestic life in London, Cardiff, and Grantham. Each notes, as well, the sorts of arrests and sentences made under DORA, such as those described by Braybon and Summerfield, in which five women arrested for being out of their houses during the Grantham curfew were given 62 days imprisonment each (109–110). It is specifically these ramifications that interest me in this chapter—not only consequential analogues of the DORA but the ways in which women's lives were circumscribed, regulated, and maintained by the Home Office during the war years.

Whether it was because of their rigorous peace campaigning or because of their perceived promiscuity that earned the nickname "khaki fever," women were singled out as a special class under DORA, especially after the March 1918 passage of Regulation 40D, seen as a pernicious revival of the Contagious Diseases Acts of 1864. Writers in *The Vote* vigorously campaigned against the regulation and argued that it represented a state ambition to punish specifically women for nationwide profligacy and corruption, as the following notice published in the June 21, 1918 issue of *The Vote* attests:

> The Regulation For Vice
>   Another urgent and important Campaign is upon us. Foiled in the attempt to revive the iniquitous provisions of the detested Contagious Diseases Acts by means of the late innocent-seeming Criminal Law Amendment Bill of unhappy memory, the men who rule us have now—by Regulation 40D of the Defence of the Realm Act—reintroduced the State Regulation of Vice in this country.
>   Long years ago the Women's Freedom League had its mind made up to oppose to the bitter end any such action.
>   Our machinery for agitation stands ready to be set in motion—money must come in freely for this renewal of the fight. . . .
>   Delay is dangerous. We must have this shameful blot upon the Statute Book, this death-knell to the moral life of Britain—as the great pioneer Josephine Butler termed it—withdrawn at once. (295)

The regulation was particularly noxious because compulsory examinations—and the attendant communal scorn, cultural blame and criminal reprimand—fell exclusively upon women. Woollacott explains that "the government, the police and military authorities sought to control women in order to control the problem of VD among the troops" ("Khaki Fever" 333). Though 32 out of every 1000 British soldiers were carrying venereal disease by 1917, Regulation 40D "made it illegal for a woman afflicted with VD to have intercourse with a serviceman, . . . [and] a woman suffering from VD could be arrested for having sex with her husband, even if he had infected her in the first place" (De Groot 235). Because Regulation 40D led to the unabashed criminalization of women and authorized compulsory medical examinations of female suspects, it prompted alarm and rancor among activists who rightfully saw its passage as a malicious return to nineteenth-century interdictions against women's behavior. While masquerading as a security measure during wartime, the regulation worked to inculpate women and to identify them (whether offenders or not) as likely moral outlaws and social deviants.

Rhetoric of this sort was nothing new in 1915. It echoed the very cultural anxieties that surfaced about women's morality during nineteenth- and early twentieth-century feminist campaigns for suffrage. Sir Almroth

Wright, for example, in a treatise against women's suffrage, argued that women's notions of morality were at best personal and domestic. A sense of *public* morality, though instinctive even to working-class men on the sinking *Titanic,* he argued, was not a natural component of women's characters, he wrote in *The Unexpurgated Case Against Woman Suffrage.* "Woman feels no interest in, and no responsibility towards, any abstract moral ideal" (108), he argued, and added that women's "systematic attempts to extort, under the cover of the word 'justice,' advantage only themselves" (108). By referring to suffrage as extortion, Wright incriminates the women's legitimate work for the vote. Women who seek justice are branded unjust, and their social activism, rather than being identified with equity, is discussed publicly as felonious behavior and extortion, perpetrated by a class of social outlaws and malefactors. In this rhetorical position, the female justice seeker becomes a rogue. "One would not be very far from the truth if one alleged that there are no good women, but only women who have lived under the influence of good men" (111), Almroth Wright pressed.[3] Living in an age in which such rhetoric could be found almost anywhere, women were associated with that class of persons who needed to be watched. They needed civic guardians, they needed what Wright called "the influence of good men," lest they corrupt themselves and their race. It was this sort of misguided thinking that led to the passage of regulation 40D of DORA, which many activists saw as a revival of the nineteenth-century Contagious Diseases Act.

In an effort to reveal the injustice of the regulation, writers in *The Vote* subsequently published a test specially designed to probe social and criminal laws such as Regulation 40D for inequity:

A Famous Legislative Test invariably used by Josephine E. Butler, Rt. Hon. Sir James Stansfield, MP, Rt. Hon. James Stuart, MP, Rt. Hon. John Edward Ellis, MP, Joshua Rowntree, MP, and Henry J Wilson, MP

1. Does the legislation tend to make of any woman a special class?
2. Does it tend to place women under police control?
3. Does it tend towards the compulsory examination of women?
4. The proposals which appear to be intended fairly, will they operate fairly?

We strenuously oppose all legislation which fails in any of the four tests. (289)

Put to such a test, Regulation 40D would fail miserably. Because writers found an alarming parity between Regulation 40D and the Contagious Diseases Act of 1864, they cited in *The Vote* disturbing nineteenth-century statistics to predict what they saw as the forthcoming social incrimination of women: namely, that the number of women brought before the magistrates under the Contagious Diseases Act, for example, was very small in comparison with the number of those actually subjected to medical examination under the 1864 Act, though more than a hundred thousand of these women were examined. Moreover, of the 103,677 women examined under the Contagious Diseases Act, only 9,688 women were registered as "diseased." 86,374 of the examinations were of healthy women, then, many of whom were undoubtedly innocent, petitioners argue in *The Vote* (June 21, 1918: 289). The popular yoking of DORA Regulation 40D with the nineteenth-century Contagious Diseases Act not only suggests the offense of a regulation invented with serious repercussions for women "offenders" but identifies what opponents saw as a critical backwards movement in the culture, one that would make of women a special class of criminal. Regulation 40D produced a great deal of anxiety among women in Britain who feared the return of nineteenth-century social restrictions.

Notwithstanding articles published in *The Vote* and elsewhere, and regardless of agitation from other circles, "whatever DORA may have done, it had popular sanction," Sidney Clarke argued in 1919 (Townshend 57). Backed as it was by popular sanction, British citizens doggedly behaved under its command and devoutly suffered its political consequences.

What surprises readers of culture in retrospect is how complicit the British public was in its own regulation under the DORA. Townshend argues that Britain believed it was fighting for its life as a nation, and that not by a jury but by history would the DORA be judged (60). Larger regulations invented on behalf of national and public security, for example, were accepted with acquiescence. Tylee suggests that part of the success of the DORA lay in its ability to avert popular attention toward an outside or foreign enemy, and she uses John Sutherland's remarks about the curious popularity of the spy novel during wartime to illustrate her point. Sutherland argues that "Probably the most valuable myth spy fiction promotes is that the nation's security service is wholly directed against foreigners and traitors, rather than against its own dissident population" (Tylee 128; Sutherland 1001). Britain's own "dissident population" often bore the weight of DORA restrictions, since DORA regulated the hours they would work and the hours they would spend confined at home, and it affected everything from their domestic and social lives to their public and personal opinions. As such, DORA regulations increasingly worked to manage and to institutionalize the behavior, the discourse, and the ideas of British citizens.[4]

Women and girls identified as being under the spell of khaki fever, in particular, were singled out as part of Britain's dissident population even as early as 1914, since they threatened to corrupt the gender and moral orders of Britain, as Woollacott explains: "Sufferers of khaki fever were consistently described as blatant, aggressive and overt in their harassment of soldiers. This assertive behaviour by young working-class women threatened a subversion of the gender as well as the moral order" ("Khaki Fever" 326), and gave rise to mounting arguments that called for more aggressive patrols of young working-class women. Increasingly, one finds that women police patrols and other such organizations were used not so much to protect *women* as they were used to protect *men*. Lucy Bland suggests in an article on the policing of women in the First World War that "this protection of men—from venereal disease—took the form of various kinds of control over women. Women police and patrols became directly implicated in this control, sometimes against their better judgement" (23). She adds:

> In December 1914 the commanding officer of Cardiff, Colonel East, invoked DORA and imposed a curfew on women 'of a certain class' between the hours of 7 PM and 8 AM. When asked by a deputation of protesting feminists for his justification, he replied that his concern was not immorality, but protection from disease. *Votes for Women* (the paper of the United Suffragists) sarcastically retorted:
>
>> It does not seem to have occurred to the military rulers of Cardiff that in protecting the troops from the women they have failed to protect the women from the troops, or that they might have accomplished both ends by closing the streets to soldiers instead of to prostitutes. (Bland 29)

Regardless of the conundrum set forth here, there were increasing calls for the patrolling, policing, and protection of women, not only in England but in her colonies as well—in South Africa and in Ireland, for example.

Answering such calls were organizations such as Nina Boyle's Women Police Volunteers (WPV), Margaret Damer Dawson's Women Police Service (WPS), and the National Union of Women Workers' (NUWW) Women Patrols Committee. In an essay on women police in the First World War, Philippa Levine notes that "from their earliest inception, both major policewomen's groups—the NUWW patrols and the WPS—were closely associated with controlling the public and even the private behaviors of working and working-class women" (44); but while "the policing of women—their protection and their needs—centrally defined the identity of the new groups," one important distinction was that the NUWW renounced all kinds of rescue work performed in the name of social purity, hoping to "dissociate itself from female philanthropy," while the WPS "adopted a palpably interventionist approach, actively warning young girls and soldiers' wives of the moral dangers their casual or wild behaviors might engender," Levine notes (42). The self-defined role of the WPS as interventionist and preventative fell directly in line with the sort of policing that officials in the Home Office sought. Many might have agreed with Huntingdon's Chief Constable who wrote in 1914 to his Under-Secretary of State that "'real' prostitutes posed a minimal threat [to soldiers] compared with lax mothers and flighty daughters" (Levine 44).

Regulation 40D was but one of the regulations aimed specifically at British women who were thought to be prurient during the war. Other statutes restricted women's behavior, too, and sermonized the glories of personal restraint. Woollacott writes that "allegations that working-class women were drinking excessively because of the removal of the controlling presence of their husbands, and especially because of their extra income, began almost as soon as the first shot of the war was fired" (*On Her* 126). Just three months after Britain declared war, for example, "the Home Office issued orders that the wives and dependents of soldiers and sailors were to be subject to police surveillance so that any woman who was reported to be drinking excessively or behaving 'loosely' would have her separation allowance cut off," she adds. Whatever sense of social freedom wives and workers won from their entry into paid labor—what Lilian Miles recalls as a sense of being "let out of the cage"—quickly was circumscribed and flanked by DORA behavioral regulations; and the host of restrictions invented under the DORA to safeguard the nation soon grew more restricting than precautionary, more prudent than practical.

National attention towards women's drinking is a good case in point. Elizabeth Roberts notes in *An Oral History of Working-Class Women 1890–1940* that DORA measures designed to curtail women's drinking, for example, were successful because "restraint was forced upon them by government policy" (122), something that led Lindsay Rogers to argue as early as 1915 that "there can no longer be the proud boast that in time of war England leaves untouched the safeguards of the citizen against the Executive" ("The War and the English Constitution" 30). Elizabeth Roberts explains that munitions workers were partly responsible for inspiring DORA drinking measures, and writes:

> In 1915, alarmed by the adverse effect on the war effort of munition workers spending a substantial part of the increase in their wages on drink, the government, in the Defence of the Realm Acts, established a Central Control Board to take charge of licensing in those areas where it was judged that extensive drinking was impeding the war effort. These areas (which included Barrow, which had a special mention in the Report of Bad Time-

keeping) were extended until, by 1917, 38 million out of a population of 41 million were subjected to the Board's regulations. The sale of alcohol was limited to two and a half hours in the middle of the day, and three hours in the evening. At the same time the potency of beer was reduced, and the tax on spirits increased (four- to five-fold between 1914 and 1920). These measures combined to have a dramatic effect on local drinking habits, as the conviction rates and the oral evidence reveal. In 1914 the average national weekly convictions for drunkenness were 3,388; by the end of 1918 this had fallen to 444. (122)

Though statistics had no doubt fallen, women often came up with more ingenious ways to skirt DORA restrictions, and they did so in the privacy of their own homes; but because DORA regulations also gave the new Women's Police Patrols power to supervise, check, and curb civilian behavior, it was only a matter of time before women's private behavior was made susceptible to public reprimand.

One policewoman describes the conditions in Grantham after an order was issued to keep "women . . . in their houses from 8 o'clock in the evening until 7 o'clock the next morning":

A Defence of the Realm regulation gave us power to go in the women's houses and to see if the girls were in bed, and to see who was in the house. We found that women were getting large quantities of drink and entertaining the men in their houses instead of being out on the streets, and, as we pointed out to the military authority, that was doing more harm than if the women had actually been in the public houses and in the streets where people could see them. We turned hundreds of soldiers and girls out of these houses, and reported it to the military authority and to the Chief Constable, with a result that the order restricting women was taken off. (Quoted in Braybon and Summerfield 109)

One cannot help wondering where exactly the "hundreds of soldiers and girls" were "turned out" to after state-sanctioned raids of this sort or how these transgressors were treated by their communities after such an infraction.

The country was growing used to wartime restrictions in drink, restrictions that worked to reduce national consumption of alcohol at the end of the war by more than half when compared with 1914 statistics. There was the so-called Beauty Sleep order that prohibited serving officers drinks after ten P.M. By 1915, brandy was unobtainable without a medical prescription, "No Treating" laws were squarely in place,[5] and temperance canteens grew in popularity and number. By 1916, the Ministry of Munitions had taken over most of Britain's whisky distilleries. While these and other measures curbed alcohol consumption, they also worked increasingly to criminalize behavior among the civilian population, and as I have explained above, women in particular quickly began to reap the reprimand. They jeopardized their separation allowances if caught and risked criminal indictment if charged. DORA Regulation 13A was frequently invoked to order curfews on dubious or questionable women and was administered in the pubs as well as on the streets, leading to a number of convictions.

Drinking was not the only private activity regulated under DORA. Censorship, in particular, was one of the more stringent conditions of DORA, and one that extended to women in particular since so many of those behind pacifist and peace league publications were women. "When . . . the DORA ordered that all writings about the war or the making of peace be submitted to censorship before publication, the Society of Friends decided not to obey," David Mitchell notes in *Monstrous Regiment: The Story of the Women of the First World War* (327), and adds that consequently "two women were arrested for distributing *A Challenge to Militarism*, a leaflet describing the fate of COs [Conscientious Objectors] in prison" (327). Tylee notes that censorship penalties under this branch of DORA ranged from the innocuous to the severe, and explains that disciplinary measures often

> includ[ed] the possibility of six months' hard labour and the forfeit of the printer's machinery; if the case were heard by court martial the sentence could be life-imprisonment. The general wording of the regulation, which referred to the 'spread of reports likely to cause disaffection or alarm' either among the forces or the civilian population, was vague enough for police to use it to intimidate the less politically desperate. Threats or raids were usually sufficient. (120)

The phrase "'likely to' cause disaffection or alarm" meant that no real intention had to be proved, especially since any and all suspects could be held without charge under DORA. So serious was DORA censorship Regulation II.21 that it unwittingly encouraged neighbors and co-workers to spy on their relatives, friends, and acquaintances and to report on the words—spoken or published—with which they discussed the war, the culture, and the Empire. Though the severest punishment under DORA was penile servitude for life, the document provided that even the innocent could be imprisoned for up to three months: "no sentence exceeding three months' imprisonment with hard labour shall be imposed in respect of any contravention of Regulation 21 if the offender proves that he acted without any intention to cause disaffection or alarm" (DORA II.27).

One particular problem associated with DORA Regulation II.21 was the ever-increasing frequency with which antiwar rallies were held. "The British Home Office was constantly considering whether anti-war speeches were illegal under DORA," Wiltsher writes in *Most Dangerous Women*. "But most of the time they decided, like the German authorities, that it was expedient not to make martyrs. . . . Chief Constables all over the country were scribbling verbatim reports at public meetings and sending them to the Home Secretary for advice on whether to take action" (137–38). Women peace campaigners and labor activists especially found themselves muzzled by DORA censorship regulations. Irene Cooper Willis and Catherine Marshall, members of the No Conscription Fellowship, were beleaguered by police and prosecuted under the DORA; David Mitchell describes Mary Macarthur as "the undisputed spokeswoman of one and a half million otherwise voiceless women, gagged by the Defence of the Realm Act and hampered by a growing network of barbed, legal wartime wire" (*Monstrous Regiment* 259–60). Mitchell's 1965 book, and Wiltsher's 1985 *Most Dangerous Women*, effectively litanize and catalogue women's censures and arrests under DORA and remain essential sources for the study of DORA's powerful and suppressive arm.

Fear of reprimand under DORA regulations extended, as well, to writers in women's service newspapers, where workers discussed the constraint of its restrictions. In a *Shell Magazine* article titled "The I———D———. Being Some Account of its Birth and Growth," the writer mocks her own expectations of censorship under DORA, and leaves the title of her essay on the "I.D." [Inspection Department] an exaggerated mystery. She opens her essay with an embellished apologia, writing,

> If it were not for D.O.R.A. I could tell many things of how the I.D. came into being and how it grew.
> But D.O.R.A. is a severe jade, an ever present terror to those who would cast discretion to the winds and tell of things whereof they know. So I must talk circumspectly, for is it not written in the books that "a live dog is better than a dead lion." And so, for fear of D.O.R.A. I must go warily. But some things I know, and the wise, as they always do, can read between the lines, crossing the t's and putting the dots over the i's. (*Shell Magazine* 8)

Her caricature of the "sensitive document" encodes the wink-wink, nudge-nudge of typical discussions transformed and codified by civilian paranoia and fear under the scrutinizing eyes and ears of DORA.

Reading between the lines, crossing the t's and dotting the i's—these small activities drove the work of a growing legion of civilian informants.

Apart from the vigorous work of scribbling Chief Constables, civilians also became vigilant scouts for the Home Office. Anne Wiltsher reports that a Mrs. Lawrenson brought her daughter into a Holyhead police station to complain about a local priest who argued that England "shouldn't have interfered" (138), and she quotes a remonstrative letter from one William Kelly, another civilian watchdog, who wrote:

> I write these few lines to warn you of a woman called Mrs Crawford . . . this woman is causing a Terrible discontentment among the munition workers and I am just suspicious of her Being a British subject. Shall I keep in touch with this Woman for the sake of our empire. Write and let me know what to do in this case. (138)

Any war breeds civilian paranoia, and neighbors and co-workers often felt pressured to protect their homes as well as the Empire when suspicious of a likely dissident. To be sure, fear of the civilian spy would flourish again during the Second World War: one popular advertising campaign in the 1940s pictured a beautiful and seductive blonde under the warning "Keep Mum—She's Not So Dumb!" During the First World War years, however, it was the DORA that championed civilian informants, and by promoting the advocacy of vigilant betrayal it demonized civilian privacy and hastened Britain's devolution into a police state. "The new regime was nearly a dictatorship," Martin suggests. "The general effect of this new government was a movement towards state control, what some called 'collectivism' and others 'war socialism'" (81). To be sure, the new regime was neither collectivist nor socialist. There were a number of writers who feared a continual police state as a result of the success of DORA and who felt alarm at what seemed to be a growing public sanctioning of its regulatory statutes. Rose Macaulay, for example, vents her frustration in *Non-Combatants and Others* through the voice of the cynic Nicholas, who cries, "After all this Defending of the Realm, and cancelling of scraps of paper such as Magna Carta and Habeas Corpus, and ordering the press, and controlling industries and finance and food and drink, saying, 'Let there be darkness' (and there was darkness) . . . the realm will go on being defended long after it's weathered this storm" (184).

It was likely the weathering of the storm that frustrated British civilians the most, especially when compounded by anxieties automatically produced by war. With civilian mental and physical initiatives restricted by the DORA, the home front soon grew weary and dispirited of the compulsory straitjacketing. Strict military controls made it difficult for civilians to cross the Channel, for example, and "the physical area covered by martial law included not only sensitive areas of Britain near army barracks, the coast, or munitions factories, and the front-line in Flanders, but the whole extent of France from the ports and base-areas up to the trenches" (Tylee 234). Britons responded to these increasing restrictions and regulations anxiously, and their anxiety began to transform them into cynics, spies, or even hooligans, as Stephen Humphries explains below.

Humphries argues in *Hooligans or Rebels? An Oral History of Working-Class Childhood and Youth 1889–1939* that "It is significant that the two most prolonged and powerful campaigns to control hooliganism and to rehabilitate working-class youth originated during the Boer War and then World War I, when reported increases in delinquent behaviour coincided with economic and military threats to national stability" (174–75).

Protracted efforts toward civilian control and the increased criminalization of Britain's own "dissident population" under DORA indicates the severity of the martial law imposed by DORA, a severity that eventually took its toll on Britain's working-class youth as well as on its overwrought police force; and even those employed to enforce DORA began to crumble under the weight of it. Philip John Stead explains that "the additional burdens the police had to bear were aggravated by the wretched pay that they were receiving: it was barely at subsistence level, less than an agricultural laborer's; teen-age girls in munitions factories were getting three times as much as a constable on overtime with a wife and family to keep" (*The Police of Britain* 72). By midnight, August 30, 1918, "almost the whole of London's police had struck" (73) in response to overwhelming work demands brought on by DORA regulations, and to mutiny against wages that were lower than those of working-class women.[6]

As the war would progress, the "capacious umbrella of DORA" would affect and restrict civilian and domestic life more egregiously, increasingly affording the government near unlimited powers, and transporting an entire range of civilian action "so innocent in peacetime" to somewhere "beyond the legal pale" (Williams 111, 178). Though laid to rest in 1921 at the official end of the war, DORA's half life, Charles Townshend provocatively suggests, "looks to be perpetual" (80). Discussions about the watchdog paranoia that it introduced into civilian life, the compulsory behavior it demanded, and the affects of the relentless barrage of notices about what civilians could or could not do under new DORA regulations will continue to modulate our approaches to understanding civilian actions and attitudes during the war. Such a degree of government intervention into private life would have been thought intolerable before 1914, Briggs argues (277), and as we remain curious about civilian acquiescence and complicity under DORA, we also must continue to investigate the effects of this "spinster aunt" on women workers, from whom information about fatal munition factory explosions was withheld, whose houses routinely were checked and searched by police patrols, who were singled out for curfew, criminalized for consensual sexual conduct, and demoralized with real or implied threats of losing their separation allowances if they misbehaved. The "popular sanction" that backed the DORA seems born out of a cultural desire to curb and control women's behavior (sexual or otherwise) during wartime, as if the stern figure of the spinster aunt were the only one who could take the place of the usual reigning overseer, women's fathers or husbands. As we shall see in the next chapter, while women were being directed by DORA their spinster aunt about what they should *not* be doing during wartime, campaigns quickly were being mounted in the name of another formidable relative to tell them what they ought to be doing instead—making babies for Mother England.

Chapter 6

Women's Work and Maternity

WHEN MABEL POTTER DAGGETT SCRIPTED HER 1918 invocation to the women of the world to *"Fill the cradles!,"* her country was well in the throes of a massive pronatalist campaign that urged women to turn their industrial energies toward maternity, no longer to fill the wombs of shells but to fill their own wombs instead and thereby prepare to leave the factories so that returning soldiers might resume their work in industry. Daggett called it "the oldest cry in the world. 'Women wanted for maternity,'" and added that "not a captain of industry who assembles the engines of war, not a general who directs the armies, may do for his country what you can do who stand beside its cradles" (267). Pronatalism seemed to many a natural successor to women's work during a war that interrupted the race building charge of British civilians.

The number of registered births dropped each year during the war and sank by an alarming 220,000 in 1918.[1] These statistics animated the government to invent policies aimed at inspiring national fecundity. To this end, Britain's pronatalist campaign was ingeniously timed and well scripted. It was a crusade that began with the inception of a Baby Week Council, an annual Mother's Day introduced in August 1916, and an annual National Baby Week, first held in July 1917. These early campaigns urged citizens to redirect their civilian energies toward the family—their own and others'—and focused public attention on the importance of protecting babies' lives just months after the worst casualty losses in the history of warfare were felt on the battlegrounds of the Somme and at Verdun.[2]

The *Daily Chronicle* described the proposed scheme for Mother's Day and focused on civilian acts of kindness toward mothers and on "practical sympathy." By galvanizing national and communal support for mothers, propagandists hoped that women would find their familial and financial burdens less overwhelming and would consider it a national service to enlarge their families. Thus, the acts of kindness and sympathy advocated in the following clipping would become preludes to the national conscription of an army of women's bodies enlisted to rebuild the nation and empire:

> A "Mother's Day"—without flags or appeals for subscriptions—is proposed for August 8. The idea is that on this date everyone should perform a kindly act towards a needy mother, and especially those with sons at the front. Forms of practical sympathy suggested are an outing, entertainment at tea, gift of food or clothing and payment of a debt to a landlord or tradesman. (June 16, 1916; Imperial War Museum Department of Printed Books, Women's Work Microfilm Collection, Item BO2 52/5)

With motherhood glorified by the Home Office and romanticized by the press and in local communities, cultural attitudes toward mothers and children and their welfare shifted, leading one *Times* reporter to comment on the growing "cult of the child" (July 3, 1917), a cult so endemic that even the disgrace usually attached to unwed mothers and their illegitimate children was tempered during the war by emerging cultural attitudes that recognized mothers as national assets[3] and their births as national bequests.[4] Maternity had become a protected occupation, and with it women's obstetric health had become prioritized and supported in ways that women's health in the factories had never been.

The campaign for Mother's Day was a widespread success, as were the subsequent campaigns for National Baby Week. Posters and print advertisements for Baby Week appropriated the familiar rhetoric of war, as in the following example which imagines the future of the race parading in a regimental file: "SAVE THE BABIES. Re-build the Nation and Empire. 'The Race marches forward on the feet of little children.' National Baby Week." In the *Lady's Pictorial,* one columnist urged women to consider that "the greatest work for them was in the care of their children" (G. Thomas 26) and wrote during the first National Baby Week

> It seems fitting that women's attention should be turned to the importance of the baby at this juncture. After all, there is no finer work in which women can engage, no higher duty for them to perform, no way in which they can better serve the Empire than by caring for the young. (July 7, 1917)

Not only did these frequent messages work to redefine women's place in British culture, undercutting the importance of their current industrial work and encouraging their immediate vocation as child bearers, but they indicated what was to become an urgent and meddlesome welfare practice during the last two years of the war and one that would continue into the 1920s, since campaigns aimed at "protecting" women's children also worked to curb women's permanent integration into the work force. This sort of welfare, Gail Braybon argues, was "patronising, intrusive and potentially dangerous to the working class" (149), and because it would remove them from the work force, such welfare would curtail women's opportunities as wage-earners.

Britain's maternity push urged women to rebuild the race not only to replace the hundreds of thousands of sons, brothers, husbands and fathers lost to the First World War but to ensure Britain's potency and strength in preparation for what might be the next war. No doubt sensing its diminishing colonial power after the First World War, Britain sought to rebuild the race and empire through its women as well as through its girls. Sally Mitchell notes in *The New Girl* that Britain's pronatalist campaign was aimed not only at young women but at the *very* young, and worked to push a generation of girls toward motherhood. Often, the pleas carried overt racist pronouncements, as when the Countess of Warwick urged women to bear more children because "it was their 'duty to the white race'" (Braybon 119). "Duty"—so long a catchword during the war—was now being contextualized within discussions of women's roles, and their duties as mothers soon eclipsed in the popular consciousness their duties as wage earners and breadwinners.

For all this, Britain's pronatalist project was not what we might call a huge success. By 1920, the birth rate had increased only to 4 percent higher than it had been before the war, an increase that has led J. M. Winter to assert that "the post-war baby boom was really a 'boomlet,'" one that reflected "the recovery of deferred births rather than a change in strategies of family formation" (*Working Class in Modern British History* 254). Other factors affected the modest rise in birth rate, as well. An increase in the use of contraception among Britons after the war surely tempered what otherwise might have been a fertile pronatalist campaign. Though Winter is correct in pointing out that the practice of issuing condoms to soldiers for protection against venereal diseases may have popularized for many men the practice of contraception, and that women's juxtaposition with other women in the factories may have led to frank discussions of contraceptive measures (Winter 271), his description of men as users of contraception and women as discussants of contraceptive measures reduces men to actors and women to talkers.[5] One picture postcard that was popular during the war reinforces such a reduction of women.[6] It pictures six hens squatting in a henhouse. Their supervisor, a decorated rooster waving the

Union Jack, says to the hens, "Now then! less cackling there—get on with that shell-making." While this postcard supports the stereotype that women cackle like hens (and suggests that this interferes with their production), it also emblematizes Britain's pronatalist push by capturing it, importantly, in a language and situation familiar to women factory workers whose celebrated production in the factories was soon being used as a paranomasiac selling point for the pronatalist push. Pronatalists were able to appropriate and exploit a body of already-published references to women and their work in the factories, texts that sought to convince Britons early in the war that women were drawn to the factories to appease their maternal instincts.[7]

Befuddled by women's mass entry into paid labor during the war, writers who tried to explain women's attraction to factory work often relied on biological explanations and argued that women were "naturally" suited for shell production, since it involved stuffing a charge into the "wombs" of shells. Other reports suggested that women found their work in the factories sexually titillating, or that they were made "power-drunk" by it, and were thrilled by opportunities to dominate what one writer called the "massive male machinery" of the munitions plants. Their exhilaration at the work site grew out of delirium born of their new-found power and autonomy. As different as these three elements may be, all three "explanations" stemmed from one overarching belief about women's entry into paid labor, as we shall see.

Hall Caine's book, *Our Girls: Their Work For the War*, is an account of his tour through London's Woolwich Arsenal, the largest of England's three government arsenal factories, a factory that by 1916 employed well over 70,000 workers and, by the Armistice, 97,000. Mystified during his tour by the volume of women workers, Caine concluded that women were perfectly suited for munitions work, and explains, saying,

> a stronger impulse than the desire for large earnings must be operating with many to enable them to defy so much discomfort. This is not the first time that women have made munitions of war. For every war that has yet been waged women have supplied the first and greatest of all munitions— men. . . . Therefore, consciously or unconsciously, the daughters of Britain may be answering some mysterious call of their sex in working all day and all night in the munition factories. (34)

By asserting that women who work in the arsenals were "answering some mysterious call of their sex," Caine proposes an instinctive tie between munitions work and maternity and attaches to the work a purely biological lure. More important, Caine suggests that the unexpected multitudes of workers were lured to work for the arsenals specifically because the job entailed stuffing explosives into what he called the "wombs" of the shells. Caine wrote:

> But you realize that the lure of money is not the sole or yet the chief magnet that draws women to work for the war. . . . Everybody knows that somewhere the womb of the shell has to be loaded with its deadly charge. (25)

Here, Caine intimates that loading these wombs became the principle draw, the "chief magnet," that beckoned women to the factories, as if during the war more than three million British women sensed maternal voids so insufferable that they sought relief in the workshops. The equation also suggests that women were drawn to munitions plants because they were surrogate birthing centers where women produced not their usual munitions of war—that is, in Caine's terms, men—but shells.

The connection between the maternal egg and the manufactured shell surfaces even in service newspapers and souvenir magazines produced by the women munitions workers themselves. *Shell Magazine*, a service newspaper printed and published by the workers at the Newlay arsenal in Leeds, adopted in the coat of arms printed on the back cover the emblematic figure of an egg. Of course, the temptation to pun on the name of the Newlay arsenal may have been unavoidable, if not irresistible, and this may be one of the reasons behind the literal iconography of the "newly laid" shells; but the workers' coat of arms also reinforces the link between munitions work and maternity since each munitions worker, the coat of arms prescribes, must in her own way produce for the defense of the realm.

Equally revealing is the front cover of the beautifully illustrated *Shell Magazine*, which pictures a woman munitions worker seated beside a three-to-four-foot shell (see Figure 4.3); the expression on her face is alluring and suggestive. Clearly, the women workers helped to popularize the notion that woman's work at the arsenals was both sexually titillating and maternally attractive, as the front and back covers of the Newlay arsenal service newspaper suggests; but to appropriate the punning language of the workers themselves, one wonders which came first, the chicken or the egg? In other words, who began filtering this message through the ranks of women workers, and at what point did the women begin to reproduce these natalist ideologies? Did they ever believe that they were answering the "call of their sex" by generating shells for the war? Did publications that exploited analogies between maternity and factory work attempt to justify women's work in the arsenals or belittle it? Did these add to the status of women's work in industry or take away from it?

Most likely, the reports did all of these at once by asserting that women as a gendered class were *ab ovo* one thing or another. Equally important, each stems from an attempt to define working-class women—as they had been and as they were now.

Reinforcing the connection between war work and maternity, "Active mothers ensure a virile race" was one of the slogans made popular during Kitchener's great munitions drive. Harriet Stanton Blatch refers to the phrase a number of times in her 1918 book *Mobilizing Woman-Power,* a text that urges women into war service. Again, the language links munitions making with procreation and wartime activity with an incongruous counterpart, virility. The maternal shells that the women produced, the volatile and deadly "wombs" they manufactured, were not only explosively charged, but gender-charged as well; and it is the very strange language of munitions that contributes to (and likely modifies) various discourses about gender in this period of the war. Mabel Potter Daggett wrote in 1918 of her government's plea to every woman, citing the popular cry, "Fill the cradles!" (Daggett 309, 311, 318). Maternity, she wrote, had finally taken on the status of a protected industry yielding what she called "birth politics" (311). A different type of birth politics, however, seems to have driven propagandists to establish, in print and in the minds of the women workers, a link between munitions-making and maternity.

Of course, not all writers were willing to nourish or protect such a link. While many writers hailed women's war work at the arsenals by calling it a celebration of a new motherhood, groups of women pacifists denounced women's work in the arsenals. Mary Gabrielle Collins, for example, criticizes women for turning their instinctive, maternal benevolence toward the manufacturing of deadly munitions. In her poem "Women at Munition Making," she writes of a different kind of birth politics, one that metamorphoses women into institutionally trained murderers:

> Their hands should minister unto the flame of life,
>   Their fingers guide
> The rosy teat, swelling with milk,
> To the eager mouth of the suckling babe
> Or smooth with tenderness,
>   Softly and soothingly
> The heated brow of the ailing child. . . .
>   But now,
> Their hands, their fingers,
> Are coarsened in munitions factories. . . .
> 'Kill, Kill.' (Reilly 24)

Clearly, Collins denounces such a displacement of the maternal, such a cultural transformation of women's "innate" benevolence. Well before their entry into the munitions labor force, women were associated with all that was life-giving and life-preserving—even though war propaganda posters worked against these constructions and attempted to ascribe a virulent militarism onto women (see Figure 6.2).[8] Furthermore, some contemporaries felt that a woman's entry into the munitions labor force was a disavowal of her sacred duty as "pre-ordained champion for the preservation of her sons" (Hallowes, *Mothers of Men and Militarism* 32). Margaret Sackville, for example, referred to women's work in the factories as an egregiously communal fault, and in her 1916 poem "Nostra Culpa" refers to women factory workers as "mothers and murderers of mankind,"[9] a sentiment echoed by Mary Macarthur in 1917 when she argued that "women have done some wonderful work, but a baby is more wonderful than a machine gun" ("Women in Industry," *Daily News*, August 15, 1917). In *Mothers of Men and Militarism*, Mrs. F. S. Hallowes rejects the aggression attributed to women during the war and urges her contemporaries to repudiate the militancy ascribed to them. She explains:

> A sight which may be called a grim satire on women's love of militarism is to be observed among the statuary that adorns the Admiralty Arch in London. A beautiful woman, the typical and classic matron of noble proportions and Juno-like form is seen tenderly pressing to her breast—what, a baby? No—a *cannon!* (40)

Targeted and trapped in a double bind, women equally were praised for living up to their maternal duties in the factories or censured for disavowing them. Munitions work was both maternal and antimaternal, and the familiar nineteenth-century adage, "The hand that rocks the cradle rules the world," was brazenly refashioned during the war into a damning sentiment: "The hand that rocks the cradle wrecks the world" (Khan 85).

It is somehow absurd that the battle was being waged in these terms: is munitions-making maternal or isn't it? Is militarism instinctive to the female or isn't it? Is munitions making a female act? These questions are of themselves important, but both sides decidedly avoid the main issue, the "big picture," as we might call it—the war itself—and only obscure reality while pretending to probe it. Both sides draw on a notion of culturally prescribed roles for women and insist on galvanizing women's "innate" qualities. That the two sides could not agree whether those qualities were maternal or militaristic likely confounded the women workers whose nine- or twelve-hour shifts sent them home too tired to wrestle for probable answers themselves. The issue—unresolved even by the war's end—

must have produced a great deal of anxiety for women who saw their work as a living and little more.

Contemporary writers who did not seek to justify women's factory work by linking it with maternalism or to censure women for ignoring or rejecting their duties as cultural pacifists and "mothers of men" ascribed the attraction of arsenal and factory work to sexual titillation, to the physical pleasure women derived from working the "pulsing and throbbing" machinery (Caine 45). Though Caine cannot bring himself to recognize the overt phallicism of the munitions he refers to as "wombs," picture postcards from World War I exploited the phallic nature of the artillery with mass-produced images of middle-class women straddling the shells and riding orgasmically across the atmosphere (see Figure 6.1). Such visual representations offered yet another reason why women were drawn to the factories—their work there ostensibly provided sexual stimulation. While written and illustrated representations of women munitions workers vary and often conflict with and contradict other published or visual representations, the silhouette of the woman munitions worker often was disfigured by language and images that surfaced in the fiction, nonfiction, and postcard and poster art of the time. She was the subject of not only male inquiry and suspicion but male burlesque, too, and writers consistently yoked women's work in the factories with what they saw as the larger issues of maternity, sexuality, and power. At the same time, then, women's factory labor was constructed as maternally fulfilling, sexually arousing, and power-inducing, as I discuss below. Women workers increasingly bore the brunt of such sociological musings, and as each of these descriptions gained currency, and as fear about women's corruption in the work force spread, Britain's pronatalist drive profited. By the time pronatalism was in full swing, the public would have more reasons than ever to want women out of the factories and returned to the safety of hearth and home.

L. K. Yates's 1918 book on women and labor, *The Woman's Part*, is a detailed record of women's work in the factories. An arsenal supervisor for her firm's women employees, Yates suggests that the women's attraction to factory work was a sexual one, and describes an episode of work-site jealousy complicated by different shifts of day and night workers. Because she discusses the women workers' attraction to their machines in terms of a romantic and sexual liaison—as if each worker's machine were her lover—Yates carnalizes the work, eroticizes the work site, and scripts an uncanny narrative about the fetishization of the workplace. She explains:

> The women, in fact, soon get attached to the machines they are working, in a manner probably unknown to men. . . . From time to time, a girl will even

157

6.1   Erotic postacrds of women riding shells.

confess that she 'can't bear to think of someone on the night-shift working *her* machine'. An understanding has arisen between the machine and the operator which amounts almost to affection. I have often noticed the expression of this emotion in the workshops; the caressing touch of a woman's fingers, for instance, as a bore is being urged on to the job on the machine. (Yates 20)

Yates' highly charged account of her women workers clearly describes the munitions making act as a sexual exercise, an act of lovemaking in which women's caressing fingers gingerly guide the bore of the massive male machine "on to the job." Reports such as these activated cultural fears about women's promiscuity during the war, a topic of much speculation and conjecture, as I already have described in chapter 2. Because women's work in the factories was described in sexual terms and veiled in sexualized metaphors and tropes, issues surrounding women's work in the factories soon were confounded by larger fears of women's sexual laxity during the war, and their work in the factories only added to the speed of what many saw as women's quickly eroding virtue. This led to many questions about the propriety of women's work in arsenals and ordnance factories. While some writers saw women's work in the factories as maternal, others described it as justly compensated seduction, yoking women's work in the factories—however unwittingly—to the oldest profession in the world.

While some of women's other wartime occupations were considered compatible with the maternal—motherhood being the *real* oldest profession in the world—munitions work was not. In fact, the image of the benevolent mother successfully was evoked in advertising campaigns for the Red Cross, whose poster "The Greatest Mother in the World" was so successful during the First World War that it was recirculated during the Second World War with the caption, "Still the greatest mother." The Red Cross poster affirms the image of the life-giving mother, the life-sustaining nurse. Nursing as a wartime occupation was endowed with more maternal propriety than factory work, since it was held to be compatible with popular notions about appropriate women's work and appropriate maternal responses to war. Tate discusses how the image of Mother was used during the war in tank manufacturing,[10] and suggests that tanks might have been renamed *Mother* because of the pleasure, protection, and the "bizarre kind of tenderness" ("Culture of the Tank" 79) the machines promised (though the mass-produced image of "Bertha," Figure 6.2, contradicts that): "Many writers describe the Great War as a war of machines against men, with the machines always winning. The tank seems, however ineptly, to provide a shield—to protect soldiers from the terrible damage of machine-gun bullets and artillery. In short, the tank promises to reduce the hideous abjection of the war," she notes ("Culture" 78). Tate has found an excess of metaphors of birth and conception in early writings about the tank, and just as "the tank produced new ways of imagining warfare" (79), it produced new ways of imagining the figure of the mother.

Apart from the obvious class distinctions that separated nurses from factory workers, distinctions I already have described in chapter 1, another reason why munitions work was not endowed with so much propriety as nursing was that handling the shells was seen as an "impure" act. For example, the writer of the *Times* article, "Midnight at Woolwich Arsenal," refers to the Woolwich Arsenal changing room—the "shifting room"—as "a kind of temple of purification" (Sept. 1, 1916) in which workers change out of their civilian clothes to don their work outfits. This particular article is fraught with allusion: "What would Schopenhauer, with his simile of the Guelphs and Ghibellines, have said to this atmosphere of feminine *camaraderie?*" the writer asks, for example. But a Dantean allusion reveals the true hell of the women's work regardless of the overwrought allusiveness that clouds the essay. He writes: "Just on the threshold of the "Clean Side" is the "Shifting Room," a kind of temple of purification where the workers abandon, not all hope, but all hairpins, outer garments and boots, replacing them by clean caps, overalls and slippers" (Sept. 1, 1916). Here, the writer almost seems to have it backwards; that is, it would make more sense if he called the shifting room a temple of purification to which the women went *after* they worked their shifts. Then, the women could be said to be purifying themselves of the dirt, grease, and grime of the workplace, not to mention the toxic dusts and vapors that remained trapped on their skin and in their hair. Instead, he is suggesting something rather invidious by the backwards Dantean metaphor: that they arrive at work impure, and proceed deservedly through the gates of hell. It seems, then, that this *Times* reporter is charging the women with another "innate" quality, something akin to adulteration or some other kind of foulness.

Because their handling of the massive ordnance machinery characteristically was described in sexual terms, women munitions workers found themselves burlesqued as sexual conquerors. Caine refers to the machines as "male monsters" that women had "wooed and won," for example; and because such suggestive language attended the descriptions of the munitions worker's job, the women were seen as seducers and temptresses. Here is Caine's account of the seduction:

> The machines themselves seem almost human in their automatic intelligence, and, if you show a proper respect for their impetuous organisms,

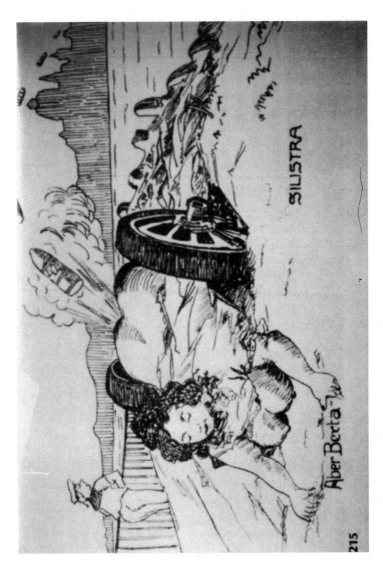

6.2 "Bertha": A shocking image of women's participation in the war.

they are not generally cruel. So the women get along very well with them, learning all their ways, their whims, their needs, and their limitations. It is surprising how speedily the women have wooed and won this new kind of male monster. (22–23)

The image of the woman munitions worker taming her machinery is one that appears frequently in munitions reports. In *Our Girls: Their Work for the War,* Caine goes so far as to draw a parallel between the size of the shell and the required analogous size of its woman handler, and implies that a larger shell necessitates a larger—what he calls a more "virile"—woman. Caine also describes the factory situation as one of "constant intercourse." A seasoned writer, Caine must have been aware of his charged and suggestive language. He writes:

> [The workers here] are chiefly occupied with the manufacture of the larger-sized shells, and are especially interesting. . . . In a huge shop, which is pulsing and throbbing with machinery, seven hundred and fifty of them are face to face and side by side. It is a stirring sight. The women are generally of larger build than we have seen before, and some of them are superb specimens of virile womanhood. . . . Constant intercourse at work appears to have given the men [workers] a high opinion of the women, of their steadiness, and power to endure. (45)

Munitions work, with its constant handling of phallic shells, somehow was seen to deflower and defile the female worker, and this may be one of the reasons why the *Times* writer refers to Woolwich's shifting room as a "temple of purification." Moreover, because women's work in the arsenals was described as a maternal act in an effort to convince women that wartime factory work was a natural extension of their maternal vocation, the job soon took on the status of a perverted and deviant maternal act; and to be sure, descriptions of the women's "constant intercourse" at work only added to the growing concern over women's work-site depravity. Arsenal "Danger Rooms," more often called "Powder Rooms" in a pernicious effort to mask the dangers of the work by punning on yet another "innate" female quality—that of primping—housed a majority of working-class women who risked the dangers of working with TNT powder so that they might earn more pay. Thus, published accounts of the women's sexual attraction to the work, of their machinated lovemaking, and so forth, conspired to place the working women, ultimately and "deservedly," at the Gates of Hell.

Complicating the extremity of the discussions of women's work in the factories and moving beyond discussions of maternity and sexuality, other writers identified elements of empowerment in the women's work and sought to explain women's attraction to the job by suggesting that their work at the factories was one big intoxicating power trip in which they threw off the yokes of capitalist and patriarchal subjugation. Women who had "tamed" the machines, women who had risen, however modestly, through the ranks of factory workers, were seen as women who hungered for power and found themselves well fed by their fast and dangerous factory work. A *Times* journalist who describes the power struggle in the factories notes that the workers have successfully enslaved the machines instead of allowing the machines to enslave them:

> The woman who feeds the lathe and the men who place the glowing steel in the jaws of the press seem to the onlooker to be but the servants of the machine, the slaves of mechanical cunning or overmastering power. The worker, he is tempted to imagine, is subordinate to the lathe or the press. . . . The truth is exactly the opposite. ("Women in Munition Works," June 24, 1918)

Descriptions such as these identify working-class women's entry into the factories as a move predicated on transcending class barriers, as one propelled by power struggles or forged on the defeat of other working-class women and men, as a deliberate and aggressive breaking of the chains of class enslavement. What distinguishes this brand of speculation and differentiates it from the previous two I have discussed—that of maternalism and sexual fulfillment—is the final piece of the trinitarian puzzle, which suggests that what women found most satisfying from their work was the power and the status that they derived from their work in the factories. There's something oddly feminist to this argument, since it implies not only that women found fulfillment in running the machines that ran the country and fueled the war, but that they recognized the potency of the metaphor that was being applied to them: they had mastered the master's machines.

Of course, all three of these explanations are preposterous. There is no biological link between manufacturing munitions and manufacturing babies, and little can be said for the sexual titillation that was to be gained from working the machines, though this sort of alarm may have stemmed from the widely discussed nineteenth-century panic over genital stimulation unwittingly introduced by foot-powered and pedal-driven sewing machines.[11] Moreover, class divisions were so clearly and defiantly marked in the factories that even the suggestion of class erosions or triumphant class reversals would be unfounded, whether one invokes Schopenhauer's simile of class camaraderie or not. All three of these explanations, however, gain currency from one overriding principle—that is, that women were *enchanted* by their work at the factories, that it held for them some sort of magical allure. Indeed, reports of women's work often evoked a bewitched or enchanted atmosphere. As we have seen from extracts printed in chapter 3, writers frequently described the women's workplace as if it were lit in a perpetually dramatic haze, as a place where women dance a never-ending quadrille on fairy dust, as a place where the evening sun lends to the women a translucent glow and endows them with a pallor so romantic that even the trees outside the factories sway to and fro in rhythmic undulation. In their attempts to explain what women found so compelling about factory work that they would shun their culturally prescribed roles as mothers and homemakers, writers and artists speculated on the unknowable by ascribing it to the incomprehensible.

It is important to see how such reports on women's work during the war were coupled with subsequent pronatalist dogma, reaching and ultimately transforming cultural opinion. As I suggest above, propagandists for the pronatalist push were able to draw from this wealth of already-published material to convince British women that their work in the factories had distracted them—enchanted them—from their duties as mothers and domestic caregivers.

To judge the victory of Britain's pronatalist campaign, then, one looks for the manifestation of its success not only in numbers and percentages, in fertility patterns and demographics, but in the ways in which the new ideology was able to transform the attitudes and behavior of British citizens. To this end, Marie-Monique Huss argues that the most important feature of the wartime ideology of the child lay in the way it successfully incorporated "the abstract and public values of patriotism with the most intimate aspects of personal and family life" (358). If during the war the DORA circumscribed public and private behavior, as I have argued in chapter 5, by the end of the war the government reached into the bedrooms of its citizens to exact new proof of civilian patriotism.

With motherhood conceptualized as a social responsibility, the ideology of motherhood and the rhetoric of maternalism filtered into daily life, and the pressure exerted on working mothers increased. They should stop working and return to their families; such was their new duty. "The implications for women of every class were serious, but above all attention was directed at the working-class mother and, to a slightly lesser extent, the 'potential' mother," Braybon notes (117). Propagandists such as Mabel Potter Daggett resounded the government's plea, the imperial charge, to every woman: "Fill the cradles!" she implores (309, 311, 318). Such an injunction is important to our understanding of working-class women in First World War Britain because it would arrest women's wage-earning and suspend their engagement in the work force.

Britain's pronatalist campaign, then, appeared to be successful on many levels: even though the gains in birth rate were modest, fertility rates did increase; infant mortality rates also decreased. Women were back at home and "protecting" their children, and jobs became available for returning soldiers. But for all this—the increased birth rate, the decreased infant mortality rate, the increased average family size and climbing marriage rates—few historians address what I find to be one of the most startling demographic statistics during the period: the rise in maternal mortality rates after the First World War. Maternal mortality rates in Britain grew from 4.17 percent in 1914 to 4.37 percent in 1919. For every thousand live births recorded in 1914, the maternal mortality rate registered at 0.95; that figure would jump to 3.81 in 1918. Though it would decrease to 1.93 per thousand live births in 1919, it would continue until the early 1930s to remain higher than it had been during the first three years of the war (Winter 136). Though Winter and others attribute the rise in working-class maternal mortality figures to the influenza epidemic that swept Britain in 1918, taking with it more British lives than the war itself, it is likely that women's poor health care in essential industries and factories contributed to the rise in postwar maternal mortality rates, too.

Those working-class women who were forced out of paid labor at the end of the war and who turned their attentions dutifully to "Re-building the Nation and Empire" were the very women exposed and susceptible to the dangerous industrial working conditions I have already described in chapter 3. Factory Inspectorate Reports as well as anecdotal evidence suggest that doctors did little to alleviate the women's pain and discomfort on the job. More than 150 women workers died from toxic jaundice due to their exposure to TNT, and hundreds more were plagued with incontinence, convulsions, menstrual irregularities, and diarrhea; or they suffered throughout their work in the factories as a result of asbestos, khaki, black powder, or lead poisoning. When the war was over, these very women were conscripted to serve their country by contributing to the next generation of Britons. Little wonder that maternal mortality rates climbed. Undaunted by the climbing figures, pronatalists found comfort in the demographic statistics of the rising birth rate and decreasing infant mortality rate. While Britain's pronatalist philosophy may have been inspired by Juno, it appears in practice to have been Machiavellian.

The increase in working-class maternal mortality rates has serious implications. It points to a scandalous area of neglect, and exposes the sobering consequences of an imperial nation aggressively determined to sustain its potency. "Fill the cradles"—at what cost? It seems too easy to attribute the rise in maternal mortality rates merely to the 1918 influenza epidemic, especially when we recall Caroline Rennles's report of what one on-site doctor said to Woolwich Arsenal canaries:

> —And I remember this doctor he was looking at us girls one day, and he'd said, "Half of you girls will never have babies," he said. "You're pulling your stomachs to pieces. And the other half are too sick, God help you." (Imperial War Museum Sound Archive, Item SR 566, Transcript 9).

Though Rennles's horrifying recollection records a conversation that took place decades ago, her words offer a speculation well worth considering by social historians and demographers.

Britain's pronatalist project likely was an unwitting precursor to the birth control push in the following decade. Only a few short years after being pushed and prodded into saving the Nation and the Empire, British women fought for birth control rights and family planning clinics, and as divorce rates began to climb after 1918, women asked for the implementation of low cost legal aid and petitioned for local access to divorce clinics and centers. It seems clear that after fulfilling their marital and maternal duties to the nation and empire, British women soon thought enough was enough and worked as advocates for national birth control policies and divorce sanctions. By 1924, for example, just six years after the end of the war, birth control clinics were springing up all over Britain, making family planning activists like Marie Stopes a household name. By the time Britain would engage in its next world war, the working-class fertility rate would plunge rapidly and the two-child family—so long a middle-class phenomenon—would become more common among the working classes (Lewis 15), a clear indication that after the fulfilling their "debt" to their country, working-class women decided it was time to begin limiting family size and to practice family planning.

The population increase so heartily sanctioned by the State led to a number of grievous welfare problems in health and housing—problems that were neither addressed nor rectified until after the war, since Britain had to remain focused on the war itself. But what Britain failed to understand and neglected to prepare for in the midst and wake of its pronatalist drive was that childbearing exacts a decidedly heavy toll on women and that the legacy of child bearing is often bad health. This is especially important to note because working-class women's health already was compromised by postwork illnesses. Lewis reminds us of the legacy of child bearing, for example, when she notes that among Marie Stopes's first 10,000 birth control patients, 1,321 of her patients had slit cervixes, 335 had serious uterine prolapses, and 1,508 had internal deformations (25), according to Stopes's 1930 report. Nearly one-third of Stopes's subjects had serious internal injuries from child bearing, figures that sustain what Mary Macarthur called the "treble strain" affecting women's lives: "child-bearing, wage-earning and household drudgery."

After the war, more women relied on contraception to limit family size; others turned to abortion, even though prosecutions for abortion had quadrupled since 1900. Between 1911, the year of the last prewar census, and 1921, the average family size in England and Wales dropped from 3.04 to 2.54; and there was a 10 percent increase in the number of families that had two, or fewer than two, children (Lewis 5). Lewis notes that "prosecutions for abortion doubled between 1900 and 1910 and doubled again during the next twenty years but this may merely indicate more vigilance on the part of the authorities rather than increasing incidence" (18). The vigilance practiced against abortionists was an attempt to prosecute practitioners for what at the time was covertly being identified as a crime against the empire, and as the incidence of abortion rose, it threatened the gains made in the wake of the postwar baby "boomlet" and robbed the state of potential national assets.

As I have tried to show, the affinities between Britain's pronatalist ideology and the precursory assessments of women's work in the factories were predicated on cultural assumptions about women's roles in British society. While traditionalists wanted to redirect women to culturally assigned and "protected" domestic spheres, pronatalists wanted to metamorphose potential workers into potential mothers. Both movements exploited patriarchal hegemony—moral, political, and cultural values that sought to define, regulate, and maintain women's societal roles in terms of their vocation as mothers, not as workers.

Yet in spite of the extremity of the pronatalist dogma, and despite the publicity given to women factory workers during the First World War, by the end of the war over 825,000 women were working in munitions factories in England alone (Dewar 14)—a staggering figure, and one described as conservative by other historians who estimate it at well over 900,000, for example (Griffiths 14). At the height of the munitions feat, advertisers capitalized on the growing popularity of munitions work by filtering the image of the munitions worker into campaigns that advertised other facets of war service, importantly romanticizing the image of the typical working-class munitions girl but not removing from the stereotype the damning characteristics that justified her status and place in British society.

Sharon Ouditt notes that "just as the officer class in the army was privileged over the cheery British Tommy, class informed the hierarchy of labour in munitions factories. . . . The propaganda, in order to justify the privileges of middle- and upper-class women, insists on reproducing the stereotyped view of their social inferiors" (84). To this end, in *Our Girls, Their Work for the War* Caine ascribes the hysterical behavior during air raids to munitions workers named "Alice and Annie and Rose" (72), whose delirium can only be regulated by the "iron hand" of an educated lady supervisor. Thus, while glorifying the image of the working-class woman, the propaganda essentially reinforces cultural assumptions about her, and serves the dual purposes of calling working-class women into the factories and satirizing them at the same time, making them "adorable" in the same sense that Roland Barthes contemptualizes the word (18–21), and making them ridiculous.

So popular had the image of the working-class woman become that she soon competed with the successful figure of the mother in advertising campaigns. Just as earlier propagandists had evoked the image of the mother successfully, war service ads began to evoke the image of the working-class woman with the same hoped-for success, carefully yoking once more women, their work in the factories, and maternity. Famed poster-maker James Montgomery Flagg created an agricultural poster for the American war service board: punning on the munitions drive, the poster asks "Will you have a part in victory?" and urges women to make "Every Garden a Munition Plant." Though Flagg's poster illustrates a middle-class woman sowing seeds and dressed in an American flag, his punning sets up a fundamental and linguistic link between women's war efforts in the arsenals and women's war efforts in the home. In other words, whether a woman is a munitions worker or not, the poster decrees that women characteristically churn out munitions in everything they do, from procreation to gardening, thus squeezing women into the role of maternal generators and suggesting that wartime women are frustrated unless they are producing, manufacturing, or generating something—be it men, munitions, or cucumbers.

Flagg's poster, a number of First World War postcards, Caine's and Yates's speculations on the biological or sexual attraction of munitions work, Aston Webb's statuary in the Admiralty Arch—each documents the general confusion, the widespread consternation and prevailing fear over women's success in the factories. By cleverly insisting that women were destined to work in munitions factories to answer "some mysterious call of their sex," by suggesting that the work was sexually gratifying, power-inducing, or enchanting, writers and artists successfully assured a steady stream of volunteers while ensuring continuous production and output at the same time. Even more important, they produced a body of written materials from which pronatalists could draw when it came time to urge women out of the factories and rezone them to an idealized version of domesticity, one that was drawn as comfortable, familiar, protected. Such homes rarely existed for working-class women, who could remember all too well how their insufficient prewar wages exacerbated the strain of running a household. Maintaining a family often meant stretching a small income, as Woollacott points out: "Some working-class wives experienced World War I, at least in part, as a liberation from the grind of eking out an inadequate weekly income" (*On Her* 123). Thus, the messages that glorified domesticity and were so full of sound and fury increasingly worked to anachronize Victorian cultural prescriptions, no longer permitting the sentimentality of hearth and home. Like the pronatalist drive itself, the language and images employed by Caine, Yates, Webb, Flagg, and others objectified and commodified women. It reduced them to breeders—manufacturers and producers of spare parts—and sexual fiends, or brute conquerors. It's a wonder that all of these assumptions weren't unraveled by their own contradictions.

Chapter 7

Demobilization and the Cost of War

I F WE AGREE WITH WINSTON CHURCHILL'S STATEMENT that "the story of the human race is War," then as this part of the story drew to a close, working-class women found their lives transformed in a number of ways. Many working-class women were now without partners, or without fathers or brothers as a result of war casualties that were made up of a majority of working-class soldiers.[1] Others lost mothers, fathers, sisters, brothers or friends to workplace accidents, or to the influenza epidemic that quickly spread across Britain. During the war, women's standard of living had increased, bringing to them and their families the benefits of better health and nutrition, and allowing them to contend with the near-60 percent rise in the food bill, which cost the average working-class family about £2 per week. Their homes most likely were equipped with a modest number of new purchases that helped to improve their living conditions. But as they and their nation were anticipating the end of this terrible war, more than three million working-class women were beginning to sense, as well, that their work in Britain's arsenals and factories was drawing to a close.

Winter argues that the classic aim of historical scholarship is "the replacement of mythology or vague memory by painstakingly-researched and documented historical analysis" (*The Working Class in Modern British History* ix), but one needs to be particularly mindful of the way even these historical analyses can create myth. Not that I have any pretence to more accurate historical information, but I would like to broaden the aspects of representation concerning the aftermath of the

First World War. Many choose to tell this part of the story by focusing on inimical consequences—by pointing, for example, to the numbers of depressed and displaced women workers after the end of the war, but there are ways to tell the same story without focusing on what some have seen as the victimization of the women workers, which has become, of late, part of the *new* mythology of this war, and has contributed to an even newer gendering of tragedy.

Historians such as Joanna Bornat, Deborah Thom, and Meta Zimmeck have written recuperative histories of working women from this period by focusing on the women's triumphs rather than on their disappointments, though each is mindful that such disappointments did in fact exist for many women, especially in the early years of the war. Though women entered the factories at tremendous rates and worked long shifts at skilled, semi-skilled, and unskilled work, they rarely earned as much as their male co-workers and likely saw them earning twice as much as they did. Though working-class women joined labor unions by the thousands during the war, few were able to break through the patriarchal stratifications of the unions, nor were the unions successful in protecting women members from work-site injuries or fatalities. Class stratifications were no less severe at the work site, where working-class women were assigned *de facto* jobs appropriate to their class and were as rarely selected for supervisory roles in the factories as forewomen or overlookers as they were assigned jobs as factory charge hands. At the Woolwich Royal Arsenal, for example, job descriptions were written up according to class and printed out to aid those interviewing and recruiting women for munitions jobs.[2] Because class played an essential role in preordaining the level and severity of working-class women's participation, these experiences contributed to a sense of working-class fatalism at the beginning of the war, when many women applied for the first time for work and found their ability to work for wages at will circumscribed by class restraints and predicated on nineteenth-century hiring practices.

But by changing perspectives a bit, we learn to formulate different questions about the women's working class during this period. In her discussion of women and unions, for example, Thom points out that the frequently speculated upon question, "Why did so few women join unions?" ought to be reformulated to ask "Why did so many of them join, and join against such considerable odds?" (261). Such reformulations are urgently necessary. Just as the privileging of male experiences of the war and the attention to anthologized responses of male writers advances a particularly male gendering of tragedy, the focusing of attention specifically on the dispirited and despondent members of the women's working class after the war promotes a female gendering of tragedy. This sort of traditional treatment of women's labor illustrates Elizabeth Garnsey's point that an "unbalanced analysis produces unbalanced conclusions" (234) and works to evict and erase further from history the triumphs of the women's working class.

The millions of women workers who had so quickly, enthusiastically, and powerfully answered Britain's civilian call to arms were, within a year of the war's end, demobilized from the workplace, reassigned to the old "humdrum," as needlewoman Jane Cox referred to women's prewar lives, were dismissed not merely as wage earners but as manufacturers and builders of their nation. Even though working-class women were recognized and rewarded for participating in their culture's enterprises during the war, their lives quickly were redefined and circumscribed by resurgent notions of women's prewar traditional roles. To understand this period effectively, the figures of these women need to be more fully "coaxed from the shadows" of history, as Meta Zimmeck illustrates in an essay on women clerks in Britain from 1850 to 1914 (170). Once they stand before us, she suggests, issues that previously have dominated historical debate fall by the wayside in the women's presence. It is then that we realize, as Zimmeck so articulately conveys, that these women workers were not the tools of their employers, nor were they the puppets of labor unions or other political groups that sought their membership. In fact, Zimmeck notes, the women liked their jobs, they liked being engaged in work, and they often "leapt at the chance" to seek work that paid the best rates. She adds that women's rise in the work force often is discussed as a trend that hastened the proletarianization of the work force. Disagreeing with such an assumption, Zimmeck writes that once the women workers are coaxed from out of the shadows of cause-and-effect history,

they turn out to have been prepossessing creatures, not simpletons or tools of employers or oppressors of men. They were quite simply human beings with all the hopes, talents, foibles and failings of the species. They leaped at the opportunity to work outside the home. They struggled under conditions which were often difficult, exhausting and demoralizing. They worked hard and gave satisfaction, and indeed the quality of this work is visible to all who rummage through the archives—faultless and beautifully set-out typing done at speeds comparable with today's on machines of almost surreal primitiveness without benefit of tipp-ex. They enjoyed this work as much as they could and were proud of their skills. They searched for the best jobs and the best employers. If necessary, they stood up for their rights with tact, dignity and energy. They certainly did not plot the doom of male clerks. If the transformation of clerical work is viewed through women's eyes, the issue of proletarianization, which has hitherto dominated historical debate, seems somewhat ephemeral. . . . Some male clerks went to the wall because the prop on which they depended for their superiority, the exclusion of a large number of competent persons (women) from eligibility for clerical posts, was removed. Some women benefitted from the opportunities afforded. Was this proletarianization or was it simply the cost of social justice? (170)

Zimmeck's question on the cost of social justice echoes the question raised in 1919 by Dr. Anna Howard Shaw, and if the transformation of First World War industrial labor is viewed through women's eyes, we begin to find an answer not only to Shaw's question, "What was the cost of this war in women?" but "What was the significance of women in this war?"

One of the significant social changes wrought by the First World War was the effect it had on diluting what was an already-crippling sense of class fatalism before the war. Willy Goldman mourned in *East End, My Cradle*, for example, that while working-class fathers knew that they were inured to their fates, their sons had to learn the hard way—through years and decades of alignment with work—that they were inured to their fates as well (60–62). If working-class men were constrained by fatalism, and inured to their fates as manual laborers, then I argue that the First World War taught working-class women that they were not inured to their fates as housewives, no matter how real, no matter how glorious, were "The Pleasures of Housewifery," as Joanna Bourke discusses them in *Working Class Cultures 1890–1960: Gender, Class and Ethnicity* (64–71).

Not only were women freer to work outside the home and to engage in the cultural (and financial) enterprises of war, but they benefited from the change, as well, and often exploited the serendipitous occasion of women's mass labor by moving quickly to new jobs, changing employers, switching jobs within factories, or taking employment at different work sites. For the first time working-class women found a degree of mobility in the workplace, even when leaving certificate policies were in place and strictly enforced.[3] They found themselves as workers a much sought-after commodity, and although they soon would find themselves unable to command such power in a surplus labor market—especially during the demobilization years—their experiences as workers for those four years surrendered a great deal to them. As they reintegrated themselves (or, more accurately, were directed to reintegrate themselves) to the domestic sphere, they took with them all of what they had learned as temporary workers, and this would affect their lives, and their culture, in significant ways.

Social historian Asa Briggs acknowledges in *A Social History of England* that women's roles were extended during the war, though he is quick to add that regardless, women "were not to transform politics" (283). With that sentiment, Briggs implies that women's entry into and departure from the work force ended where it began and offered little personal transformation for the women or for British culture. He writes:

> The role of women had been greatly extended during the war: some had worked as nurses at the front, far more at the bench in munitions factories, and many others in offices and in occupations hitherto closed to them. Yet by 1921 they constituted exactly the 29 per cent of the workforce that they had done ten years before, and despite the vote they now had they were not to transform politics. (283)

But Briggs's assessment is terribly wrong: women did transform politics, though little can be gleaned of this from merely comparing percentage numbers in the work force.[4] First of all, the composition of the 29 percent had shifted during the war: it was not the same work force but a transformed one. More women workers were hired and working at skilled and semi-skilled levels, and were aligned with trade unions. Though many of them entered the workplace to fill in for a father or brother serving at the front and found themselves paired with other women workers hired to divide the tasks—and salary—of one man's job, they quickly proved themselves capable beyond their culture's imagining and worked to challenge the ineffectiveness of Britain's iniquitous dilution scheme, which sanctioned employers to pay two or three women workers the sum of one man's wages. They also helped collapse the myth of apprenticeship and exposed the workplace exploitation of apprentices who remained underpaid for years while being "trained." By learning and performing difficult, usually apprenticed, tasks within a few short weeks of training, women proved themselves to be savvy and industrious understudies. The best of these workers—especially if they were single women or widows—kept their jobs after the war at great expense. The criticism and reprimands they received for remaining in the work force after the war were nearly as insufferable as the antagonism the women suffered when they entered the work force at the beginning of the war, bearing out Karl Marx's polemical statement that "history repeats itself; the first time as tragedy, the second as farce."

When the war ended, many women remained on the job and fought to put into place policies that jealously guarded their jobs from other interlopers seeking work, especially other women. Joanna Bourke identifies a number of postwar initiatives that women workers fought for, policies such as the 1921 resolution scripted by women civil service workers that asked for the banning of married women from their job (104–105). As Bourke notes, this particular resolution remained in place until 1946. While women's upholding of the presumptuous marriage ban is clearly not an example of women's solidarity, it is an example of women fighting for themselves, of women protecting their own personal right to work, and as such represents a significant departure from their prewar attitudes and the ways in which women viewed their own right to work. Class and gender solidarity would come soon enough for these women, who now were caught in the classic workplace struggle in which workers rage against each other rather than against management.

Within a few years, the politicism so many women had gained from their association with work and with labor and trade unions during the war would propel them in the 1920s and 1930s to crusade for workers' rights, especially during the serendipitous but calamitous resurgence of Anglo-Marxism in the late 1920s and early 1930s.[5] Moreover, women would exhibit their politicism in other ways, by petitioning for a national fluency about birth control and by seeking institutional practices and policies that would back up such programs.[6] After participating so obediently in Britain's pronatalist campaign—during which more women lost their lives in childbirth than they had in previous recent generations—women would insist that the demands upon them stop. It is absurd to argue, as Briggs does, that women did nothing during and after the war to transform the politics of Britain—not only absurd but dead wrong. It is a sentiment that adds insult to injury by wiping away in one sweeping gesture any and all traces of the women's politicism from the records of the past, and it exacerbates an already-limited version of working-class women's lives during and after the First World War.

Apart from these differences in the 29 percent of the work force made up by women in 1911 and the 29 percent made up by women in 1921, the women workers' ideologies differed from those they upheld and systematically sustained at the beginning of the First World War. Labor laws put into effect during and immediately after the war affected the ways workers performed their jobs; salaries changed; rates of pay and wage figuration changed. Because so much of Briggs's analysis of postwar Britain centers on the "New Poor," what he calls the economically displaced middle class, his attention focuses on the middle class's attempts to work within the constraints of new labor laws and employment policies. As I have argued, this sort of academic attention to the middle class is always at the expense of the working class, who not only benefited from the postwar reorganization of labor but who played a role in transforming those policies and labor regulations. The women's work force was a transformed one *because* of their efforts, not in spite of them; it was an ideologically educated work force and one less prone to be bound by class fatalism than it had been before the war. Though it was a time in history when "women were at once so close and yet so far from wielding real power" at the work site (Gordon et al. 55), it was a felicitous moment nonetheless and one that would reap social consequences in the decades to follow. It is inaccurate to represent these years and these experiences as altogether degenerative to working-class solidarity, as devolutionary to women's status, or as aiding and abetting the proletarianization of skilled labor. None of these changes is obvious when historians quote only percentage figures. Though the numbers may look the same—29 percent in 1911, 29 percent in 1921—it was an ideologically different women's working class. This remains essential to our understanding of the women's working class in the demobilization years.

Social gains made by women during the war quickly were stabilized as the nation tried to reinvent itself after the First World War; but it is important to realize these gains were neither suspended nor rescinded in the aftermath of war. Though women's wage earning possibilities were curbed by postwar policies that sought to prioritize employment opportunities for returning soldiers, many working-class women did remain employed in British industries after the war. Many of those who didn't stay on the job fell into despair—"I cried me eyes out when I left, that was the sort of life I led," Amy Elizabeth May commented in her oral history (Imperial War Museum Sound Archive, Item SR 684, Reel 4); but those who did remain in the factories put into place policies that protected them during the postwar reshuffling of British society, regardless of the pressure from outside sources to give up their jobs to returning men.

Working-class lives, like the lives of every Briton, were affected in significant and consequential ways by postwar reshuffling, but it was not all doom and gloom; in fact, some women were happy to be off the work, glad to return to their roles as housewives and mothers, a role endowed with much glory and self-satisfaction, as Joanna Bourke has suggested (62–70). Others were pleased to be done with the long hours, eager to be off TNT work, or looking forward to the cessation of their years-long coughs, their jaundiced appearances, their come-and-go incontinence, their pale eyes and worn countenances. Likely they looked forward, as well, to the day when they could exhibit—without cultural reprimand—the exuberance they had found during the war years, when they could act happy without being reminded that this was an unhappy time, when they could be self-satisfied without facing charges of being smug, when they could treat themselves or their families to niceties thought unimaginable or undeserved before the war without risking rebuke. They looked forward to life returning to "normal" with a prescience learned during the war that their lives, like their culture, would never be the same; and they fully recognized that they had been transformed in the process, and that their personal transformations would lead to a metamorphosing of their nation and of their place in it.

Having been put to the test during the war, working-class women anticipated being put to the test after it, as well. They wrote in their service newspapers about their willingness to construct a new Empire without reproducing what one writer called the "faults of the past," as this excerpt from "My Country" attests:

> The task of re-constructing the social fabric of the Empire as it existed before the war would have been a gigantic one, but to re-build so that the faults of the past may not be reproduced, is a task appalling in its magnitude. It cannot be accomplished in a few weeks or a few months, it cannot be accomplished by legislation alone, nor can it be accomplished by the few; it can only be accomplished by the patient and earnest efforts of the many to solve the problems which must arise in a spirit of broadminded justice and tolerance. (*Shell Magazine* 43)

Similarly, an editorial in the *Dornock Souvenir Magazine* confirms that "Despite occasional appearances to the contrary, we are all prepared to admit that we have had a very happy time here. For most of us our work at Dornock has been a complete new education likely to prove of enormous value in years to come" (4).

Clearly the women recognized the value of their experiences as workers from 1914 to 1918–19 and looked forward to putting their new knowledge to work as they helped to construct a new postwar nation. If women's contributions were neither so quick nor so dramatic as some historians would have them be, "Even the War," Rebecca West reminded D. H. Lawrence, "called more for obedience in its soldiers than for aggression and independence" (*The Gender of Modernism* 586). So, too, did industry, which had its own set of culturally constructed behavioral mandates. It demanded that its women workers produce at mind-boggling speeds, in freezing room temperatures, under poor lighting, and amid dangerous and life-threatening workplace conditions all that was needed to fuel, and ultimately to end, the war. That there was little time to do anything else is no surprise—and it certainly should not invite, or be a cause for, censure.

In spite of the behavioral acquiescence exacted from working-class women, they successfully participated in changing "the faults of the past" without reproducing them and without internalizing the myth of their victimization. As Gertrude Stein would write 15 years after the war in her *Autobiography of Alice B. Toklas,* "they say that an awful lot of people were killed in the war but it seems to me that an extraordinary large number of grown men and women have suddenly been born" (190).

Conclusion

"How can we linger over books we feel the author was not compelled to write?"

—*George Bataille, Preface,* Le Bleu de Ciel

THE AMERICAN POET MURIEL RUKEYSER SAID THAT SHE wrote her 1942 biography of physicist Willard Gibbs because it was a book she needed to read (xiv). More than two decades later, she would write in her poem "The Speed of Darkness" that "The universe is made of stories/ not of atoms" (231), thereby fusing her Gibbs project with her office as poet. *Working-Class Culture, Women, and Britain, 1914–1921* is a book I needed to read; it is a book I've been looking for in library stacks and on bookstore shelves since the late 1980s when I became interested in this period, and one that grew out of that same "moment of rage" that George Bataille suggests every real book grows from. I do not mean to suggest that there is not already a body of scholarship on women and the First World War. In fact, since the 1970s, scholars have written histories from below that place women at the center of the story of the First World War, and I fully acknowledge my debt to these studies. But many of these histories from below don't go deep enough: issues of class must enter squarely into the picture and become an extension of the focus on gender. Academic attention to working-class women during the war has been slow in coming. To reanimate the stories of working-class women in Britain during the war, I have tried to coax them from the shadows of history, knowing full well that to ask life of them is as dangerous an enterprise as asking life of words, since in both instances the writer runs the risk of being crushed by them (Auster 21).

But the women workers on whom I have concentrated would not allow themselves to be crushed. They became their own publicists when necessary and championed their own heroism and exploits in their service publications, not only expecting that their experiences would merit equal notice in the popular press but becoming the agents of their own publicity when they sensed their culture's sad indifference to anything but the sensational. The following example from *Shell Chippings,* a service newspaper written and compiled by the "Lady Operators, Bootle," illustrates the women's call for equal attention:

> We've had songs about the Trenches
> And songs about the Fleet
> But what about the saucy girls
> Who come tripping down the street
> Every morn, to catch the tram car
> In the hail, rain, snow, or sleet? (Vol 1 No. 1: 7)

Yes, what about them? They worked for years in essential industries performing difficult and physically demanding jobs. Coming off their long night shifts, many women stepped right onto meat queues or other ration lines, according to worker Elsie McIntyre, who notes that often one worker would pass another on her way home only to hear, "Have you heard? They've got a little bit of margarine at Gallows or Maypole!" and with that, she'd surrender her off time to stand in queue (Transcript 13). Even in such hard times, the women were able to keep their sense of humor about the daily difficulties, and joked amid the troubles about familiar ration lines, for example, or voiced their frustration over the rationing system lightheartedly, as in the poem "Cards," published in a service newspaper and pseudonymously signed "Carrie Canteen":

> We've cards for meat and butter
>   And sugar for our tea
> They say a bread card's coming
>   Amen, so let it be.
> But mournfully I ponder
>   When I shuffle up the pack
> Another card or two, and then—
>   A Cardiac attack! (*Cardonald News* Vol. 2, No. 1)

Obviously spirited, the women also were brave, and many of them lost or risked their lives working for the war effort. They performed their work under primitive conditions, some using old and dangerous machines housed in even older and more dangerous factories. The TNT dust on the factory floors nearly killed them because even though they were issued masks or respirators at work, or were supplied with barrier creams to protect their skin, many of them liked to sing on the job, and the dust got in through their mouths and burned the backs of their throats. Their physical appearances were altered by their work as well; hundreds of workers turned yellow as a result from working with TNT, or their teeth were rotted by TNT dust, or their hair became bleached at the front from bending over hot acid tanks. Many of the workers were overcome by gaseous fumes in the factories, and daily had to manage heavy production schedules or fill quotas under such conditions. For all this, their production on the job was phenomenal, and without their labor, Britain would not have been able to fuel and win its "war to end war."

More than 300 women were diagnosed with toxic jaundice from their factory work, and over 100 of them died as a result of it. Other illnesses were grievously misdiagnosed by doctors. Prophylactic measures invented to "protect" women workers in factories were innocuous, and measures to contain the wanton TNT dust were ineffective. Hundreds more women workers were killed or wounded in war service from accidents on the job, accidents that were described axiomatically as "inevitable." Equally as compelling are the stories of women workers who were punished for violating health and safety regulations, such as those who were found with matches, pins, or hairpins during frequent on-the-job searches. Factory supervisors were rightfully strict in enforcing regulations against workers found with these items, since these might spark a fire in the factory, but the mandated 28-day prison sentence without the option of a fine seems, even now, rather severe and incriminating. The ending of Anna Smith's 1919 poem resounds with a pronouncement of relief at what she no longer will have to endure as her work in the factory draws to a close. She writes:

No more we'll be searched by the Bobby.
No more kharki trousers we'll wear,
No more will we breathe in the Acid,
That rose in great fumes in the air—
"No more!" "No more!" (*Dornock Souvenir Magazine* 65)

Smith's poem anticipates both an ending and a new beginning, and like many of her co-workers, she was prepared to leave her factory at war's end and looked forward to returning home after spending four uninterrupted years at work.

Others, however, wanted to remain on the job, and were angered by reports of their likely dismissal which seemed, to them, rotten with cultural ingratitude. Caroline Rennles describes the day she and thousands of other women workers marched to the Houses of Parliament to demand the right to keep their jobs:

Thousands of us—it must've been two or three thousand—walked over the bridge, protesting that we'd been thrown out. We went right up to the door of the Houses of Parliament and before you could say 'Jack Robinson' there were hundreds of policemen on horseback dispersing us. And I saw one Irish girl who was with us, she pulled the reins down on a horse. We ran for our life, we ran down the Embankment, everywhere, from these policemen. But that was the beginning of our dole: Lloyd George gave us that. We was all thrown out, as much as to say, 'Well, that's it—it's finished.' (Imperial War Museum Sound Archive, Item SR 566, Reel 4)

With women's ability to work at will curbed by hiring policies that sought to ease returning soldiers back into the work force, working-class women found themselves with fewer choices than they had been used to having of late and fewer options than they had grown fond of delighting in. Equally important, they had invested themselves greatly in the war and the war enterprise, and they were proud of their work. They held tightly to the memories of their years at various work sites, in canteens and lodging facilities, though these memories would become more romanticized as the women grew nostalgic and protective about their experiences. Woollacott explains the intensity of the women's attachment to the factories by suggesting that "For the women who made the munitions of war, it was their war, a war in which they had been caught up and were centrally involved" (*On Her* 14). In many ways, it *had* been their war. It was a war that was fought to protect them, they often were told, and because it was billed as the "war to end war," and as the "war for peace," it was a war that was waged to shield them and their children from ever having to experience something like it again. Their complicity in this national project would malign them, though, and would raise questions about women and militancy that remain the subjects of conjecture today.

John Stevenson suggests in *British Society 1914–1945* that

> The danger of social history . . . has been the tendency to drift into descriptive history, of how people lived and spent their days with little or no attempt to analyze why their lives, their beliefs, their activities were what they were. (10)

Even though such descriptive methodologies are ultimately useful and interesting, we can speculate on why working-class women's lives "were what they were" during the First World War. Robert Roberts argues in *The Classic Slum* that the "war . . . undoubtedly snapped strings that had bound [working-class women] in so many ways to the Victorian age" (162). It also introduced financial and personal autonomy into many women's lives. Apart from these gains, women's limited suffrage after the war, as well as the passage of the 1919 Sex Disqualification Removal Act, gave to many women the right to vote, the right to hold most public offices, and the right to enter professions from which they had been previously banned. But these privileges did not extend to most working-class women, especially the majority of those workers who, under thirty and not university-educated, could not benefit from the 1918 suffrage act. Though women of the working class had earned certain freedoms in the culture, these were deliriously hard-won. During the war, the culture frowned upon their mass entry into the work force, scowled at their wages and spending, sat by indifferently as women were hurt, wounded, or killed by their work, acquiesced to DORA regulations invented to enforce behavioral mandates for women, and characterized the women's work at the factories in sexual terms, burlesquing them as sexual conquerors, temptresses, or perverted Juno figures.

The women's well-earned shopping sprees were deemed socially irresponsible and were looked upon as radical and dangerous indulgences, even though shopkeepers in working-class districts reported a rise in the purchase of necessities—in children's better shoe and boot sales, for example, and in soap sales. These figures run counter to the notion of the frivolous and self-indulgent working-class shopper. The women, in fact, were thrifty, and saved part of their wages in on-site savings schemes, or used them charitably, to send parcels to soldiers, to contribute to weekly Bench to the Trench Funds, or to support war charities. When they weren't doing this, they were working eight-, nine-, or ten-hour shifts, or were on their way home to their "second" jobs as householders, where they tried to turn slim rations or uninviting war substitutes into presentable and edible masterpieces. These experiences conspired to produce the *why* that Stevenson appeals for; these are some of the reasons why "their lives . . . were what they were."

Moreover, working-class women had gained a sense of entitlement, a class assertiveness as a result of their work and solidarity, and no longer were constrained by the class fatalism that burdened their fathers. Their triumphs as temporary workers brought them temporary status, and if they weren't so successful in homogenizing class differences—a difficult enough proposition for any worker—they were more successful in surprising their culture, in astonishing them with their output, their athleticism on the job, their endurance, and their quickly learned and perfected work skills. For the duration, these millions of women did their part on the benches of well over a hundred factories, arsenals, and workshops, and as eagerly as they claimed their part, they made sure to exact their claim by documenting their lives, their work, their attitudes, and their unyielding strength as a class of workers.

If it was the work itself that branded them as sexual temptresses, as contemporaries argued, or the work itself that seemed to devastate and overturn Britain's social order and hasten working-class women's devolution into hell, as one writer predicted in the *Times*, then it would be that same work that would redeem them, they knew. As one worker argued in her factory's souvenir magazine, the solidarity of the women would come to frustrate even Lucifer, and if working-class women were on a course straight to hell, they'd better take a copy of *Dornock Souvenir Magazine* with them, she advised—not for protection, but as proof of the women's collective salvation. She ends her poem with an imperious stanza that describes "Auld Nick's" likely disappointment:

> But aiblins, if to Hell we go,
> We'll tak' a copy doon below;
> I'll bet Auld Nick cries, "O Hell O!—
> Damn Dornock!" (37)

Armed with their service magazines, their gold-plated service badges, their civilian medals of bravery, and other emblems that validated the severity of their war contributions, these women were fully convinced as they left their jobs in 1918 and 1919 that they had made history. And they had.

Notes

Introduction

1. Apart from the nearly three million women who worked in industry, another two million women worked in other facets of war service as nurses with the FANY (First Aid Nursing Yeomanry), as volunteer ambulance drivers, as nurses with the VAD (Volunteer Aid Detachment), in army service with the QMAAC (Queen Mary's Army Auxiliary Corps), in naval service with the WRNS (Woman's Royal Naval Service), or in air force service with the WRAF (Women's Royal Air Force). These women came from a higher social class than those who worked in industry. Thousands of women also worked in organizations such as the Women's Emergency Corps, the Women's Volunteer Reserve, the Central Committee on Women's Employment, the Women's Police Volunteers, the Women's Land Army, the Women's National Land Service, the Women's Forage Corps, the Women's Hospital Corps or the Women's Legion, or they worked as tram conductors, driver-mechanics, parts cleaners and polishers, cooks, clerks, waitresses, or canteen operators.

2. See Jim Sharpe's review essay "History From Below" in *New Perspectives on Historical Writing*, ed. Peter Burke (University Park: Pennsylvania State Press, 1991), pp. 24–41.

3. Jane Marcus describes volunteer ambulance driver Helen Zinna Smith and her companions in her Afterword to Smith's novel *Not So Quiet . . .* :

> They, like V.A.D. (Volunteer Aid Detachment) nurses, have actually paid for the privilege of serving at the Front, their patriotic upper-class families proud to sacrifice daughters as well as sons for the war effort, providing their passage money and their uniforms, sending packages of cocoa and carbolic body belts to keep off the lice. ("Corpus/Corps/Corpse" 243)

4. Allyson Booth, *Postcards From the Trenches: Negotiating the Space Between Modernism and the First World War* (New York: Oxford University Press, 1996); Gail Braybon, *Women Workers in the First World War, The British*

Experience (Totowa, NJ: Barnes and Noble, 1981); Gail Braybon and
Penny Summerfield, *Out of the Cage: Women's Experiences in Two World
Wars* (London: Pandora Press, 1987); Helen Cooper, Adrienne Munich,
and Susan Squier, ed., *Arms and the Woman: War, Gender and Literary
Representation* (Chapel Hill: University of North Carolina Press, 1989);
Claire Culleton, "Gender-Charged Munitions: The Language of World
War I Munitions Reports," *Women's Studies International Forum* 11.2
(1988): 109–16; Claire Culleton, "Irish Working-Class Women and World
War I" in *Representing Ireland: Gender, Class, Nationality,* ed. Susan Shaw
Sailer (Gainesville: University of Florida Press, 1997): 156–80; Claire Cul-
leton, "Working Class Women's Service Newspapers and the First World
War," *Imperial War Museum Review* 10 (1995): 4–12; Jean Gallagher, *The
World Wars Through the Female Gaze,* Carbondale: Southern Illinois Uni-
versity Press, 1998; Dorothy Goldman, Jane Gledhill, and Judith Hattaway,
Women Writers and the Great War (New York: Twayne, 1995); Margaret
Higonnet, Jane Jenson, Sonya Michel, and Margaret Weitz, ed., *Behind the
Lines: Gender and the Two World Wars* (New Haven: Yale University Press,
1987); Angela Ingram, "Un/Reproductions: Estates of Banishment in Eng-
lish Fiction after the Great War" in *Women's Writing in Exile,* ed. Mary
Lynn Broe and Angela Ingram (Chapel Hill: University of North Carolina
Press, 1989), 325–48; Angela Ingram and Daphne Patai, ed., *Rediscovering
Forgotten Radicals: British Women Writers 1889–1939* (Chapel Hill: University of North Carolina Press, 1993); Nosheen Khan, *Women's Poetry of
the First World War* (Lexington: University Press of Kentucky, 1988); Lyn
Macdonald's four books of eyewitness accounts and survivor testimonies
(*1914, Somme, The Roses of No Man's Land,* and *They Called it Passchen-
daele*); Jane Marcus, "Corpus/Corps/Corpse: Writing the Body In/At War"
in *Arms and the Woman,* Cooper et al., ed., pp. 124–67; Jane Marcus, "The
Asylums of Antaeus: Women, War, and Madness: Is There a Feminist
Fetishism?" in *The Difference Within: Feminism and Critical Theory,* ed.
Elizabeth Meese and Alice Parker (Amsterdam: John Benjamins, 1989),
pp. 49–83; Jane Marcus, "The Nurse's Text: Acting Out an Anaesthetic Aes-
thetic" in *We That Were Young* by Irene Rathbone (New York: Feminist
Press, 1989), pp. 467–98; Sharon Ouditt, *Fighting Forces, Writing Women:
Identity and Ideology in the First World War* (London: Routledge, 1994);
Pam Schweitzer, ed., *What Did You Do in the War, Mum? Women Recall
Their Wartime Work* (London: Age Exchange Theatre Trust, 1993); Trudi
Tate, ed. *Men, Women, and the Great War: an Anthology of Stories* (Man-
chester: Manchester University Press 1995); Trudi Tate, *Modernism, His-
tory and the First World War* (Manchester: Manchester University Press,
1998); Claire Tylee, *The Great War and Women's Consciousness: Images of
Militarism and Womanhood in Women's Writings, 1914–64* (Iowa City:
University of Iowa Press, 1990), and Angela Woollacott, *On Her Their
Lives Depend: Munitions Workers in the Great War* (Berkeley: University of
California Press, 1994).

5. Gagnier discusses these differences in chapters 1 and 4 of her book *Subjectivities*. She suggests:

> Although some working people wrote to understand themselves, with the characteristic splitting of the subjective self from the objective world that gave rise to the intense introspectivity of literary artists, most wrote unselfconsciously, without the introspective or aesthetic ends that characterized the literary artists of Woolf's generation. They wrote to record lost experiences for future generations, to raise money, to warn others, to teach others, or to relieve or amuse themselves. One pragmatic William Tayler, footman to a wealthy London widow in 1837, wrote his autobiographical journal "to improve my handwriting" (i.e., as an exercise in practical self-help for social mobility).
>
> Such pragmatic uses of literacy have little to do with the literary aesthetic as it is represented in literature departments or with the autobiographical canon in particular, which has centered on such extraordinary spiritual lives as Augustine's or Rousseau's *Confessions* (for comparatists) and Carlyle's *Sartor Resartus* or Newman's *Apologia Pro Vita Sua* (for Victorianists). Criteria we may deduce from such canons include a meditative and self-reflexive sensibility; faith in writing as a tool of self-exploration; an attempt to make sense of life as a narrative progressing in time, with a narrative typically structured upon parent-child relationships and familial development; and a belief in personal creativity, autonomy and freedom for the future. This is autobiography as the term is usually employed by literary critics, and . . . it is also compatible, if not identical, with bourgeois subjectivity, the dominant ideology of the nineteenth and at least the first half of the twentieth century. (39)

Importantly, to avoid wrestling with messy distinctions between literary autobiographies and other "non," "sub," or "extra" forms of literary self-representation, Gagnier adds that she considers "all autobiography as rhetorical projects embedded in concrete material situations" (40).

Linda Anderson discusses Vera Brittain's *Testament of Youth* as an example of middle-class autobiography that blurs the distinction between individual and public history in her book *Women and Autobiography in the Twentieth Century: Remembered Futures* (76–100), and reminds us that Virginia Woolf noted in her diary that Brittain's book was "A very good book of its sort. The sort, the hard anguished sort, that the young write; that I could never write. Nor has anyone written that kind of book before. Why now? What urgency is there on them to stand bare in public? She feels that these facts must be made known, in order to help—what? herself partly I suppose. And she has the social conscience" (Anderson 76; Woolf, *Diary* IV, 177).

6. Owen 55–56, Sassoon 100, Wilson 677.

7. It is important to point out at this juncture that one must be mindful of not making what Arthur Marwick calls "the quick jump" when discussing the working class; he writes: "I cannot myself accept the quick jump so often made by which occupation suddenly becomes equated with class" ("Images of Class," 216). While women were taking jobs at a rate of 21,700 a month in 1915 (Woollacott 17), women who entered the work force by taking working-class jobs were not all working class women; and their experiences on the bench must be treated differently from those who before 1914 were members of Britain's working class. Equally important, their history need not eclipse that of their working-class co-workers.

8. Here the contrast in representations is worth discussing, since class and its attendant stereotypes figure into these two illustrations of British and Irish women. Racial attitudes, too, bear out in the illustrations. The British mother in the poster appears sophisticated. Her emotions are under control. She has two lovely and well-behaved children at her side whom she comforts as they gaze out of a window in their home and watch a regiment of orderly, armed British soldiers marching off to war. The mother's and daughter's hair is pulled back neatly into a bun. The daughter's shoulders are covered, draped in a shawl.

In dramatic contrast, the poster aimed at recruiting Irish soldiers seems a parody of the British poster. It, too, pictures a parental figure who holds the hands of two children, but in this case it is a father, presumably the Irish counterpart to the British father who in the other poster has gone off to fight. The threesome gaze across the sea at Belgium, and with their backs to the poster's viewer, we cannot tell whether they are moved or unmoved by the scene. The poster's foreground pictures the stereotype of an Irish peasant woman. Her hair flies wildly in the wind. Not a shawl but a tartan scarf barely covers her shoulders. Here another gender reversal takes place: in contrast to the armed soldiers in the British poster, it is she who holds a rifle while her emasculating rhetoric—"For the Glory of Ireland, Will you go or must I?"—attempts to shame her male companion into joining up. Her rhetoric also trivializes (and thereby profanes) the prayerful supplication "For the glory of God."

Importantly, as he is drawn, the Irish male figure seems a derision of the British soldiers pictured in the "Women of Britain say—GO!" poster. He, too, wears a hat, a coat, trousers, and boots, but his "uniform" is shabby and worn. His hands are cupped firmly and ineffectually into the pockets of his jacket, and instead of a gun, he has tucked under his arm a blackthorn walking stick, a shillelagh. Except for the fact that there are no Irish "apes" in this poster—a detail often featured in derisive British representations of the Irish—this recruitment poster couldn't be more offensive.

Chapter 1

1. Imperial War Museum (IWM) Sound Archive, Item SR 705, Reel 4. In my bibliography, the number that follows each oral history's item number

refers to the number of reels that make up the taped interviews. "Item SR 705/06" means that six tapes make up the interview.

2. The IWM Sound Archive collection is of vast significance to my project. Margaret Brooks, in her essay on the collection, explains its genesis:

> In 1974 the Museum's Department of Sound Records began to record the reminiscences of civilians who undertook war work during the First World War. The project embraced a variety of areas of employment. . . . but the frame of reference for this article is women's industrial work, specifically, munitions and ordnance. The Museum holds interviews with about a hundred women in this type of employment. . . .
> The contributors were located through letters to the press in areas which had held wartime factories—such as Leeds, Coventry, Southampton, East London—and through organisations involved in recording oral history. . . . The aim was to record individual experiences rather than obtain an historic overview. The resulting tapes are comparable as sources to personal letters; most of the contributors had not kept wartime letters nor published written reminiscences. (4)

3. Jane Lewis explains in *Women in England 1870–1950* that within male-dominated society, the boundaries of change primarily are set by men, and that historically, women's lives have been defined by men. She explains:

> male doctors defined female sexuality, male scientists defined women's intellectual ability, male legislators their legal capacity, male employers and trade unionists their position at work and husbands their degree of personal, emotional and financial security. (xi)

4. The Report of the Working Classes Cost of Living Committee showed that "larger proportions of the household budget were being spent on food and clothes in 1918 than in 1914" (Woollacott 121). Moreover, members of the working class were purchasing more high-quality goods than they had before the war: one boot firm reported in 1918 that it couldn't "keep up with the demand for high-quality boots in poor neighborhoods, where before the war, only the cheapest boots were sold" (Woollacott 121–22). Trevor Wilson writes that during the war "there was an abnormal demand for children's shoes . . . children were better fed and better clothed than ever before" (152) and notes an unprecedented rise in soap sales at the time, too (724).

5. See Paul Johnson's essay "Credit and Thrift and the British Working Class, 1870–1939," in *The Working Class in Modern British History*, ed. Jay Winter (Cambridge: Cambridge University Press, 1983: 147–70).

6. Even though the National Health Insurance (NHI) Act of 1911 guaranteed each insured worker's access to general practitioners, the insurance rarely

extended to the worker's dependents who were usually women and children, Lewis notes in *Women in England 1870–1950* (24). Women householders at the time of the NHI Act often were reluctant to spend the money necessary to maintain their own health, since they were responsible for looking after the family budget while their husbands worked. Once women began earning their own money, though, it seems that they felt more justified in contracting a medical diagnosis.

7. Andrew Davies, *Leisure, Gender and Poverty. Working-Class Culture in Salford and Manchester, 1900–1939* (Buckingham: Open University Press, 1992).

8. "Workers' Demand for Rations," *Times*, December 17, 1917.

9. J. M. Winter, *The Great War and the British People*, 216.

10. Winter, *The Great War and the British People*. See his section titled "The Paradox of the Great War," chapters 4–7, in which Winter identifies a central paradox of the war, namely that the First World War, "a conflict of unprecedented human costs[,] was also the occasion of an improvement in conditions which made [Britain] a healthier place in which to live" (215).

11. Butt continued, saying,

> the French have found that [women's] employment in munition factories has been highly successful and that women possess not only the aptitude, but also the stamina necessary for the work. That our own women are equally capable I see no reason to doubt. . . .
> In addition to the demand for women's labor in various war industries, it should not be forgotten that their services are also needed as shop assistants, clerks and so forth. Various peace industries must be kept going, for it is these which must pay for the war in the long run. (3)

12. Such hierarchies were firmly established in the factories. At Woolwich Arsenal, for example, canteen work was considered ideal for former charwomen, while assistant forewomen or principal overlookers should be drawn from the ranks of former teachers or university women (IWM Department of Printed Books, Women's Work Microfilm Collection Item #MUN 29).

13. See Woollacott, *On Her Their Lives Depend*, pp. 37–58.

14. Clarke, IWM Sound Archive, Item SR 774/04. Other workers complained about high rents, as well. Beatrice Lee, for example, who worked during the war making bags for shells at Scarborough Bag Factory and also as a crane driver at Yorkshire Copper Works, recalls that she paid £3 a week for lodging; her rent was so high that she had to take money out of the bank to pay it (IWM Sound Archive, Item SR 724/06, Reel 3).

15. Britain's propaganda and recruiting campaigns were rarely sources of amusement in Ireland and were thought, in fact, to be particularly offensive. In such campaigns, for example, Irish recruits were promised a sizeable weekly separation allowance of 12s. 6d., payable to mothers, wives, sisters, or anyone else dependent upon the soldier's wages. In addition to the separa-

tion allowance, wives and children of recruited Irish soldiers were guaranteed free entrance to the Dublin Zoo, a boon found to be ludicrous and insulting by vigilant antirecruiting parties throughout Ireland (O'Brien 254).

16. Remington was in Ireland when the Armistice came but says that she and her husband could not safely celebrate because they feared the repercussions. Here she describes constant anxieties brought on by Sinn Féin:

> Everything had to be very quiet because you see the Sinn Féin had got such a hate on the British by that time. It was the British Army just like it is now, the British officers; and if ever we were asked out to dinner in the evening by Irish families—and we were frequently—these wretched people they would do anything to harm you, and they used to string ropes across the road in the dark, and we went out in jaunting cars, to try and trip up the horses and upset you out of the jaunting car. (IWM Sound Archive, Item SR 511, Reel 7)

Chapter 2

1. Trevor Wilson discusses the "large measure of public approval and support" of "the unwritten law" in *The Myriad Faces of War*, p. 723.

2. IWM Department of Printed Books, Women's Work Collection Item LR 118/3 describes the Bench to the Trench Fund as follows: "each worker would subscribe a nominal weekly fee to enable the Fund to send out Parcels of food clothing etc. to all workmates who had joined H. M. Forces and proceeded overseas."

3. At the Woolwich factory, for example, positions were reserved for members of certain social classes: assistant forewoman and principal overlooker positions, for example, often went to university women; overlooker positions were given to educated women; the position of charge hand went to capable ordinary factory workers, and so forth. One memorandum notes that former charwomen might best be placed in the factory canteen (IWM Department of Printed Books, Women's Work Collection, Item MUN 29).

4. Some of the immediate effects of England's declaration of war on August 4, 1914 was panic food-buying. As Christopher Martin explains, business was phenomenal at the beginning of the war:

> Grocers reported eight days' business in one day, some shops selling out completely. People carried off car loads of food, or brought dustbins and tubs to load with groceries. Angry poor women snatched parcels from the rich; shop delivery vans were held up and robbed. Gradually there was an official appeal to housewives: "Act as you always act." (*English Life in the First World War* 9)

5. Arthur Marwick discusses the length of women's skirts in his 1965 *The Deluge: British Society and the First World War*, noting that "Most striking of all

was the change in women's dress; for, however far politicians were to put the clocks back in other steeples in the years after the war, no one ever put the lost inches back on the hems of women's skirts" (111).

6. Woollacott writes: "Of the women who worked in munitions factories in World War I, many (certainly hundreds, perhaps upward of a thousand) were killed and others were maimed, poisoned, or injured in the processes of making explosives, filling shells, and working with fast, heavy machinery" (9).

Chapter 3

1. Two women medical officers whose findings were published in *The Lancet* on August 12, 1916 reported on the effects of TNT on women workers in the munitions factories. They described the following symptoms as being directly caused by work in munitions:

> Throat and/or chest tight, swollen and burning; coughing, sometimes a thick yellow phlegm with a bitter taste; pain round the waist and in abdomen; nausea, vomiting, constipation at first, then diarrhoea; rashes and eruptions on the skin. These could in turn lead to toxic symptoms: digestive, as in the irritative stage in jaundice; circulatory, giddiness, hot and cold flushes, swelling etc.; cerebral, drowsiness, loss of memory, disorders of sight; delirium, coma and convulsions.

2. Braybon notes that "a limited number of women were awarded state compensation for ill health caused by TNT, but it was difficult to prove [to the satisfaction of authorities] that TNT was responsible" (152 n. 103).

3. "Woman's Year. Extension of Her Work in 1915." *Times*, Jan. 3, 1916.

4. Isabella Clarke also discusses an incident at White and Poppe's just before the Armistice when another friend lost her hand in an accident (Reel 4).

5. Gail Braybon discusses one of the many ironies that becomes apparent researching working class women's lives during this period. In her chapter on pronatalism she writes that while "[t]he government was not prepared to step in to protect women working with TNT or aircraft dope, or make sure that they received financial reward for the risk they ran" (141), it was prepared to insist that women's health was essential to the longevity of the Empire, and that the working-class woman should "relish the role of 'mother of the race'" (149).

Chapter 4

1. The editor of *The Bombshell* explains in the premiere issue that the impulse to publish a factory newspaper stemmed from the workers' desire to document their war service and to promote unity among the various classes in the factory:

Owing to the present shortage of paper it is undoubtedly a some-what inopportune time for starting a new Magazine; but the 'pros' and the 'cons' of the matter have been very carefully weighed, and it is felt that the advantages of having a home-produced Magazine turn the scale against the disadvantages. And so the idea, long considered, has at length matured and the result . . . you now hold in your hands.

It need hardly be said that this Magazine is not intended for any particular section of the N. P. F. [National Projectile Factory] . . . One of its foremost aims is to promote a feeling of unity among all the different classes of Staff and Employees; to ask them

> "To set the Cause above renown
> And love the game beyond the prize,"

and to make everyone realise that Staff, Foremen, Operators, Gaugers, Toolsetters, Checkers—are all working for one common purpose and should be animated by one common desire. . . .

Of one thing I am sure—that in retrospect these days which have brought so many of the women of England among sights and scenes once never dreamed of—into an atmosphere of grub screws, and C Spanners and Cutting Compound and . . . trousers—will take upon themselves in after years a glamour and romance all their own. And it is hoped that "The Bombshell" will be a more tangible reminder of them than that unreliable gentleman Mr Memory.—C. K. W. (16)

2. For histories of trench and other kinds of newspapers produced by men at the front, see Malcolm Brown's "O What a Jolly Old War: Service Newspapers" in *The Imperial War Museum Book of the First World War* (London: Sidgwick and Jackson), 1991, pp. 263–271; Martin Taylor's "*The Open Exhaust* and some other trench journals of The First World War," in *The Imperial War Museum Review* 5 (1990):18–27; and J. M. Winter's chapter "Popular Literature and Trench Journalism" in *The Great War and the British People*, 285–89.

3. The breadth and scope of the eventual full exhibit at the Crystal Palace did not please everyone associated with women's war work, and indeed, the displeased vented their anger in later service newspapers, such as the following condemnation printed in 1921 in an issue of the *Old Comrades' Association Gazette*, a publication of Queen Mary's Army Auxiliary Corps (QMAAC):

> Several QMAAC exhibits which were promised for the women's war service section of the museum have not materialised and the result is that QMAAC do not make nearly such a good show at the Crystal Palace as some of the other services. (No. 8, Feb. 1921: 1)

4. Women's factory newspapers can also be found at other collections: the University of Tulsa, for example, houses copies of *The Shell Magazine* and the *Dornock Souvenir Magazine* in its Special Collections archives.

5. This particular letter, first published in a June 1917 issue of *Bombshell*, is reprinted in several other factory newspapers practically word for word. It was either a form letter sent from the front, or just as likely, was plagiarized from *Bombshell* by editors of other factory newspapers who altered the names and local allusions to make the letter appear more genuine. See, for example, *Cardonald News* 1.33 (Dec. 21, 1917).

6. The factory records at H. M. Factory, Gretna, record that for every 100 women workers "36 had been formerly in domestic service; 20 had lived at home; 15 had already served as Munition workers; 12 had already worked in ordinary factories; and 5 had been shop assistants while the remaining 12 had been laundry workers, farm hands, dressmakers, school teachers or clerks" (Imperial War Museum Department of Printed Books, Women and Work Microfilm Collection, Item 1 4/8 Journals).

7. Malcolm Brown, p. 263.

8. Malcolm Brown, p. 263. *The Open Exhaust,* for example, a publication of 358 Company, MT, ASC, Repair Shop, had a distinct advantage over its contemporaries, Martin Taylor explains, in that "it was type-set and printed in France by Joly-Thulliez of St Omer, although the zinco line blocks for the illustrations were made by Holloway & Sons of Bristol" (*"The Open Exhaust"* 25).

9. *Cardonald News* Vol. 1, No. 35, Friday, January 11, 1918; *Cardonald News* Vol. 1, No. 38, Friday, February 1, 1918.

10. The coats of arms are interesting in themselves and warrant brief description here. The cover page of *WRNS Magazine,* for example, displays an elaborate insignia that frames an illustration of a wren atop an anchor. Above the bird's head, the Royal Crown is flanked by the dates 1917 and 1919, and on both sides of the bird stands a column of four heraldic shields. On the left column, from top to bottom, the shields contain a pair of crossed feathers, a sea shell, a steering wheel and crossed keys; in the right column, an envelope, a star, crossed mallets, and a bolt of lightning pierced by an arrow. The motto across the entire bottom reads "Never at Sea," a clever and perhaps playful reminder of the women's landlubber roles during the war but one that asserts their reliability as well, as the phrase "never at sea" is meant to suggest.

Most of the eight items that frame the emblematic bird, anchor and crown are easily connected with the WRNS (the star for navigation, for example) except for the crossed feathers, which the writers explain carry a mythological symbolism (*WRNS Magazine,* Imperial War Museum Department of Printed Books, Women and Work Collection, Item WRNS 19/1): according to Norse legend, "a Syren tried to lure men to sea. A charm was tried to capture the siren but she escaped in the form of a wren. Hence, wrens are killed in the hope of destroying the siren. The feathers of the bird are plucked and preserved as a preservation from death by shipwreck." In a related side note, the writer points out the fortuitous association between the WRNS and their director, Dame Kathleen Furze, noting the tradition of St. Stephen's Day in Ireland, when men and boys kill wrens and carry them about on furze-bushes from house to house. The writer also notes that once upon a time, "all the birds were very cold so they asked for a volunteer to fly to the sun and bring back warmth. The tiny wren volunteered but he came back burnt. All the other birds, in their gratitude, gave him one of their feathers—except the owl" (11).

The *Bombshell* has a similarly interesting coat of arms, one that contains a shovel, a mallet and a broom crossed above a trolley carrying munitions. Its motto reads "Flagrante Bello." Similarly, the coat of arms on the last page of *Shell Magazine* (Figure 4.6) emblematizes the women's work at the Newlay arsenal. Punning on the word "newly laid," it pictures in one quadrant a number of hens laying not eggs but munitions. In another section of the coat of arms, a woman munition worker emerges from a newly laid egg, already dressed and ready for work.

11. Christopher Martin notes in *English Life in the First World War* that the women's new affluence led to a number of changes: they more frequently wore powder and makeup, and purchased silk stockings and shorter skirts (six inches off the ground): "sales of jewelry, silk-stockings, fur coats and the status symbol, the piano, were rising rapidly" (82), he notes. Martin fails to connect the women's increased use of cosmetics with their likely desire to camouflage their yellowed skin, a result of protracted work in the TNT danger rooms.

12. See Paul Thomas Murphy, *Toward a Working-Class Canon: Literary Criticism in British Working-Class Periodicals, 1816–1858* (Columbus: Ohio State University Press, 1994).

13. Murphy's description of the utility of art in working class periodicals differs greatly from that described more than half a century before the First World War. In 1858 Margaret Oliphant denounced working class periodicals, complaining that the working classes preferred to read contemptible low-grade fiction (Bristow 12).

14. In this case, the literary allusion might also serve to encode the wink-wink nudge-nudge of a sexual subculture running through the WAAC, since Shakespeare's Rosalind is also the cross-dressed Ganymede, who tries the limits of gender fixity by flirting with and ultimately transgressing gender boundaries. Jayne Marek notes in *Women Editing Modernism* that many little magazines published during modernism used techniques of "indirection or 'absence'" to express lesbianism and queer desire and that by keeping their prose intentionally vague but sexually suggestive, "what is left out," she explains, "allows the reader to assume the 'ecstasy' . . . what is left out also protects the speakers while still expressing an aspect of their personal relationship" (91).

15. During the great munitions drive, letter-writers lodged a campaign in the press so that soldiers might be eligible for a Trench Ribbon after completing 100 days in the trenches (See "A Trench Ribbon. The Popularizing of the Infantry," *Times*, May 18, 1916). No such civilian medal of honor existed for

women industrial workers. Though many of them spent four uninterrupted years in the arsenals, their only medal of honor was their service badge, which many of them paid to have gold-plated.

16. "We've had songs about the Trenches/And songs about the Fleet/But what about the saucy girls/Who come tripping down the street/Every morn, to catch the tram car/In the hail, rain, snow or sleet?" Six stanzas follow. *Shell Chippings*, Vol. 1, No. 1 (1916): 7.

17. Trudi Tate in fact concludes in her study *Modernism, History and the First World War* that the distinction between war writing and modernism begins to dissolve after 1914, and that modernism emerges as a strange but important form of war writing.

18. Captain F. J. Roberts quoted in Beaver's Introduction to the facsimile edition of the *Wipers Times* (xiii); E. M. Delafield is quoted from her "Preface" to Irene Rathbone's novel *We That Were Young* (viii).

19. The following description of the cordite process, issued by H. M. Factory, Gretna, can help us understand the severity of the cordite "candy" women workers chewed with regularity during their shifts:

> The actual making of cordite consists of the following operations. At the ACID SECTION of the Factory, Sulphuric and Nitric Acids are manufactured and mixed in suitable proportions. In the NITRO-COTTON SECTION this mixed acid is used to convert suitably prepared Cotton Waste into Nitro Cotton. The NITROGLYCERINE SECTION is engaged in manufacturing N-G by the intersection of the mixed acid with refined Glycerine. The Nitro Cotton and the N-G are then mixed in certain proportions forming what is technically known as Paste. At the CORDITE SECTION this Paste is treated with Ether, Alcohol and Mineral Jelly and pressed into Cords from which Cordite derives its name. (IWM Department of Printed Books, Women's Work Microfilm Collection Item MUN 14/8)

> A mock advertisement in the *Dornock Souvenir Magazine* recommends two other uses for cordite that go beyond its usual application. The mock advertisement reads:

> SALE! SALE! SALE!
> Post-war Great Sale. Genuine Bargains.
> Try our Famous Gretna Blend R. D. B. Cordite.
> Best and goes farthest.
> Try it in your BATH,
> Try it for TIRED FEET. (47)

20. Nathalie Blondel finds similar commentary in Frances Bellerby's novel *Hath the Rain a Father?*, set during the First World War. Bellerby's deliberate dis-

tortion of the "Tinker, tailor, soldier, sailor, rich man, poor man, beggar man, thief" counting game "point[s] to the extent to which war ravages even innocent children's ditties" (170), Blondel argues. "[It's] Like counting prune-stones," Bellerby's character thinks. "Infant, Child, Adolescent, Soldier, Corpse."

21. During characteristic searches, guards checked the women for matches, hairpins, needles, metal buttons, and other items that might spark or start fires in the arsenal danger rooms. An example of the severe, consequential, punishments is that factory authorities imposed 28-day prison sentences without the option of a fine upon workers caught with matches. Lilian Miles recalls the day her best friend was caught with a match leftover from the previous night's blackout. Imprisoned for the usual 28 days, the friend "never got over it. She died a few months later. She was twenty," Miles told the interviewer (Imperial War Museum Sound Archive, Item SR 854, Transcript 10).

22. Woollacott notes further that "Anonymously, women in factories making helmets, gas masks and other items which they knew would be opened by a solider at the front would write notes expressing support, even giving their names and addresses in order to initiate a correspondence" ("Sisters and Brothers in Arms" 138).

Chapter 5

1. Arthur Marwick notes in *The Deluge: British Society and the First World War* that civilians felt so encumbered by certain DORA restrictions that a committee was established to arbitrate civilian compensation requests:

> In the spring of 1915 the Government appointed a permanent commission to adjudicate upon claims for compensation made by individuals who felt they had suffered loss from Government action under D.O.R.A. In its decisions the Commission showed a consistent lack of generosity, though it must be said that many of the cases brought before it showed great triviality and lack of public spirit on the part of the claimants. (139)

2. John Turner refers to the DORA nine times but by name only, not in any general discussion of its impact on the culture (*British Politics and the Great War: Coalition and Conflict 1915–1918* [New Haven: Yale UP, 1992]); Asa Briggs's recently revised *A Social History of England* has one sentence on the DORA (London: Weidenfeld and Nicholson, 1994); Gerard De Groot's scant discussion of the DORA is more descriptive than analytical in *Blighty: British Society in the Era of the Great War* (London: Longman 1996); Samuel Hynes's 1990 work *A War Imagined* contains no discussion of the DORA, as well; and Ian Hogg fails to enter it in his *Dictionary of World War I* (Oxford: Helicon 1994).

3. Not surprisingly, in *The Unexpurgated Case* Wright resorts to cultural stereotypes to condemn women suffragists, and argues that women should not be allowed to vote, nor be expected to select among candidates, because any woman "spends her life halting between . . . two opinions, eternally shilly-shallying" (126). To drive home the point of women's dangerous political hesitancies, Wright places suffragists alongside some of the most potentially dangerous bedfellows he can think of—Irish nationalists. Women who continue to cry out for suffrage, he argues, or women who continue to bemoan their economic or physiological difficulties when all they've got to do is emigrate from their social class into a more humble one (157), are like Irish nationalists who continue to agitate for a separate Parliament for Ireland even after the settlement of the land question and the granting of old age pensions (157–58). Of course, Wright misses the point completely about a separate Parliament for Ireland, and this is important, since he introduces it into his discussion of women and the vote. Ireland had her own Parliament from 1295 to 1800, but England restricted its legislative authority by Poyning's Law, enacted in 1494, and by the Sixth of George I, enacted in 1719. When these were repealed in 1782, an independent Irish Parliament came into existence and lasted until 1800 when the Act of Union severed it. After legislating justice and inculcating public and national accountability in Ireland for more than five centuries, the Irish Parliament was dismembered in a 138 to 96 vote in the British House of Parliament. The motion later passed in the Irish House but only because William Pitt had promised Archbishop of Dublin John Thomas Troy and other members of the Catholic hierarchy that passage of the Act of Union would move King George III to grant Catholic emancipation. The Irish House passed the motion in March of 1800 but would wait another 29 years for Catholic emancipation. Many still wait for settlement of the land question. I point this out because Wright thinks that Irish politicism is no longer necessary "after the settlement of the land question and the granting of old age pensions" (157–58); since he uses this choleric analogue to fuel his argument against women's suffrage—that women (like the Irish) ought not to agitate for the vote because they have won sufficient progress—his wrongheadedness needs attention, and his palliative for women with economic difficulties, that they emigrate to a lower social class, seems incorrigible.

Wright's outrageous yoking of political bedfellows—British suffragists and Irish nationalists—also works to masculinize women suffragists, since the bulk of Irish agitators were male. Sensationalizing suffrage by juxtaposing it with dangerous, and thought by the British to be immoral, Irish nationalist campaigns is another way of treating women's suffrage as a menace to social purity and as a threat to the morality of the Empire; moreover, it was one other way to insist that women had the potential to be moral outlaws and social deviants.

4. The DORA worked increasingly as a tool to manage intellectual as well as physical behavior, as Claire Tylee notes in *The Great War and Women's Consciousness:*

Almost immediately on the declaration of war in August 1914, the British government resolved on two means of promoting the War which were to be decisive for British culture: censorship and propaganda. Defence of the Realm Acts were slipped through Parliament, and a secret Bureau of Propaganda was established. By these means the government strengthened and institutionalised the management of ideas, which had previously been exercised more loosely under the Obscene Publications Act of 1857. This Act had been used to control sexual, political and religious dissent. Under DORA direct political censorship was more rigorously enforced, and the penalties were more stringent. (252)

5. Trevor Wilson notes that anti-treating laws were often taken to the extreme: "'treating' (that is, the purchase of a drink for another person) was prohibited, it being held that much public drunkenness among soldiers was caused by the generosity of misguided patriots. The application of this ban became general. A man might be prosecuted (and this did happen) for buying a drink for his own wife" (153).

6. Of course, by failing to point out here that working-class women's wages were significantly lower than those of working-class men's—usually by half—Stead aligns himself with the constable's misdirected sense of injustice. A more appropriate way to phrase the pay inequity would be to point out that even the lowest-paid workers in munition factories were getting three times as much as a constable on overtime, thereby removing gender from his statement entirely, especially since class bias sustained so much of the rhetoric of the 1918 police strike.

Chapter 6

1. While the birth rate held at about 880,000 per year before the war, it reached a low of 660,000 in the last year of the war. J. M. Winter notes that

Fluctuations in the birth rate were more severe than were variations in the marriage rate during the First World War. From a level of approximately 24 births per 1,000 population in 1910–13, the birth rate dropped 10 per cent in each of the first two years of the war. By 1917, the birth rate had descended to 17.8 per 1,000, which was the lowest on record, only to fall still further to 17.7 in the last year of the war. (Winter 253)

What pronatalists failed to mention in their fertility push was an alarming statistic that ultimately would temper the success of their campaign: that three-quarters of the men who died or were killed in the war were under age 30 and unmarried (Winter 256).

2. John Williams notes in *The Home Fronts* that by May 1916, "it was reported . . . that the Christian name 'Verdun' was frequently being given at British baptisms: a recognition of the fearful and prolonged struggle being waged by the French around that beleaguered citadel" (123).
3. The author of the *Daily News* article "Mothers and Children" wrote, "This war is bringing home to many of us the value of the mother as a national asset" (June 16, 1917).
4. By 1918, 6 percent of all births were illegitimate, J. M. Winter notes. This indicates an increase in illegitimate births; before the war, illegitimate children made up 3 percent (253).

Tosh, a character in Helen Zenna Smith's 1930 novel of the First World War, *Not So Quiet . . .*, invents a "war alphabet" that reconceptualizes the cultural attitude towards illegitimacy. Smith writes, "Yesterday she compiled a war alphabet: B for Bastard—obsolete term meaning war-baby. . . . I for Illegitimate—(see B). . . . V for Virgin—a term of reproach (ask any second loot) . . ."(160). In her Afterword to Smith's novel, Jane Marcus interestingly points out that "Tosh's alphabet inscribes the complicity of motherhood and war" (282).

5. See Winter 270–71.
6. Picture postcards were more or less "invented" during World War I as a means of sending personal photos or other photographic reproductions through the mail with cost and time efficiency. Postcard representations of women, then, were not the brainchild of a settled or standardized industry trying to outdo its competitors by supplying a hungry or worse, complacent audience with increasingly outrageous depictions. Rather, World War I cards are among the earliest pictorial postcards and as such are more disturbing since they represent early mass-produced images not only of working-class women but of the World War I woman in general who is subject to male fantasy.
7. See Culleton, "Gender-Charged Munitions: The Language of World War I Munitions Reports," *Women's Studies International Forum* 11.2 (1988): 109–116.
8. In her discussion of the popular "Women of England Say 'Go!'" poster, Tylee notes that it was only second in popularity to the "Kitchener Wants You" poster, and adds:

> These were not statements of the same degree of veracity. Kitchener himself initiated the idea of a volunteer army. There was no referendum to establish what women said. The poster seems designed as much to convince women of what to say, as to convince men that they were saying it. Actually many women tried to get their sons out of the army. Others were agitating to prevent conscription. Still others were working for a negotiated settlement to the War. It is only very recently that the suppressed history of this political dissent has been recovered, and related to the pre-War women's analysis of militarism and its debasing effects. (257)

9. Margaret Sackville, *The Pageant of War* (London: Simpkin, Marshall Kent and Co., 1916), p. 39.

10. Strangely enough, images of the mother also were appropriated into descriptions and discussions of military tanks during the First World War regardless of the obvious incongruity between nurturing mothers and murderous 28-ton tanks. Trudi Tate has explained that when the so-named *Little Willie* tank was replaced by a larger model, the *Big Willie*, it instantly was renamed *Mother*. The tank, however, was manufactured and supplied to British troops in male, female, and hermaphrodite versions. She explains:

> Mother came in two forms: male and female. (There were also 'hermaphrodite' tanks.) The sex of the tank was determined by relatively minor variations: the male was a little larger and weighed 28 tons; the female weighed 27 tons. The male had two kinds of guns; the female only one (though both carried a total of six guns). Perhaps most significantly from the crew's point of view, in the early models the male had a narrow door in the side, allowing men to escape, with difficulty, if the tank caught fire. The female by contrast had only a small trap door, just two foot high, out of which it was almost impossible to escape. This was soon modified, but in the earliest tanks, being inside a female Mother was one of the men's worst nightmares: it was a place in which they could be trapped and burned alive. Tank driver Jenkin notes [in *A Tank Driver's Experiences*] that the men 'most favoured the male Mothers.' (*Modernism, History and the First World War* 136)

Another version of Tate's chapter appeared as "The Culture of the Tank" in *Modernism/Modernity* 4.1 (1997): 69–87.

11. Karen Offen describes the grand upheaval instigated by the introduction of the bi-pedal sewing machine in Europe that was argued to produce in women workers "involuntary masturbation resulting from the play of the machine" (97). Offen notes that

> Despite the higher earning possibilities for women, turnover among machine operators was high, and some women workers in the workshops complained of fatigue, ill health, and assorted physical problems. The most sensational claim was that extended use of the machine produced extensive vaginal discharges, sometimes hemorrhages, and extreme genital excitement, due to rubbing of the thighs during operation of the double pedal mechanism that then powered the machines used in industrial production. (94)

The documents that Offen translates in her essay worked to spread fear about the moral laxity of working-class women and sought to regulate at the same time their sexuality. The continental attention focused on women workers in the sewing industry also curbed their wage-earning possibilities, which nearly doubled after the introduction of the pedal-driven sewing machine. Offen suggests that because the industry began to pay higher wages due to increased production, male workers sought to displace women on the machines and used the "evidence" of sexual titillation to send them back to their protected domestic spheres. Perhaps the same motives were at work during the First World War. See "'Powered by a Woman's Foot': A Documentary Introduction to the Sexual Politics of the Sewing Machine in Nineteenth-Century France," *Women's Studies International Forum* 11.2 (1988): 93–101.

Chapter 7

1. Winter, *The Great War and the British People,* 282.
2. See Braybon and Summerfield, 77.
3. Braybon and Summerfield note that

   > One other thing is very striking about women's memories of work, and that is the ease with which they changed jobs, even when the leaving certificate was still in operation. Many of them did three, or even four, different jobs during the war, while others moved between factories or areas. . . . This mobility was quite unknown for women before the war, and goes a long way to explaining why so many of them found jobs they liked in the end. Their labour was actually in demand—a rare thing for women workers. (71)

4. Sallie Heller Hogg quotes different statistics—that by 1921 women made up 31 percent of the work force whereas they had made up 32 percent a decade earlier (487).
5. See Chushichi Tsuzuki's essay "Anglo-Marxism and Working-Class Education," *The Working Class In Modern British History,* ed. Jay Winter (Cambridge: Cambridge University Press, 1983, pp. 187–99).
6. Lewis notes, for example, that during the interwar years, birth control was discussed more freely than ever, and that "women in the Labour Party made sure that resolutions asking for the provision of birth control information via local authority clinics came before the Party's Annual Conference in 1925, 1926 and 1927" (20).

Works Cited

"A Trench Ribbon: The Popularising of the Infantry." *The Times*, May 18, 1916.

Anderson, Linda. *Women and Autobiography in the Twentieth Century: Remembered Futures*. London: Prentice Hall, 1997.

Ardis, Ann L. *New Women, New Novels: Feminism and Early Modernism*. New Brunswick: Rutgers University Press, 1990.

Aronowitz, Stanley. *The Politics of Identity: Class, Culture, Social Movements*. New York: Routledge, 1992.

Auster, Paul. *The Art of Hunger: Essays, Prefaces, Interviews and "The Red Notebook."* New York: Penguin Books, 1993.

"Baby Week." *The Times*, July 3, 1917.

Banta, Martha. *Taylored Lives: Narrative Production in the Age of Taylor, Veblen, and Ford*. Chicago: University of Chicago Press, 1993.

Barthes, Roland. *A Lover's Discourse. Fragments*. Trans. Richard Howard. New York: Hill and Wang, 1978.

Batty, Reverend B. Staunton. Letter. Imperial War Museum Department of Printed Books, Item MUN 34 2/2.

Beaver, Patrick. "Introduction." *The Wipers Times. Facsimile of the Famous Trench Newspaper, incorporating the New Church Times, The Kemmel Times, the Somme Times, the B.E.F. Times, and the Better Times*. London: Peter Davies, 1973.

Beetham, Margaret. *A Magazine of Her Own?: Domesticity and Desire in the Woman's Magazine 1800–1914*. London: Routledge, 1996.

Best, Richard. "Housing Associations, 1890–1990." *A New Century of Social Housing*. Ed. Stuart Lowe and David Hughes. Leicester: Leicester University Press, 1991. 142–58.

Bethke Elshtain, Jean. *Women and War*. Chicago: University of Chicago Press, 1995.

Blackwell, Trevor, and Jeremy Seabrook. *Talking Work: An Oral History*. London: Faber and Faber, 1996.

Bland, Lucy. "In the name of protection: the policing of women in the First World War." *Women-in-Law: Explorations in Law, Family and Sexuality*. Ed. Brophy and Smart. London: Routledge and Kegan Paul, 1985. 23–49.

Blatch, Mrs. Harriet Stanton. *Mobilizing Woman-Power*. New York: The Woman's Press, 1918.

The Bombshell. The Official Organ of the National Projectile Factory Templeboro. 1.1 (March 1917); 1.4 (June 1917).

Boone, Joseph Allen. *Libidinal Currents: Sexuality and the Shaping of Modernism.* Chicago: University of Chicago Press, 1998.

———. *Tradition Counter Tradition: Love and the Form of Fiction.* Chicago: University of Chicago Press, 1987.

Booth, Allyson. *Postcards from the Trenches. Negotiating the Space Between Modernism and the First World War.* New York: Oxford University Press, 1996.

Bornat, Joanna. "Lost Leaders: Women, Trade Unionism and the Case of the General Union of Textile Workers 1875–1914. *Unequal Opportunities.* Ed. Angela John. Oxford: Basil Blackwell, 1985. 207–33.

Bourdieu, Pierre. *Distinction: A Social Critique of the Judgement of Taste.* Trans. Richard Nice. Cambridge, MA.: Harvard University Press, 1984.

Bourke, Joanna. *Dismembering the Male: Men's Bodies, Britain and the Great War.* London: Reaktion Books Ltd., 1996.

———. *Working Class Cultures in Britain 1890–1960: Gender, Class, Ethnicity.* London: Routledge, 1994.

Bradbury, Frank. Oral History. Imperial War Museum Sound Archive, Item SR 675/04.

Braybon, Gail. *Women Workers in the First World War: The British Experience.* London: Croon Helm, 1981.

Braybon, Gail and Penny Summerfield. *Out of the Cage: Women's Experiences in Two World Wars.* London: Pandora Press, 1987.

Briggs, Asa. *A Social History of England.* 2nd ed. London: Weidenfeld and Nicholson, 1994.

Bristow, Joseph. *Empire Boys: Adventures in a Man's World.* London: Harper Collins, 1991.

Brookes, Mrs. Sophia. Letter to Miss Agnes Conway. September 10, 1919. Imperial War Museum Department of Printed Books, Item 34 2/3.

Brooks, Margaret. "Women in munitions 1914–1918: the oral record." *Imperial War Museum Review* 5 (1990): 4–17.

Brophy, Julia and Carol Smart, ed. *Women-in-Law: Explorations in Law, Family and Sexuality.* London: Routledge and Kegan Paul, 1985.

Brown, Malcolm. *The Imperial War Museum Book of the First World War: A Great Conflict Recalled in Previously Unpublished Letters, Diaries and Memoirs.* London: Sidgwick and Jackson, 1991.

Bunce, Mr. Letter to Miss Agnes Conway. Undated. Imperial War Museum Department of Printed Books Item 34 2/4.

Burke, Peter. "History of Events and the Revival of Narrative." *New Perspectives on Historical Writing.* Ed. Peter Burke. University Park: Pennsylvania State University Press, 1991. 233–48.

———. "Overture: the New History, its Past and its Future." *New Perspectives on Historical Writing.* Ed. Peter Burke. University Park: Pennsylvania State University Press, 1991. 1–23.

————. *Sociology and History*. London: Allen and Unwin, 1980.

Burke, Peter, ed. *New Perspectives on Historical Writing*. University Park: Pennsylvania State University Press, 1991.

Caine, Sir Hall. Letter. Imperial War Museum Department of Printed Books, Item MUN 5/2.

————. *Our Girls: Their Work for the War*. London: Hutchinson, 1917.

Cardonald News. Mar 1917; Oct. 5, 1917; Vol. 1, No. 33 (Dec. 21, 1917); Vol. 1, No. 35 (Jan. 11, 1918); Vol. 1, No. 36 (Jan. 18, 1918); Vol. 1, No. 37 (Jan. 25, 1918); Vol. 1, No. 38 (Feb. 1, 1918); Vol. 1, No. 39 (Feb. 8, 1918); Vol. 1, No. 40 (Feb. 15, 1918); Vol. 1, No. 42 (Mar. 1, 1918)-Vol. 2, No. 9. Imperial War Museum Department of Printed Books, Item VII/21–46.

Cardonald Souvenir Magazine. Jan. 1919. Imperial War Museum Department of Printed Books, Item VII 46.

Carry On. The Armstrong Munition Workers' Christmas Magazine. Newcastle-on-Tyne, Christmas 1916. Imperial War Museum Department of Printed Books, Item VII/13.

Chinn, Carl. *Poverty Amidst Prosperity. The Urban Poor in England 1834–1914*. Manchester: Manchester University Press, 1995.

————. *They Worked all their Lives: Women of the Urban Poor in England, 1880–1939*. Manchester: Manchester University Press, 1988.

Chisholm, Mairi. Oral History. Imperial War Museum Sound Archive, Item SR 771/02.

Christie, Dame Agatha. Oral History. Imperial War Museum Sound Archive, Item SR 493.

Clarke, Isabella. Oral History. Imperial War Museum Sound Archive, Item SR 774/04.

Clarke, J., C. Critcher and R. Johnson, ed. *Working-Class Culture: Studies in History and Theory*. New York: St. Martin's Press, 1980.

The Clincher. The House Journal of Castle Mills. Feb. 1918; April 1918; June 1919. Imperial War Museum Department of Printed Books, Item 27/3.

The Clincher Magazine. The House Journal of the North British Rubber Company, Ltd. Mills Edinburgh: Scotland. Vol. 2, No. 3 (March 1919). Imperial War Museum Department of Printed Books, Item 27/8.

Coates, Donna. "The Best Soldiers of All: Unsung Heroines in Canadian Women's Great War Fictions." *Canadian Literature* 151 (1996): 66–99.

Collins, Mary Gabrielle. "Women at Munition Making." *Scars Upon My Heart: Women's Poetry and Verse of the First World War*. Catherine Reilly, ed. London: Virago Press, 1981.

Connolly, James. *James Connolly: Selected Writings*. Ed. P. Beresford Ellis. New York: Monthly Review Press, 1973.

Cooke, Miriam and Angela Woollacott, ed. *Gendering War Talk*. Princeton: Princeton University Press, 1993.

Cooper, Helen, Adrienne Munich, and Susan Squier, ed. *Arms and the Woman: War, Gender and Literary Representation*. Chapel Hill: University of North Carolina Press, 1989.

"The Cordite Process." Imperial War Museum Department of Printed Books, Item MUN 14/8.

Cosens, Monica. *Lloyd George's Munitions Girls.* London: Hutchinson and Co., 1916.

Cox, Jane. Oral History. Imperial War Museum Sound Archive, Item SR 705/06.

C. R. O. Bulletin, War Souvenir number Christmas 1918 (Journals Collection). London: Imperial War Museum Department of Printed Books.

Culleton, Claire A. "Gender-Charged Munitions: The Language of World War I Munitions Reports." *Women's Studies International Forum* 11.2 (1988): 109–116.

———. "Irish Working Class Women and World War I." *Representing Ireland: Gender, Class, Ethnicity.* Gainesville: University Press of Florida, 1997: 156–80.

———. *Names and Naming in Joyce.* Madison: University of Wisconsin Press, 1994.

———. "Working Class Women's Service Newspapers and the First World War." *Imperial War Museum Review* 10 (1995): 4–12.

Daggett, Mabel Potter. *Women Wanted: The Story Written in Blood Red Letters on the Horizon of the Great War.* New York: George Doran Co., 1918.

Dancyger, Irene. *A World of Women: An Illustrated History of Women's Magazines.* Dublin: Gill and Macmillan, 1978.

Davidoff, Leonore, and Belinda Westover. "From Queen Vic to the Jazz Age: Women's World in England, 1880–1939." *Our Work, Our Lives, Our Words. Women's History and Women's Work.* London: Macmillan, 1986. 1–35.

Davidoff, Leonore, and Belinda Westover, ed. *Our Work, Our Lives, Our Words. Women's History and Women's Work.* London: Macmillan, 1986.

Davies, Andrew. *Leisure, Gender and Poverty. Working-Class Culture in Salford and Manchester, 1900–1939.* Buckingham: Open University Press, 1992.

De Groot, Gerard. *Blighty: British Society in the Era of the Great War.* London: Longman, 1996.

Delafield, Elizabeth. "Preface." *We That Were Young* by Irene Rathbone. New York: Feminist Press, 1989. vii–viii.

Dewar, A. B. George. *The Great Munitions Feat 1914–1918.* London: Constable and Company, 1921.

"Dilution and Greater Output." *The Times,* June 24, 1918.

Dornock Souvenir Magazine. 1916–1919. McFarlin Library, Special Collections, University of Tulsa.

Drotner, Kirsten. "Schoolgirls, Madcaps, and Air Aces: English Girls and Their Magazine Reading Between the Wars." *Feminist Studies* 9.1 (Spring 1983): 33–52.

Edwards, Julia. *Women of the World: The Great Foreign Correspondents.* Boston: Houghton Mifflin, 1988.

Ellis, Alec. *Public Libraries and the First World War.* Upton: Ffynnon Press, 1975.

Ellis, P. Berresford. *A History of the Irish Working Class.* London: Gollancz Ltd., 1972.

Farlow, Elsie May. Oral History. Imperial War Museum Sound Archive, Item SR 773/03.

Femia, Joseph V. *Gramsci's Political Thought. Hegemony, Consciousness and the Revolutionary Process.* Oxford: Clarendon Press, 1981.

Foxwell, A[gnes] K[ate]. *Munitions Lasses: Six Months as Principal Overlooker in Danger Buildings*. London: Hodder and Stoughton, 1917.

Fussell, Paul. *The Great War and Modern Memory*. New York: Oxford University Press, 1975.

Gagnier, Regenia. *Subjectivities: A History of Self-Representation in Britain, 1832–1920*. New York: Oxford University Press, 1991.

Galbraith, Gretchen R. *Reading Lives. Reconstructing Childhood, Books, and Schools in Britain, 1870–1920*. New York: St. Martin's Press, 1997.

Gallagher, Jean. *The World Wars Through the Female Gaze*. Carbondale: Southern Illinois University Press, 1998.

Gardner, Martin, ed. *The Annotated Alice*. New York: Wings Books, 1960.

Garnsey, Elizabeth. "Women's Work and Theories of Class Stratification." *Sociology* 12 (1978): 223–243.

Gilbert, Sandra M. "Soldier's Heart: Literary Men, Literary Women and the Great War." *Signs* 8.3 (Spring 1983): 422–50.

Giles, Judy. "Playing Hard to Get: Working Class Women 1918–40." *Women's History Review* 1 (1992): 239–55.

———. *Women, Identity and Private Life in Britain, 1900–1950*. New York: St. Martin's Press, 1995.

Ginns, George. Oral History. Imperial War Museum Sound Archive, Item SR 775/05.

"Girl Munition Workers: Health and a Twelve-Hours Day." *The Times*.

"Girl's Masquerade: Two Years as a Male Worker." *The Times*, Jan. 21, 1918: 3.

Godber, Lily Maud. Oral History. Imperial War Museum Sound Archive, Item SR 693/07.

Goldman, Dorothy, Jane Gledhill, and Judith Hattaway. *Women Writers and the Great War*. New York: Twayne Publishers, 1995.

Goldman, William. *East End, My Cradle*. London: Faber and Faber, 1940.

Gordon, Linda, Persis Hunt, Elizabeth Pleck, Rochelle Goldberg Ruthchild, and Marcia Scott. "Historical Phallacies: Sexism in American Historical Writing." *Liberating Women's History: Theoretical and Critical Essays*. Ed. Berenice A. Carroll. Urbana: University of Illinois Press, 1976. 54–74.

Gould, Jenny. "Women's Military Service in First World War Britain." *Behind the Lines: Gender and the Two World Wars*. Ed. Margaret Higonnet et al. New Haven: Yale University Press, 1987. 114–125.

Gramsci, Antonio. *Selections from the Prison Notebooks of Antonio Gramsci*. Ed. and trans. Quintin Hoare and Geoffrey Nowell Smith. New York: International Publishers, 1971.

Green, Barbara. *Spectacular Confessions: Autobiography, Performative Activism, and the Sites of Suffrage 1905–1938*. London: Macmillan, 1997.

Gretna Factory Records. Imperial War Museum Department of Printed Books, Item JOURNALS I 4/8.

Griffiths, Gareth. *Women's Factory Work in World War I*. Phoenix Mill: Alan Sutton Publishing Inc., 1991.

Hallowes, F. S. *Mothers of Men and Militarism*. London: Headley Brothers, 1915.

Hamilton, Peggy. *Three Years or the Duration: The Memoirs of a Munition Worker, 1914–18*. London: Peter Owen, 1978.

Hanley, Lynne. *Writing War: Fiction, Gender, and Memory*. Amherst: University of Massachusetts Press, 1991.

Hart, Mildred. Letter to Agnes Conway. October 24, 1918. Imperial War Museum Department of Printed Books Item 34 2/5.

Haste, Cate. *Rules of Desire. Sex in Britain: World War I to the Present*. London: Chatto and Windus, 1992.

Heathorn, Stephen. "'Let us remember that we, too, are English': Constructions of Citizenship and National Identity in English Elementary School Reading Books, 1880–1914." *Victorian Studies* 38.3 (Spring 1995): 395–427.

Hibberd, Dominic. *The First World War*. London: Macmillan, 1990.

Higonnet, Margaret, Jane Jenson, Sonya Mitchell, and Margaret Weitz, ed. *Behind the Lines: Gender and the Two World Wars*. New Haven: Yale University Press, 1987.

Himmelfarb, Gertrude. "Some Reflections on the New History." *American Historical Review* 94.3 (June 1989): 661–70.

Hobsbawm, Eric. *On History*. New York: New Press, 1997.

Hogg, Ian V. *Dictionary of World War I*. Chicago: NTC Publishing Group, 1997.

Hogg, Sallie Heller. "The Employment of Women in Great Britain, 1891–1921." Ph.D. Thesis, Oxford University, 1967.

Home Service Corps Review. Vol. 1, Nos. 1–19, 21, 22; Vol. 2, Nos. 23–30, 32, 33. Imperial War Museum Department of Printed Books Item VOL. CORPS 6/4–37.

Hopkins, Eric. *The Rise and Decline of the English Working Classes. 1918–1990*. London: Weidenfeld and Nicolson, 1991.

Humphries, Stephen. *Hooligans or Rebels? An Oral History of Working-Class Childhood and Youth 1889–1939*. Oxford: Basil Blackwell, 1981.

Huss, Marie-Monique. "Pronatalism and the Popular Ideology of the Child in Wartime France: the Evidence of the Picture Postcard." *The Upheaval of War: Family, Work and Welfare in Europe, 1914–1918*. Ed. Richard Wall and Jay Winter. Cambridge: Cambridge University Press, 1988. 329–67.

Hynes, Samuel. *A War Imagined: The First World War and English Culture*. London: The Bodley Head, 1990.

"In Self-Defence, By a Munition Girl." *Daily Express* Nov. 1, 1917.

Ingram, Angela. "Un/Reproductions: Estates of Banishment in English Fiction After the Great War." *Women's Writing in Exile*. Ed. Mary Lynn Broe and Angela Ingram. Chapel Hill: University of North Carolina Press, 1989. 325–48.

Ingram, Angela, and Daphne Patai, ed. *Rediscovering Forgotten Radicals: British Women Writers 1889–1939*. Chapel Hill: University of North Carolina Press, 1993.

John, Angela V., ed. *Unequal Opportunities. Women's Employment in England 1800–1918*. Oxford: Basil Blackwell, 1985.

Johnson, Paul. "Credit and Thrift and the British Working Class, 1870–1939." *The Working Class in Modern British History*. Ed. Jay Winter. Cambridge: Cambridge University Press, 1983. 147–170.

Joyce, Patrick, ed. *The Historical Meanings of Work*. Cambridge: Cambridge University Press, 1987.

Kaplan, Caren. "Resisting Autobiography: Out-Law Genres and Transnational Feminist Subjects." *De/Colonizing the Subject: The Politics of Gender in Women's Autobiographies*. Ed. Sidonie Smith and Julia Watson. Minneapolis: University of Minnesota Press, 1992. 115–138.

Kessler-Harris, Alice. *Out to Work: A History of Wage-Earning Women in the United States*. New York: Oxford University Press, 1982.

Kewley, Ivy. Oral History. Imperial War Museum Sound Archive, Item SR 3154. Transcript.

Khan, Nosheen. *Women's Poetry of the First World War*. Lexington: University Press of Kentucky, 1988.

Kipling, Rudyard. *The Complete Verse*. London: Kyle Cathie Limited, 1990.

Lee, Beatrice. Oral History. Imperial War Museum Sound Archive, Item SR 724/06.

Levine, Philippa. "'Walking the Streets in a Way No Decent Woman Should': Women Police in World War I." *Journal of Modern History* 66 (1994): 34–78.

Lewis, Jane. *Women in England 1870–1950: Sexual Divisions and Social Change*. Bloomington: Indiana University Press, 1984.

"Lonely Girl Workers." *The Times*, Apr. 17, 1918.

Lorber, Judith. *Paradoxes of Gender*. New Haven: Yale University Press, 1994.

Lowe, Stuart. "Introduction: One Hundred Years of Social Housing." *A New Century of Social Housing*. Ed. Stuart Lowe and David Hughes. Leicester: Leicester University Press, 1991. 1–12.

Lowe, Stuart and David Hughes, ed. *A New Century of Social Housing*. Leicester: Leicester University Press, 1991. 142–58.

Macdonagh, Michael. *In London During the Great War: The Diary of a Journalist*. London: Eyre and Spottiswoode, 1935.

Macdonald, Lyn. *The Roses of No Man's Land*. New York: Atheneum, 1989.

Made in the Trenches. Composed Entirely from Articles and Sketches Contributed by Soldiers. Sir Frederick Treves, Bt., and George Goodchild, ed. London: George Allen and Unwin, 1916.

Marcus, Jane. Afterword. "Corpus/Corps/Corpse: Writing the Body In/At War." *Not So Quiet: Stepdaughters of War* by Helen Zinna Smith. New York: Feminist Press, 1989. 241–300; Rpt. in *Arms and the Woman: War, Gender and Literary Representation*. Ed. Helen Cooper et al. Chapel Hill: University of North Carolina Press, 1989. 124–167.

———. Afterword. "The Nurse's Text: Acting Out an Anaesthetic Aesthetic." In *We That Were Young* by Irene Rathbone. New York: Feminist Press, 1989. 467–98.

———. "Asylums of Antaeus: Women, War and Madness—Is There a Feminist Fetishism?" *The Difference Within: Feminism and Critical Theory*. Ed. Elizabeth Meese and Alice Parker. Amsterdam: John Benjamins, 1989: 49–83; Rpt. in *The New Historicism*. Ed. Aram Veeser. New York: Routledge, 1989. 132–51.

Marek, Jayne E. *Women Editing Modernism: "Little" Magazines and Literary History*. Lexington: University Press of Kentucky, 1995.

Martin, Christopher. *English Life in the First World War*. London: Wayland, 1974.

Marwick, Arthur. *The Deluge: British Society and the First World War.* Boston: Little, Brown and Company, 1965.

Marwick, Arthur. "Images of the working class since 1930." *The Working Class in Modern British History.* Ed. J. M. Winter. Cambridge: Cambridge University Press, 1983. 215–231.

May, Amy Elizabeth. Oral History. Imperial War Museum Sound Archive, Item SR 684/05.

McIntyre, Elsie. Oral History. Imperial War Museum Sound Archive, Item SR 673/09.

Megill, Allan. "Recounting the Past: 'Description,' Explanation and Narrative in Historiography." *American Historical Review* 94.3 (June 1989): 627–53.

"Midnight at Woolwich Arsenal. The Happy Canteens." *The Times,* Sept. 1, 1916: 9d.

Miles, Lilian. Oral History. Imperial War Museum Sound Archive, Item SR 854/04.

Mitchell, David. *Monstrous Regiment: The Story of the Women of the First World War.* New York: Macmillan, 1965.

Mitchell, Sally. *The New Girl: Girls' Culture in England, 1880–1915.* New York: Columbia University Press, 1995.

"Mothers and Children." *Daily News,* June 16, 1917.

Murphy, Paul Thomas. *Toward a Working-Class Canon: Literary Criticism in British Working-Class Periodicals, 1816–1858.* Columbus: Ohio State University Press, 1994.

"1916 Woman, The." *The Times,* May 18, 1916: 9.

O'Brien, Joseph. *Dear Dirty Dublin: A City in Distress 1899–1916.* Berkeley: University of California Press, 1982.

Offen, Karen. "'Powered by a Woman's Foot': A Documentary Introduction to the Sexual Politics of the Sewing Machine in Nineteenth-Century France." *Women's Studies International Forum* 11.2(1988): 93–101.

Old Comrades' Association Gazette [QMAAC]. 6 (Dec. 1920); 8 (Feb. 1921). Imperial War Museum Department of Printed Books.

Oral History Recordings. War Work, 1914–1918 [catalogue]. London: Imperial War Museum, 1980.

Ord, Ruby Adelina. Oral History. Imperial War Museum Sound Archive, Item SR 044. Transcript.

Ouditt, Sharon. *Fighting Forces, Writing Women: Identity and Ideology in the First World War.* London: Routledge, 1994.

Owen, Wilfred. *The War Poems.* Ed. Jon Silkin. London: Sinclair-Stevenson, 1994.

Paget, Elma K. *The Woman's Part.* Papers for Wartime, no. 3. London: Oxford University Press, 1914.

Pankhurst, [E.] Sylvia. *The Home Front.* London: Hutchinson, 1932.

Playne, Caroline. *Britain Holds On, 1917–18.* London: Allen and Unwin, 1933.

Potter, Jane. "'A great purifier': The Great War in Women's Romances and Memoirs 1914–1918." *Women's Fiction and the Great War.* Ed. Raitt and Tate. Oxford: Oxford University Press, 1997. 85–106.

Prins, Gwyn. "Oral History." *New Perspectives on Historical Writing.* Ed. Peter Burke. University Park: Pennsylvania State University Press, 1991: 114–139.

Programme. Special Service for Munition and War Workers. St. Paul's Cathedral, April 20, 1918. Imperial War Museum Department of Printed Books, Item VII/2.

"Proposed scheme for Mother's Day." *Daily Chronicle,* June 30, 1916. Imperial War Museum Department of Printed Books, Item BO2 52/5.

Pugh, Martin. *Women and the Women's Movement in Britain 1914–1959.* New York: Paragon House, 1993.

Raitt, Suzanne and Trudi Tate, ed. *Women's Fiction and the Great War.* Oxford: Oxford University Press, 1997.

Rathbone, Irene. *We That Were Young.* New York: Feminist Press, 1989.

Reilly, Catherine. *English Poetry of the First World War: A Bibliography.* London: G. Prior, 1978.

————, ed. *Scars Upon My Heart: Women's Poetry and Verse of the First World War.* London: Virago Press, 1981.

Remington, Alice Christobel (née Procter). Imperial War Museum Sound Archive, Item SR 511/08.

Rennles, Caroline. Oral History. Imperial War Museum Sound Archive, Item SR 566/07. Transcript.

Riquelme, John Paul. *Teller and Tale in Joyce's Fiction.* Baltimore: Johns Hopkins University Press, 1983.

Robert, Krisztina. "Gender, Class and Patriotism: Women's Paramilitary Units in First World War Britain." *International History Review* 19.1 (Feb. 1997): 54–65.

Roberts, Elizabeth. *An Oral History of Working-Class Women 1890–1940.* Oxford: Basil Blackwell, 1984.

Roberts, Robert. *The Classic Slum: Salford Life in the First Quarter of the Century.* Harmondsworth: Penguin Books, 1973.

Rogers, Lindsay. "The War and the English Constitution." *The Forum,* July 1915.

Rukeyser, Muriel. *A Muriel Rukeyser Reader.* Ed. Jan Heller Levi with an Introduction by Adrienne Rich. New York: W. W. Norton & Company, 1995.

Rumbold, Emily. Oral History. Imperial War Museum Sound Archive, Item SR 576. Transcript.

Rumney, Mrs. Mary Millicent. Imperial War Museum Sound Archive, Item SR 739/05.

Sackville, Margaret. *Collected Poems.* London: 1939.

Sassoon, Siegfried. *The War Poems.* London: Faber and Faber, 1983.

Saywell, Shelley. *Women in War.* New York: Viking Press, 1985.

Scharlieb, Dr. Mary. Report. *The Times,* May 5, 1916.

Schweitzer, Pam, L. Hilton, and J. Moss, ed. *What Did You Do in the War, Mum?* London: Age Exchange, 1985.

Scott, Bonnie Kime, ed. *The Gender of Modernism: A Critical Anthology.* Bloomington: Indiana University Press, 1990.

Scott, Joan W. "The Evidence of Experience," *Critical Inquiry* 17.4 (Summer 1991): 773–97.

————. "Experience," *Feminists Theorize the Political.* Ed. Judith Butler and Joan Scott. New York: Routledge, 1992. 22–40.

————. "History and Women," *Learning About Women*. Ed. Conway et al. 1991. 93–118

————. "History in Crisis? The Others' Side of the Story." *American Historical Review* 94.3 (June 1989): 680–92.

————. "Rewriting History." *Behind the Lines: Gender and the Two World Wars*. Ed. Margaret Higonnet et al. New Haven: Yale University Press, 1987. 19–30.

————. "Women's History." *New Perspectives on Historical Writing*, Ed. Peter Burke. University Park: Pennsylvania State University Press, 1991. 42–66.

Shakespeare, William. *As You Like It. The Norton Shakespeare*. Ed. Stephen Greenblatt et al. New York: W. W. Norton and Co., 1997.

Sharpe, Jim. "History from Below." *New Perspectives on Historical Writing*. Ed. Peter Burke. University Park: Pennsylvania State University Press, 1991. 24–41.

Shaw, Dr. Anna Howard. *What the War Meant to Women*. New York: League to Enforce Peace, 1919.

Shell Chippings. A Six Eight Munition Magazine. An Anniversary Souvenir of Women's Work in a Munition Factory. Written and Compliled by the Lady Operators. Bootle. Vol. 1, no. 1 (Sept. 1916). Imperial War Museum Department of Printed Books, Item VII/14.

The Shell Magazine. An Original Souvenir by the Employées of the National Ordnance Factory. No. 1 [Nov. 1917?] n.p., Newlay, Leeds. McFarlin Library, Special Collections, University of Tulsa.

Shover, Michelle J. "Roles and Images of Women in World War I Propaganda." *Politics and Society* 5.3 (1975): 469–89.

Soloway, Richard A. "Eugenics and Pronatalism in Wartime Britain." *The Upheaval of War: Family, Work and Welfare in Europe, 1914–1918*. Ed. Richard Wall and Jay Winter. Cambridge: Cambridge University Press, 1988. 369–88.

Souvenir of Cardonald National Projectile Factory. 1915 . . . 1919. Cardonald: 1919. Published by private subscription at the Factory (Glasgow). Imperial War Museum Department of Printed Books, Item 12/6.

Stead, Philip John. *The Police of Britain*. New York: Macmillan, 1985.

Stein, Gertrude. *The Autobiography of Alice B. Toklas*. New York: Vintage Books, 1990.

Stevenson, John. *British Society 1914–1945*. London: Allen Lane 1984.

Summerfield, Penny. "Gender and War in the Twentieth Century." *International History Review* 19.1 (Feb. 1997): 3–15.

Sutherland, John. *Best Sellers: Popular Fiction of the 70's*. London: Routledge, 1981.

Tate, Trudi. "The Culture of the Tank, 1916–1918." *Modernism/Modernity* 4.1 (1997): 69–87.

————. *Modernism, History and the First World War*. Manchester: Manchester University Press, 1998.

Tate, Trudi, ed. *Men, Women, and the Great War. An Anthology of Stories*. Manchester: Manchester University Press, 1995.

Taylor, A. J. P. *English History 1914–1945*. New York: Oxford University Press, 1965.

Taylor, Martin. "*The Open Exhaust* and some other trench journals of the First World War." *Imperial War Museum Review* 5 (1990): 18–27.

———. "'You Smug-Faced Crowds': Poetry and the Home Front in the First World War." *Imperial War Museum Review* 3 (1988): 87–96.

Taylor, Pam. "Daughters and mothers—maids and mistresses: domestic service between the wars." *Working-Class Culture: Studies in History and Theory.* Ed. J. Clarke. New York: St. Martin's Press, 1980. 121–139.

Thom, Deborah. "The Bundle of Sticks. Women, Trade Unionists and Collective Organization Before 1918." *Unequal Opportunities.* Ed. Angela John. Oxford: Basil Blackwell, 1985. 261–89.

———. "Tommy's Sisters." *Patriotism: The Making and Unmaking of British National Identity.* Ed. Ralph Samuel. London, 1989. 144–57.

———. "Women and Work in Wartime Britain." *The Upheaval of War: Family, Work and Welfare in Europe, 1914–1918.* Ed. Richard Wall and Jay Winter. Cambridge: Cambridge University Press, 1988. 297–326.

Thomas, Elsa. Oral History. Imperial War Museum Sound Archive Item SR 676/08. Transcript.

Thomas, Gill. *Life on All Fronts. Women in the First World War.* Cambridge: Cambridge University Press, 1989.

Townshend, Charles. *Making The Peace: Public Order and Public Security in Modern Britain.* Oxford: Oxford University Press, 1993.

Tratner, Michael. *Modernism and Mass Politics.* Stanford: Stanford University Press, 1995.

Truphet, Lily Maud. Oral History. Imperial War Museum Sound Archive, Item SR 693/07.

Tuck, Lillian Annie. Oral History. Imperial War Museum Sound Archive, Item SR 854/04.

Turner, John. *British Politics and the Great War: Coalition and Conflict 1915–1918.* New Haven: Yale University Press, 1992.

Tylee, Claire M. *The Great War and Women's Consciousness. Images of Militarism and Womanhood in Women's Writings, 1914–64.* Iowa City: University of Iowa Press, 1990.

Verity, Laura. Oral History. Imperial War Museum Sound Archive, Item SR 864/08.

Vicinus, Martha. *Independent Women: Work and Community for Single Women 1850–1920.* Chicago: University of Chicago Press, 1985.

Vincent, David. *Literacy and Popular Culture. England 1750–1914.* Cambridge: Cambridge University Press, 1989.

The Vote. Advertisement. June 21, 1918, p. 295.

The Vote. "A Famous Legislative Test." June 21, 1918, p. 289.

The WAAC Magazine. 3 (Jan. 1919); 4 (March 1919). Imperial War Museum Department of Printed Books Item Army 3 26/13.

Walker, Dora M. *With the lost generation, 1915–1919, from a V.A.D.'s Diary.* Hull: A. Brown and Sons Ltd., 1970.

Wall, Richard, and Jay Winter, ed. *The Upheaval of War: Family, Work and Welfare in Europe, 1914–1918*. Cambridge: Cambridge University Press, 1988.

The War Worker. Vol. I, nos. 1–11, vol. II, no. 2 (June 1917–July 1918 incomplete). London: Imperial War Museum Department of Printed Books.

"War-Time Housing Problem." *The Times*, May 18, 1916.

Watson, Janet S. K. "Khaki Girls, VADs, and Tommy's Sisters: Gender and Class in First World War Britain." *International History Review* 19.1 (Feb. 1997): 32–51.

We Are the Arsenal Girls. A BBC Film Production. Yesterday's Witness Series, Women at War. London: British Broadcasting Series. Imperial War Museum Department of Film.

"The Week in Paris." *The Times*, July 22, 1918.

West, Rebecca. Letter. *The Gender of Modernism: A Critical Anthology*. Ed. Bonnie Kime Scott. Bloomington: Indiana University Press, 1990: 584–87.

"What is Being Done." *The Times*, May 5, 1916.

The Whistle. The Journal of the Women's Police Service. 1.1 (June 1919); 1.2 (July 1919); 1.3 (Aug. 1919). Imperial War Museum Department of Printed Books, Item EMP 43/99–101.

Williams, John. *The Home Fronts: Britain, France and Germany, 1914–1918*. London: Constable and Co., Ltd., 1972.

Willis, Mr. Personal Interview, July 1990. Imperial War Museum. London.

Wilson, Trevor. *The Myriad Faces of War: Britain and the Great War, 1914–1918*. Cambridge: Polity Press, 1986.

Wiltsher, Anne. *Most Dangerous Women: Feminist Peace Campaigners of the Great War*. London: Pandora Press, 1985.

Winter, J. M. *Socialism and the Challenge of War: Ideas and Politics in Britain 1912–1918*. Routledge and Kegan Paul: Boston, 1974.

———. *The Great War and the British People*. Cambridge, MA: Harvard University Press, 1986.

———. "Unemployment, nutrition and infant mortality in Britain, 1920–50." *The Working Class in Modern British History*. Ed. Jay Winter. Cambridge: Cambridge University Press, 1983. 232–56.

Winter, J. M., ed. *The Working Class in Modern British History*. Cambridge: Cambridge University Press, 1983.

The Wipers Times. A Complete Facsimile of the Famous WWI Trench Newspaper, Incorporating the New Church Times, The Kemmel Times, the Somme Times, the B.E.F. Times, and the Better Times. Introduction, notes, and glossary by Patrick Beaver; foreword by Henry Williamson. London: Peter Davies, 1973.

"The Woman Who Works." *The Times*, Dec. 12, 1916.

"Woman's Year: An Extension of Her Work in 1915." *The Times*, Jan. 3, 1916.

"Women for Men." *The Times*, Sept. 15, 1916.

"Women in Industry." *Daily News*, August 15, 1917.

"Women in Munition Works. 'Dilution' and Greater Output." *The Times* 24 June 1918.

"Women on Overtime." Imperial War Museum Department of Printed Books, Item MUN V/2.

Woodward, Llewellyn Sir. *Great Britain and the War of 1914–1918*. London: Methuen and Co. Ltd., 1967.

Woolf, Virginia. *A Room of One's Own*. New York: Harcourt Brace Jovanovich, 1929.

———. *The Diary of Virginia Woolf*. 5 vols. Ed. Anne Oliver Bell. London: Hogarth Press, 1982; Harmondsworth: Penguin, 1983.

Woollacott, Angela. "'Khaki Fever' and its Control: Gender, Class, Age and Sexual Morality on the British Homefront in the First World War." *Journal of Contemporary History* 29 (1994): 325–47.

———. *On Her Their Lives Depend: Munitions Workers in the Great War*. Berkeley: University of California Press, 1994.

———. "Sisters and Brothers in Arms: Family, Class, and Gendering in World War I Britain." *Gendering War Talk*. Ed. Cooke and Woollacott. Princeton: Princeton University Press, 1993. 128–147.

The Woman's Leader. Aug. 13, 1920; Aug. 20, 1920; Aug. 27, 1920; Oct. 10, 1920; Oct. 17, 1920. Imperial War Museum Department of Printed Books.

"Workers' Demand for Rations." *The Times*, Dec. 17, 1917.

Wright, Sir Almroth Edward. *The Unexpurgated Case Against Woman Suffrage*. New York: Hoeber, 1913.

Wright, D. G. "The Great War, Government Propaganda and English 'Men of Letters' 1914–16." *Literature and History* 7 (1978): 70–100.

WRNS Magazine. Aug. 12, 1919; July 19, 1919. Imperial War Museum Department of Printed Books, Items WRNS 16/35 and WRNS 19/1.

Yalom, Marilyn. *Blood Sisters: The French Revolution in Women's Memory*. New York: Basic Books, 1993.

Yates, L. K. *The Woman's Part: A Record of Munitions Work*. New York: George H. Doran Co., 1918.

Zimmeck, Meta. "Jobs for the Girls: Expansion of Clerical Work for Women, 1850–1914." *Unequal Opportunities*, Ed. Angela John. Oxford: Basil Blackwell, 1985. 153–77.

Index

Abbey Wood munitions factory, 89, 94
Aldrich, Mildred, 6
Althusser, Louis, 122
Anderson, Linda, 185
antiwar rallies, 145
Armstrong Munition Factory, 117
Aronowitz, Stanley, 23–24

Baby Week Council, 149
Barnbow factory, 57, 80
Barrie, J. M., 120
Barthes, Roland, 167
Bataille, George, 177
Batty, B. Staunton, Rev., 95, 97
Beaver, Patrick, 110, 118
Bedford, Madeline Ida, 62–63
Beetham, Margaret, 9
Bellerby, Frances, 6, 194–95
Bench to the Trench Fund, 57, 181, 189
Benjamin, Walter, 60
black powder poisoning, 81
Blackwell, Trevor, 7
Bland, Lucy, 137, 141
Blatch, Harriet Stanton, 154
Blighty, 116
Blondel, Nathalie, 194–95
*Bombshell, The: The Official Organ of
    the NPF, Templeboro,* 104,
    108–9, 111, 116, 120, 124, 190,
    191, 193
Boone, Joseph, 123
Booth, Allyson, 4, 183
Bornat, Joanna, 170
Bourdieu, Pierre, 71, 118
Bourke, Joanna, 172, 173, 175

Bourne, J. M., 136, 137
Bowen, Elizabeth, 6
Bowlby, Rachel, 60
Bradbury, Frank, 69
Braybon, Gail, 2, 4, 47, 69, 76, 79,
    80–81, 83, 84, 86, 94, 137, 143,
    151, 183, 184, 190, 200
Bray Factory (Leeds), 90
Briggs, Asa, 2, 147, 172–74, 195
British Trades Union Congress (TUC),
    24, 26, 42
Brittain, Vera, 185
Broe, Mary Lynn, 4, 184
Brookes, Sophia, 97–98
Brooks, Margaret, 17, 24, 27, 77, 90,
    94, 129, 187
Brown, Malcolm, 91, 191, 192
Browning, Robert, 126
Brunner, Mond and Co. chemical
    factory, 94
Bunce, Mary, 98
Butt, Clara, 20–21, 188

Cable, Boyd, 93
Caine, Hall, 10, 31, 77, 152–53, 156,
    161, 167–68
Caley, E. S., 115
Campbell, Janet, 75
Cardonald National Projectile Factory,
    18, 87
    on-site savings bank, 18, 181
Cardonald News, 8, 108, 110, 116, 178,
    192
Cardonald Souvenir Magazine, 101,
    102

Carroll, Lewis, 114–16
Carry On, 105, 108, 117
censorship, 144–45
Central Committee on Women's
   Employment, 183
Chinn, Carl, 39
Christie, Agatha, Dame, 98
Clarke, Isabella, 40–41, 45, 80, 89, 90,
   188, 190
Clarke, Sidney, 140
Clincher, The: The House Journal of
   Castle Mills, 108
Clincher Magazine, The: The House
   Journal of the North British
   Rubber Company Ltd., 108
Collins, Mary Gabrielle, 154–55
Compton-Burnett, Ivy, 6
Connolly, James, 43
conscription, 23, 43, 145
Contagious Diseases Act, 139–40
Conway, Agnes, 97
Cooper, Helen, 4, 184
cordite, 131, 194
Cosens, Monica, 76
Cox, Jane, 17, 19, 26, 49, 92, 171, 187
C.R.O., The, 108
Culleton, Claire, 184, 198

Daggett, Mabel Potter, 2, 19, 149, 154,
   163
Davies, Andrew, 18–19, 188
De Groot, Gerard, 195
Defense of the Realm Acts (DORA),
   10, 15, 16, 25, 39, 48, 51, 76, 94,
   102, 103, 131, 135–48, 163, 181,
   195, 196–97
Delafield, Elizabeth M., 130
Derby scheme, 23
Dickens, Charles, 126–27
Doolittle, Hilda (H. D.), 6
Dornock Souvenir Magazine, 111, 127,
   129, 130, 133, 176, 179, 182,
   192, 194

Edmonton Munitions Works, 97–98

Ellis, Alec, 119
Employees Quarterly, 108
Enfield Royal Ordnance Factory, 125
Engels, Friedrich, 39

factories
   Abbey Wood munitions factory,
      89, 94
   Armstrong Munition Factory, 117
   Barnbow factory, 57, 80
   Bray Factory (Leeds), 90
   Brunner, Mond and Co. chemical
      factory, 94
   Cardonald National Projectile
      Factory, 18, 87
   Enfield Royal Ordnance Factory,
      125
   Gretna H. M. Factory, 129, 192,
      194
   Gwynne's munition factory, 91
   National Ordnance Factory, 101
   National Projectile Factories, 111,
      124, 125, 191
   National Shell Factory, 56
   Pembury factory, 92, 93, 95
   Scarborough Bag Factory, 188
   Schneider's Clothing Factory, 17,
      92
   Waltham Royal Ordnance Factory,
      125
   White and Poppe's fuse factory, 85,
      89, 190
   Woolwich Royal Ordnance Factory,
      125, 189
factory magazines, 9
factory newspapers, 8–9, 64, 101–34
   see also women's factory
      newspapers
Farlow, Elsie May, 57
Farmerette, The, 108
First Aid Nursing Yeomanry (FANY),
   3, 109, 183
Flagg, James Montgomery, 167–68
Foxwell, A. K., 78
Furze, Kathleen, 193

Fussell, Paul, 4, 6, 7, 130

Gagnier, Regenia, 6, 7–8, 185
Galbraith, Gretchen, 120
Gallagher, Jean, 4, 6, 184
Gard, Lillian, 62
Gardner, Martin, 116
Garnsey, Elizabeth, 171
Garrison Goat, 103
Geertz, Clifford, 2
Gelhorn, Martha, 6
General Union of Textile Workers, 24
Georgetown Gazette, The, 108
Gibbs, Willard, 177
Ginns, George, 69, 85, 89
Gledhill, Jane, 184
Godber, Lily Maud, 131
Goldman, Dorothy, 2, 4, 13, 36, 184
Goldman, Willy, 172
Goodchild, George, 66
Gould, Jenny, 52
Gramsci, Antonio, 25
Graves, Robert, 13
Great Munitions Push, 29, 193
Green, Barbara, 60
Greenwood, Walter, 33
Gretna H. M. Factory, 129, 192, 194
Griffiths, Gareth, 28, 33, 34, 38, 53, 73, 75, 102, 108
Gwynne's munition factory, 91

Haddon, Lisa, 79
Hall, Radclyffe, 6
Hallowes, F. S., Mrs., 155
Hamilton, Peggy, 35, 55, 62
Harbard, Ellen, 89, 94, 99
Harriet, Ellen, 61
Hart, Mildred, 97
Hattaway, Judith, 184
Hibberd, Dominic, 48
Higonnet, Margaret, 4, 6, 26, 184
Hobsbawm, Eric, 87
Hogg, Ian, 195
Hogg, Sally Heller, 200
Home Service Corps Review, 108

Hood, Thomas, 115
Howard, Jean, 124
Humphries, Stephen, 147
Huss, Marie-Monique, 163
Hynes, Samuel, 195

Ibbotson, A. H., 64
Ingraham, B. L., 136
Ingram, Angela, 4, 184
Ingram, Heather, 6
Irish Trades Union Congress, 41
Irish Transport and General Workers' Union (ITGWU), 42
Irish women workers, 39–41, 43–45
Irish Women's Workers Union, 41

Jarrow Crusade, 48
Jenson, Jane, 184
Johnson, Paul, 187

Kaplan, Caren, 7
Kelly, William, 146
Kennedy, Nell, 123
Kewley, Ivy, 69–70
Khan, Nosheen, 4, 67, 184
Kipling, Rudyard, 11, 111, 113, 116, 121

labor unions, 24–26, 29, 42, 48, 55–56, 170, 171
Labour Leader, The, 48
Labour Woman, 64
Ladies' Field, The, 108
Lady's Pictorial, 150
Langford, Beverley, 79
Larkin, James, 42
Latzko, Andreas, 67
Lee, Beatrice, 89, 188
Lee, Vernon, 6
Levine, Philippa, 137, 141–42
Lewis, Jane, 36, 47, 187–88
"Little Mother," 12–13
Lloyd George, David, 20–21, 180
Longfellow, Henry Wadsworth, 121
Lorber, Judith, 33–34

Macarthur, Mary, 75, 145, 155
Macaulay, Rose, 6, 146
Macdonald, Lyn, 4, 184
Mackintosh, E. A., 10
Manchester Guardian, 51
Mansfield, Katherine, 6
Marcus, Jane, 4, 15, 133, 183, 184, 198
Marek, Jayne, 193
Marshall, Catherine, 145
Martin, Christopher, 64, 65, 70, 91,
    135, 136, 189, 193
Marwick, Arthur, 137, 186, 189, 195
maternity, 15, 149–68
    birth rates, 197
    maternal mortality rates, 16, 18,
        164–65, 174
May, Amy Elizabeth, 19, 57, 133, 134,
    175
McIntyre, Elsie, 57–58, 63, 80, 82, 85,
    178
Meese, Elizabeth, 184
Michel, Sonya, 184
Miles, Lilian, 2, 19, 40, 81–82, 84, 88,
    142, 195
Mitchell, David, 144, 145
Mitchell, Sally, 4, 70, 151
Morning Post, The, 52
Mossband Farewell Magazine, 111
Mother's Day, 149–50
Munich, Adrienne Auslander, 4, 184
Murphy, Paul, 121–22, 193

National Baby Week, 149–50
National Health Insurance Act,
    187–88
national leaving certificate policies, 20
National Ordnance Factory, 101
National Projectile Factories, 111, 124,
    125, 191
National Register, 23
National Shell Factory, 56
National Union of Women Workers
    (NUWW)
    Women Patrols Committee, 141
"New Girl," 4–5

Newlay Arsenal, Leeds, 153
Nichols, Robert, 4
No Conscription Fellowship, 145
NTF Souvenir, 108

O'Brien, Joseph, 42
Obscene Publications Act, 197
Offen, Karen, 199–200
Old Comrades' Association Gazette,
    108, 191
Oliphant, Margaret, 193
oral narratives, 2, 9, 17, 35, 41, 43, 57,
    63, 68, 69, 72, 79, 81, 85, 87, 88,
    89, 99, 118, 130, 131, 133, 134,
    142, 175
Ord, Ruby, 38, 68, 69
Ordnance Works, *see* Royal Ordnance
    Works
Ouditt, Sharon, 4, 18, 38, 166, 184
Owen, Wilfred, 4, 10, 65, 67, 185

pacifism, 16, 52, 103, 110, 156
Pankhurst, Emmeline, 20–21
Pankhurst, Sylvia, 67, 135
Parker, Alice, 184
Parliamentary Recruitment
    Committee, 11
Patal, Daphne, 184
Patriotic Gazette, The, 108
patriotism, 13, 20, 40, 44, 82, 83, 84
Peg's Paper, 123
Pembury factory, 92, 93, 95
Playne, Caroline, 76, 91
Poole, Dorothy, 31
Proctor, Alice, 99

Queen Mary, 90
Queen Mary's Army Auxiliary Corps
    (QMAAC), 10, 69–70, 109, 183,
    191

Raitt, Suzanne, 6
Rathbone, Irene, 184
rationing, 19, 58, 70, 122
Red Cross, 158

Remington, Alice Christobel, 45, 189
Rennles, Caroline, 35–36, 45, 80,
    87–88, 89, 91, 118, 165, 179
Report of the War Cabinet Committee
    on Women in Industry, 28, 30
Rhys, Jean, 6
Richardson, Dorothy, 6
"Right to Serve," 20–21
Riquelme, John Paul, 126
Roberts, Elizabeth, 142
Roberts, F. J., 130, 194
Roberts, Robert, 34, 120, 180
Rogers, Lindsay, 142
Rosenberg, Isaac, 4
Rossiter, Clinton, 136
Royal Ordnance Factory
    at Enfield, see Enfield Royal
        Ordnance Factory
    at Waltham, see Waltham Royal
        Ordnance Factory
    at Woolwich, see Woolwich Royal
        Ordnance Factory
Royal Ordnance Works, 40–41, 57
Rukeyser, Muriel, 177
Rumbold, Emily, 72
Russell, Bertrand, 137

Sackville, Margaret, 12, 155, 199
Sailer, Susan Shaw, 184
Sassoon, Siegfried, 4, 10, 64–65, 67,
    185
Saywell, Shelley, 22
Scarborough Bag Factory, 188
Scharlieb, Mary, 79–80
Schneider's Clothing Factory, 17, 92
Schweitzer, Pam, 4, 184
Scott, Joan, 6, 70–71
Seabrook, Jeremy, 7
service newspapers, 79, 99–100, 110
    see also women's service
        newspapers
Sex Disqualification Removal Act, 181
Shakespeare, William, 122–24, 193
Sharpe, Jim, 183
Shaw, Anna Howard, 14, 172

Shell Chippings, 107, 108, 115, 120–21,
    127, 177, 194
Shell Magazine, 64, 101, 106, 110, 116,
    117, 125, 128, 145, 153, 192, 193
Sinclair, May, 6
Sinn Féin, 41, 44, 189
Slades Green, 89
Smith, Anna, 133, 179
Smith, Helen Zinna, 183, 198
social freedom, 18
Spencer, Edward, 129
Squier, Susan Merrill, 4, 184
Stead, Phillip John, 147, 197
Stein, Gertrude, 6, 176
Stevenson, John, 56, 180–81
Stopes, Marie, 165
Summerfield, Penny, 2, 26, 47, 69, 76,
    79, 80–81, 84, 86, 94, 137, 143,
    184, 200
Sutherland, John, 140

Tate, Trudi, 4, 6, 7, 159, 184, 194,
    199
Tawney, R. H., 65
Taylor, A. J. P., 137
Taylor, Martin, 9, 12, 66–67, 103, 191
Taylor, William, 185
Thom, Deborah, 15, 24, 170
Thomas, Elsa, 85
TNT poisoning, 80–91, 97, 127, 129,
    161, 164, 175, 178–79, 190
Townshend, Charles, 136–37, 147
trench journalism, 4
trench newspapers, 6, 102–3, 110, 134,
    191
trench poetry, 4
Treves, Frederick, 66
Truphet, Lily Maud, 88
Tsuzuki, Chushichi, 200
Tuck, Lillian Annie, 63
Turner, John, 195
Tylee, Claire, 4, 6, 137, 140, 184, 196

Verity, Laura, 19, 56, 90
Vicinus, Martha, 5

Volunteer Aid Detachment (VAD), 3, 98–99, 109, 183

Vote, The, 138–40

WAAC Magazine, 108, 112, 115, 122, 124

Wallace, Stuart, 137

Waltham Royal Ordnance Factory, 125

Ward, Humphrey, Mrs., 6

Webb, Aston, 167–68

Webb, Beatrice, 30

Weitz, Margaret, 184

West, Gabrielle, 44, 45, 92, 93, 95

West, Rebecca, 176

Wharton, Edith, 6

Whistle, The: The Journal of the Women's Police Service, 108

White and Poppe's fuse factory, 85, 89, 190

Williams, Joan, 91

Williams, John, 12, 32, 46, 197

Willis, Irene Cooper, 145

Wilson, Trevor, 6, 10, 23, 59, 137, 185, 187, 189, 197

Wiltsher, Anne, 137, 145, 146

Winter, J. M., 19, 151, 188, 191, 197, 198, 200

Wipers Times, 102, 110, 194

Wolff, Janet, 60

Woman's Leader, The, 108

Woman's Royal Naval Service (WRNS), 109, 113–14, 132, 183

Women Police Service (WPS), 141–42

Women Police Volunteers (WPV), 141

Women's Army Auxiliary Corps (WAAC), 3, 68–70, 109, 193

Women's Committee for the Council of National Defense, 14

Women's Dreadnought, 39

women's emancipation, 26

women's factory newspapers, 101–34

    Bombshell, The: The Official Organ of the NPF, Templeboro, 104, 108–9, 111, 116, 120, 124, 190, 191, 193

Cardonald News, 8, 108, 110, 116, 178, 192

Cardonald Souvenir Magazine, 101, 102

Carry On, 105, 108, 117

Clincher, The: The House Journal of Castle Mills, 108

Clincher Magazine, The: The House Journal of the North British Rubber Company Ltd., 108

Dornock Souvenir Magazine, 111, 127, 129, 130, 133, 176, 179, 182, 192, 194

Mossband Farewell Magazine, 111

Old Comrades' Association Gazette, 108, 191

Shell Chippings, 107, 108, 115, 120–21, 127, 178, 194

Shell Magazine, 64, 101, 106, 110, 116, 117, 125, 128, 145, 153, 192, 193

Wipers Times, 102, 110, 194

Women's Emergency Corps, 183

Women's Forage Corps, 183

Women's Freedom League, 138

women's health, 18, 38, 75–100, 150, 164–65, 169

Women's Hospital Corps, 183

women's industry newspapers, 9, 43

Women's Labor League Congress, 28

Women's Land Army, 3, 109, 183

Women's Legion, 183

women's magazines, 9

Women's National Land Service

Women's Police Patrols, 143

Women's Police Service, 92

Women's Police Volunteers, 183

Women's Royal Air Force (WRAF), 183

women's service newspapers, 101–34, 176

    C.R.O., The, 108

    Employees Quarterly, 108

    Farmerette, The, 108

    Georgetown Gazette, The, 108

Home Service Corps Review, 108
Ladies' Field, The, 108
NTF Souvenir, 108
Patriotic Gazette, The, 108
WAAC Magazine, 108, 112, 115, 122, 124
Whistle, The: The Journal of the Women's Police Service, 108
Woman's Leader, The, 108
WRNS Magazine, 108, 130, 192
women's sexuality, 18, 61, 68–69, 71, 148, 156–62, 167–68, 181, 182, 187, 200
Women's Social and Political Union, 20
women's suffrage, 21, 52, 139, 181, 196
Women's Trade Union League, 27, 75
Women's Volunteer Reserve, 183
Woodward, Llewellyn, 137
Woolf, Virginia, 6, 46, 60, 185
Woollacott, Angela, 4, 27, 37, 39, 44, 56, 71, 83, 84, 93, 138, 141, 142, 168, 180, 184, 186, 187, 188, 190, 195

Woolwich Royal Arsenal, 77, 80, 81, 86, 89, 94, 117–18, 152, 159, 161, 165, 170, 188
Woolwich Royal Ordnance Factory, 125, 189
working women
  in clothing and textile manufacturing, 1, 38, 39, 56, 92, 102, 123, 132, 192
  in munitions, 1, 31, 35, 37, 38, 39, 43, 52–55, 57, 59, 63, 71, 76, 78–85, 89–96, 102, 117–18, 125, 131, 132, 142, 146, 152–62, 166–67, 180, 188, 192
Wright, Almroth, 138–39, 196
Wright, C. W., 64
WRNS Magazine, 108, 130, 192

Yates, L. K., 156–58, 168
Yeats, William Butler, 124–25
Yorkshire Copper Works, 188
Young, George, 23

Zimmeck, Meta, 170–72